McDougal Littell
Algebra 2

Larson   Boswell   Kanold   Stiff

Notetaking Guide

The Notetaking Guide contains a lesson-by-lesson framework that allows students to take notes on and review the main concepts of each lesson in the textbook. Each Notetaking Guide lesson features worked-out examples and Checkpoint exercises. Each example has a number of write-on lines for students to complete, either in class as the example is discussed or at home as part of a review of the lesson. Each chapter concludes with a review of the main vocabulary of the chapter. Upon completion, each chapter of the Notetaking Guide can be used by students to help review for the test on that particular chapter.

Copyright ©2007 by McDougal Littell, a division of Houghton Mifflin Company.
All rights reserved.

Permission is hereby granted to teachers to reprint or photocopy in classroom quantities the pages or sheets in this work that carry a McDougal Littell copyright notice. These pages are designed to be reproduced by teachers for use in their classes with accompanying McDougal Littell material, provided each copy made shows the copyright notice. Such copies may not be sold and further distribution is expressly prohibited. Except as authorized above, prior written permission must be obtained from McDougal Littell, a division of Houghton Mifflin Company, to reproduce or transmit this work or portions thereof in any other form or by any other electronic or mechanical means, including any information storage or retrieval system, unless expressly permitted by federal copyright laws. Address inquiries to Manager, Rights and Permissions, McDougal Littell, P.O. Box 1667, Evanston, IL 60204.

ISBN 13: 978-0-618-73693-5
ISBN 10: 0-618-73693-X

56789-MDO-10 09 08

Contents
Algebra 2 Notetaking Guide

1 Equations and Inequalities
- **1.1** Apply Properties of Real Numbers 1–3
- **1.2** Evaluate and Simplify Algebraic Expressions 4–6
- **1.3** Solve Linear Equations 7–9
- **1.4** Rewrite Formulas and Equations 10–12
- **1.5** Use Problem Solving Strategies and Models 13–15
- **1.6** Solve Linear Inequalities 16–19
- **1.7** Solve Absolute Value Equations and Inequalities 20–23
- Words to Review 24–25

2 Linear Equations and Functions
- **2.1** Represent Relations and Functions 26–29
- **2.2** Find Slope and Rate of Change 30–32
- **2.3** Graph Equations of Lines 33–36
- **2.4** Write Equations of Lines 37–39
- **2.5** Model Direct Variation 40–42
- **2.6** Draw Scatter Plots and Best-Fitting Lines 43–45
- **2.7** Use Absolute Value Functions and Transformations 46–50
- **2.8** Graph Linear Inequalities in Two Variables 51–53
- Words to Review 54–56

3 Linear Systems and Matrices
- **3.1** Solve Linear Systems by Graphing 57–60
- **3.2** Solve Linear Systems Algebraically 61–64
- **3.3** Graph Systems of Linear Inequalities 65–67
- **3.4** Solve Systems of Linear Equations in Three Variables 68–71
- **3.5** Perform Basic Matrix Operations 72–75
- **3.6** Multiply Matrices 76–79
- **3.7** Evaluate Determinants and Apply Cramer's Rule 80–84
- **3.8** Use Inverse Matrices to Solve Linear Systems 85–88
- Words to Review 89–91

4 Quadratic Functions and Factoring

- 4.1 Graph Quadratic Functions in Standard Form 92–95
- 4.2 Graph Quadratic Functions in Vertex or Intercept Form 96–98
- 4.3 Solve $x^2 + bx + c = 0$ by Factoring 99–101
- 4.4 Solve $ax^2 + bx + c = 0$ by Factoring 102–104
- 4.5 Solve Quadratic Equations by Finding Square Roots 105–107
- 4.6 Perform Operations with Complex Numbers 108–111
- 4.7 Complete the Square 112–115
- 4.8 Use the Quadratic Formula and the Discriminant 116–119
- 4.9 Graph and Solve Quadratic Inequalities 120–124
- 4.10 Write Quadratic Functions and Models 125–128
- Words to Review 129–131

5 Polynomials and Polynomial Functions

- 5.1 Use Properties of Exponents 132–134
- 5.2 Evaluate and Graph Polynomial Functions 135–137
- 5.3 Add, Subtract, and Multiply Polynomials 138–140
- 5.4 Factor and Solve Polynomial Equations 141–143
- 5.5 Apply the Remainder and Factor Theorems 144–146
- 5.6 Find Rational Zeros 147–149
- 5.7 Apply the Fundamental Theorem of Algebra 150–153
- 5.8 Analyze Graphs of Polynomial Functions 154–156
- 5.9 Write Polynomial Functions and Models 157–159
- Words to Review 160–161

6 Rational Exponents and Radical Functions

- 6.1 Evaluate nth Roots and Use Rational Exponents 162–164
- 6.2 Apply Properties of Rational Exponents 165–168
- 6.3 Perform Function Operations and Composition 169–172
- 6.4 Use Inverse Functions 173–175
- 6.5 Graph Square Root and Cube Root Functions 176–179
- 6.6 Solve Radical Equations 180–183
- Words to Review 184

Algebra 2
Notetaking Guide

7 Exponential and Logarithmic Functions

- **7.1** Graph Exponential Growth Functions 185–188
- **7.2** Graph Exponential Decay Functions 189–191
- **7.3** Use Functions Involving e 192–194
- **7.4** Evaluate Logarithms and Graph Logarithmic Functions 195–198
- **7.5** Apply Properties of Logarithms 199–201
- **7.6** Solve Exponential and Logarithmic Equations 202–205
- **7.7** Write and Apply Exponential and Power Functions 206–209
- Words to Review 210

8 Rational Functions

- **8.1** Model Inverse and Joint Variation 211–214
- **8.2** Graph Simple Rational Functions 215–217
- **8.3** Graph General Rational Functions 218–220
- **8.4** Multiply and Divide Rational Expressions 221–223
- **8.5** Add and Subtract Rational Expressions 224–227
- **8.6** Solve Rational Equations 228–230
- Words to Review 231

9 Quadratic Relations and Conic Sections

- **9.1** Apply the Distance and Midpoint Formulas 232–234
- **9.2** Graph and Write Equations of Parabolas 235–237
- **9.3** Graph and Write Equations of Circles 238–240
- **9.4** Graph and Write Equations of Ellipses 241–243
- **9.5** Graph and Write Equations of Hyperbolas 244–247
- **9.6** Translate and Classify Conic Sections 248–252
- **9.7** Solve Quadratic Systems 253–256
- Words to Review 257–258

10 Counting Methods and Probability

- **10.1** Apply the Counting Principle and Permutations 259–262
- **10.2** Use Combinations and the Binomial Theorem 263–267
- **10.3** Define and Use Probability 268–271
- **10.4** Find Probabilities of Disjoint and Overlapping Events 272–274
- **10.5** Find Probabilities of Independent and Dependent Events 275–278
- **10.6** Construct and Interpret Binomial Distributions 279–283
- Words to Review 284–285

11 Data Analysis and Statistics
- 11.1 Find Measures of Central Tendency and Dispersion 286–289
- 11.2 Apply Transformations to Data 290–291
- 11.3 Use Normal Distributions 292–294
- 11.4 Select and Draw Conclusions from Samples 295–297
- 11.5 Choose the Best Model for Two-Variable Data 298–300
- Words to Review 301–302

12 Sequences and Series
- 12.1 Define and Use Sequences and Series 303–306
- 12.2 Analyze Arithmetic Sequences and Series 307–310
- 12.3 Analyze Geometric Sequences and Series 311–314
- 12.4 Find Sums of Infinite Geometric Series 315–317
- 12.5 Use Recursive Rules with Sequences and Functions 318–320
- Words to Review 321–322

13 Trigonometric Ratios and Functions
- 13.1 Use Trigonometry with Right Triangles 323–326
- 13.2 Define General Angles and Use Radian Measure 327–330
- 13.3 Evaluate Trigonometric Functions of Any Angle 331–335
- 13.4 Evaluate Inverse Trigonometric Functions 336–338
- 13.5 Apply the Law of Sines 339–343
- 13.6 Apply the Law of Cosines 344–347
- Words to Review 348–349

14 Trigonometric Graphs, Identities, and Equations
- 14.1 Graph Sine, Cosine, and Tangent Functions 350–353
- 14.2 Translate and Reflect Trigonometric Graphs 354–357
- 14.3 Verify Trigonometric Identities 358–361
- 14.4 Solve Trigonometric Equations 362–365
- 14.5 Write Trigonometric Models 366–367
- 14.6 Apply Sum and Difference Formulas 368–371
- 14.7 Apply Double-Angle and Half-Angle Formulas 372–374
- Words to Review 375

1.1 Apply Properties of Real Numbers

Goal • Study properties of real numbers.

Your Notes

VOCABULARY

Opposite _____

_____

Reciprocal _____

SUBSETS OF REAL NUMBERS

The real numbers consist of the _____ numbers and the _____ numbers. Two subsets of the rational numbers are the _____ (0, 1, 2, 3...) and the _____ (−3, −2, −1, 0, 1, 2, 3...).

Rational Numbers
- Can be written as quotients of integers
- Can be written as decimals that terminate or repeat

Irrational Numbers
- Cannot be written as quotients of integers
- Cannot be written as decimals that terminate or repeat

Example 1 Graph real numbers on a number line

Graph the real numbers $-\frac{13}{5}$ and $\sqrt{6}$ on a number line.

Solution

Note that $-\frac{13}{5} =$ _____. Use a calculator to approximate $\sqrt{6}$ to the nearest tenth: $\sqrt{6} \approx$ _____. So, graph $-\frac{13}{5}$ between _____ and _____ and graph $\sqrt{6}$ between _____ and _____.

```
<---|---|---|---|---|---|---|---|---|--->
   -4  -3  -2  -1   0   1   2   3   4
```

Lesson 1.1 • Algebra 2 Notetaking Guide 1

Your Notes

PROPERTIES OF ADDITION AND MULTIPLICATION

Let a, b, and c be real numbers.

Property	Addition	Multiplication
_____	$a + b$ is a real number.	ab is a real number.
Commutative	$a + b =$ _____	$ab = ba$
Associative	$(a + b) + c$ $= a + (b + c)$	$(ab)c =$ _____
Identity	$a + 0 = a$, _____ $= a$	$a \cdot 1 = a$, _____ $= a$
Inverse	$a + (-a) =$ ___	$a \cdot \frac{1}{a} = 1, a \neq 0$

The following property involves both addition and multiplication.

Distributive $a(b + c) =$ ____ $+$ ____

Example 2 *Identify properties of real numbers*

Identify the property that the statement illustrates.

a. $(6 \cdot 3) \cdot 2 = 6 \cdot (3 \cdot 2)$ _____ property of _____

b. $21 + (-21) = 0$ _____ property of _____

✓ **Checkpoint** Complete the following exercises.

1. Graph the numbers $-3.2, \frac{3}{4}, \sqrt{5}, -2, -\frac{1}{2}$.

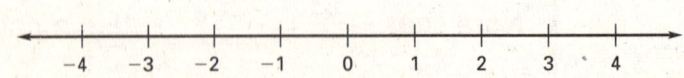

2. Identify the property that $10(6 + 8) = 10(6) + 10(8)$ illustrates.

Your Notes

DEFINING SUBTRACTION AND DIVISION

Subtraction is defined as _____. The opposite, or _____, of any number b is $-b$. If b is positive, then $-b$ is negative. If b is negative, then $-b$ is positive.

$a - b = a + (-b)$ Definition of subtraction

Division is defined as _____.
The reciprocal, or _____, of any nonzero number b is $\frac{1}{b}$.

$a \div b = a \cdot \frac{1}{b}, b \neq 0$ Definition of division

Example 3 Use properties and definitions of operations

Show that $9 + (b - 9) = b$.

$9 + (b - 9)$

$= 9 + [b + (\underline{})]$ Definition of subtraction

$= 9 + [(\underline{}) + b]$ Commutative property of addition

$= [9 + (-9)] + b$ _____ property of addition

$= \underline{} + b$ Inverse property of addition

$= \underline{}$ Identity property of addition

✓ **Checkpoint** Use properties and definitions of operations to show that the statement is true.

3. $5(a \div 5) = a$

Homework

1.2 Evaluate and Simplify Algebraic Expressions

Goal • Evaluate and simplify expressions involving real numbers.

Your Notes

VOCABULARY

Power

Variable

Term

Coefficient

Identity

ORDER OF OPERATIONS

Step 1	First, do operations that occur within _____.	$1 + 7^2 \cdot (5 - 3)$
Step 2	Next, evaluate _____.	$= 1 + 7^2 \cdot 2$
Step 3	Then, do multiplications and divisions from _____.	$= 1 + 49 \cdot 2$
Step 4	Finally, do additions and subtractions from _____.	$= 1 + 98$
		$= 99$

Your Notes

Example 1 Evaluate an algebraic expression

Evaluate $-6y^2 - 11y + 34$ when $y = -5$.

Solution

$-6y^2 - 11y + 34$

$= -6(\underline{})^2 - 11(\underline{}) + 34$ Substitute -5 for y.

$= -6(\underline{}) - 11(\underline{}) + 34$ Evaluate the power.

$= \underline{} + \underline{} + 34$ Multiply.

$= \underline{}$ Add.

✓ **Checkpoint** Evaluate the expression.

1. $3a - 16$ when $a = 7$

2. $2y^2(y - 10)$ when $y = 3$

TERMS AND COEFFICIENTS

In an expression that can be written as a sum, the parts added together are called _____.

A term that has a variable part is a _____.
A term that has no variable part is a _____.

When a term is a product of a number and a power of a variable, the number is called the _____ of the power.

Your Notes

Example 2 *Simplify by combining like terms*

a. $11x - 5x$
b. $2(y + 5) - 3(y - 9)$
c. $14x - 6y + 5x + 13y$

Solution

a. $11x - 5x = (\underline{})x$ Distributive property

         $= \underline{}$ Add coefficients.

b. $2(y + 5) - 3(y - 9)$

    $= 2y + 10 - 3y + 27$ Distributive property

    $= (\underline{}) + (\underline{})$ Group like terms.

    $= \underline{} + \underline{}$ Combine like terms.

c. $14x - 6y + 5x + 13y$

    $= (\underline{}) + (\underline{})$ Group like terms.

    $= \underline{} + \underline{}$ Combine like terms.

✓ **Checkpoint** Simplify the expression.

3. $11n - 6 + 14 - 2n$	4. $2a^3 - 6a^2 + 5a^3$
5. $6(x - 4) - 3(x + 11)$	6. $-15y + 12x + 2y - 7x$

Homework

1.3 Solve Linear Equations

Goal • Solve linear equations.

Your Notes

VOCABULARY

Equation

Linear equation

Solution

Equivalent equations

TRANSFORMATIONS THAT PRODUCE EQUIVALENT EQUATIONS

_____ Property of Equality	Add the same number to each side.	If $a = b$, then $a + c = b + c$.
Subtraction Property of Equality	_____ the same number from each side.	If $a = b$, then $a - c = b - c$.
Multiplication Property of Equality	Multiply each side by the same nonzero number.	If $a = b$ and $c \neq 0$, then ____ = ____
Division Property of Equality	_____ each side by the same nonzero number.	If $a = b$ and $c \neq 0$, then $a \div c = b \div c$.

Lesson 1.3 • Algebra 2 Notetaking Guide

Your Notes

> **Example 1**   *Solve an equation with a variable on one side*
>
> Solve $\frac{3}{4}x + 15 = 33$.
>
> **Solution**
>
> $\frac{3}{4}x + 15 = 33$ Write original equation.
>
> $\frac{3}{4}x =$ _____   Subtract _____ from each side.
>
> $x = \dfrac{}{}(18)$ Multiply each side by _____, the reciprocal of $\frac{3}{4}$.
>
> $x =$ _____   Simplify.
>
> The solution is _____.
>
> **CHECK**   Check $x =$ _____ in the original equation.
>
> $\frac{3}{4}x + 15 = \frac{3}{4}(\underline{}) + 15 =$ _____ $+ 15 =$ _____ ✓

✓ **Checkpoint** Solve the equation. Check your solution.

1. $15a - 6 = 9$	2. $\frac{5}{6}y + 3 = 13$

Lesson 1.3 • Algebra 2 Notetaking Guide

Your Notes

Example 2 Solve an equation using the distributive property

$3(3x - 2) = 7(4x + 3) - 31x$ Original equation

___ $- 6 =$ ___ $+ 21 - 31x$ Distributive property

$9x - 6 =$ ___ $+ 21$ Combine like terms.

___ $- 6 = 21$ Add ___ to each side.

___ $=$ ___   Add ___ to each side.

$x =$ ___   Divide each side by ___ and simplify.

The solution is ___.

CHECK Check $x =$ ___ in the original equation.

$3\left(3 \cdot \underline{} - 2\right) \stackrel{?}{=} 7\left(4 \cdot \underline{} + 3\right) - 31 \cdot \underline{}$ Substitute ___ in for x.

$3(\underline{}) \stackrel{?}{=} 7(\underline{}) - \underline{}$ Simplify.

___ $=$ ___ ✓   Solution checks.

✓ **Checkpoint** Solve the equation. Check your solution.

3. $4(x - 6) = 3(x + 2)$

4. $3(x + 4) = -2(x - 7) - 15x$

Homework

1.4 Rewrite Formulas and Equations

Goal • Rewrite and evaluate formulas and equations.

Your Notes

VOCABULARY

Formula

Solve for a variable

Example 1 *Rewrite a formula with two variables*

Solve the formula $C = 2\pi r$ for r. Then find the radius of a circle with a circumference of 26 meters.

Step 1 Solve the formula for r.

$C = 2\pi r$ Write original circumference formula.

$\dfrac{\quad}{\quad} = r$ Divide each side by ____.

Step 2 Substitute the given value into the rewritten formula.

$r = \dfrac{\quad}{\quad} = \dfrac{\quad}{\quad} \approx \underline{\quad}$ Substitute ____ for C and simplify.

The radius of the circle is about ____ meters.

✓ **Checkpoint** Complete the following exercise.

1. Solve the temperature formula $F = \dfrac{9}{5}C + 32$ for C. Then convert the temperature of 85° Fahrenheit into degrees Celsius.

Your Notes

Example 2 Rewrite a formula with three variables

Solve the formula $A = \ell \cdot w$ for ℓ. Then find the length of a rectangle with a width of 11 feet and an area of 187 square feet.

Solution

Step 1 Solve the formula for ℓ.

$A = \ell \cdot w$ Write area formula.

$\underline{} = \ell$ Divide both sides by ____.

Step 2 Substitute the given value into the rewritten formula.

$\ell = \dfrac{}{}$ Substitute ____ for A and ____ for w.

$= \underline{}$ Simplify.

The length of the rectangle is ____ feet.

✓ **Checkpoint** Complete the following exercises.

2. Solve the formula $P = 2\ell + 2w$ for w. Then find the width of a rectangle with a length of 9 meters and a perimeter of 32 meters.

3. Solve the distance formula $d = rt$ for t. Then find the time it takes to travel the distance of 135 miles at a rate of 30 miles per hour.

Your Notes

Example 3 *Rewrite a linear equation*

Solve $5x - 4y = 9$ for y. Find y when $x = -3$.

Step 1 Solve the equation for y.

$5x - 4y = 9$	Write original equation.
$-4y = 9$ ____	Subtract ____ from each side.
$y = -\_\_ + \_\_$	Divide each side by ____.

> When dividing each side of an equation by the same number, remember to divide every term by the number.

Step 2 Substitute the given value into the equation.

| $y = -\_\_ + \_\_(-3)$ | Substitute -3 for x. |
| $y = \_\_$ | Simplify. |

Example 4 *Rewrite a nonlinear equation*

Solve $8y + xy = 10$ for y. Find y when $x = -6$.

Step 1 Solve the equation for y.

$8y + xy = 10$	Write original equation.
____ $y = 10$	Distributive property
$y = \dfrac{10}{\boxed{}}$	Divide each side by ____.

Step 2 Substitute the given value into the equation.

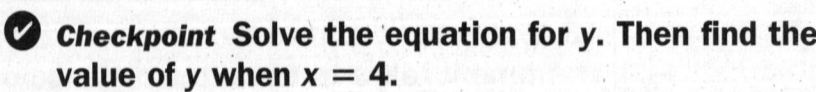

$y = \dfrac{10}{\boxed{}} = \_\_$ Substitute -6 for x.

✓ **Checkpoint** Solve the equation for y. Then find the value of y when $x = 4$.

| 4. $2y + 6x = 14$ | 5. $3y - 4xy = 26$ |

Homework

Lesson 1.4 • Algebra 2 Notetaking Guide

1.5 Use Problem Solving Strategies and Models

Goal • Solve problems using verbal models.

Your Notes

VOCABULARY

Verbal model

Example 1 Use a formula

A bus travels at an average rate of 55 miles per hour. The distance between Chicago and San Francisco is 2130 miles. How long would it take for the bus to travel from Chicago to San Francisco?

Solution

Use the distance formula for distance traveled as a verbal model.

| Distance (miles) | = | Rate (mi/h) | · | Time (hours) |

_____ = _____ · t

An equation for this situation is _____ = _____ t. Solve for t.

_____ = _____ t   Write equation.

_____ ≈ t   Divide each side by _____.

The amount of time it would take to travel from Chicago to San Francisco is about _____ hours.

CHECK You can use unit analysis to check your answer.

_____ miles ≈ $\dfrac{\boxed{} \text{ miles}}{\text{hour}}$ · _____ hours

Your Notes

✓ **Checkpoint** Complete the following exercise.

> 1. In Example 1, how fast is the bus traveling if it takes 22 hours to travel from San Francisco to Colorado Springs, a distance of 1335 miles?

Example 2 Look for a pattern

The table shows the height h of a jet airplane t minutes after beginning its descent. Find the height of the airplane after 9 minutes.

Time (min), t	0	1	2	3	4
Height (ft), h	35,000	32,000	29,000	26,000	23,000

Solution

The height decreases by 3000 feet per minute.

35,000   32,000   29,000   26,000   23,000
　　−3000　　−3000　　−3000　　−3000

You can use this pattern to write a verbal model for the height.

Height (feet)	=	Initial height (feet)	−	Rate of descent (feet/min)	·	Time (min)

h = _____ − _____ · t

An equation for the height is h = _____ − _____ t.

So, the height after 9 minutes is

h = _____ − _____ (_____) = _____ feet.

14   Lesson 1.5 • Algebra 2 Notetaking Guide

Your Notes

Example 3 — Draw a diagram

You want to paint five 1 foot wide stripes on the wall. There should be an equal amount of space between the ends of the wall and the stripes and between each pair of stripes. The wall is 14 feet long. How far apart should the stripes be?

Begin by drawing and labeling a diagram, as shown at the right.

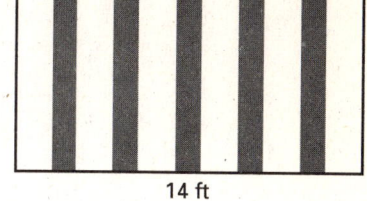

From the diagram, you can write and solve an equation to find x.

$x + 1 + x + 1 + x + 1 + x + 1 + x + 1 + x = 14$ Write equation.

$\underline{}x + \underline{} = 14$ Combine like terms.

$\underline{}x = \underline{}$ Subtract ___ from each side.

$x = \underline{}$ Divide each side by ___.

The stripes should be painted _____ feet apart.

✓ **Checkpoint** Complete the following exercises.

2. If a jet airplane descends at the rate given in the table, what is its height after 8 minutes?

Time (min), t	0	1	2	3	4
Height (ft), h	36,000	32,800	29,600	26,400	23,200

3. In Example 3, how far apart do the stripes need to be painted if you are only going to put 4 stripes on the wall?

Homework

1.6 Solve Linear Inequalities

Goal • Solve linear inequalities.

Your Notes

VOCABULARY

Linear inequality

Compound inequality

Equivalent inequalities

Example 1 *Graph simple inequalities*

a. Graph $x \leq 4$.   b. Graph $x > -2$.

Solution

a. The solutions are all real numbers _____ or _____ 4. A _____ dot is used in the graph to indicate 4 is a solution.

```
←—+——+——+——+——+——+——+——+——+→
  -2  -1   0   1   2   3   4   5   6
```

b. The solutions are all real numbers _____ -2. An _____ dot is used in the graph to indicate -2 is not a solution.

```
←—+——+——+——+——+——+——+——+——+→
  -4  -3  -2  -1   0   1   2   3   4
```

✓ **Checkpoint** Graph the inequality.

1. $x \leq -1$	2. $x > -3$
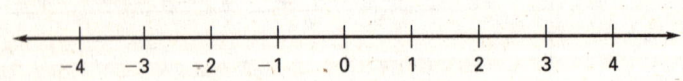	

16 Lesson 1.6 • Algebra 2 Notetaking Guide

Your Notes

Example 2 Graph compound inequalities

a. Graph $-3 < x < 1$.
b. Graph $x < -1$ or $x \geq 1$.

Solution

a. The solutions are all real numbers that are _____ than _____ and _____ than ___.

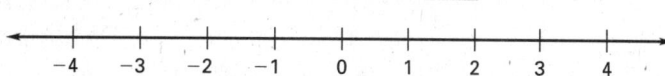

b. The solutions are all real numbers that are _____ than _____ or _____ or _____ to ___.

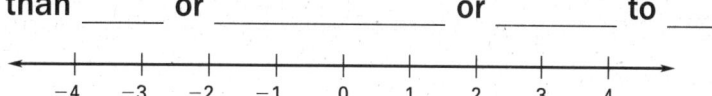

✓ **Checkpoint** Graph the inequality.

3. $x \leq 0$ or $x > 2$

TRANSFORMATIONS THAT PRODUCE EQUIVALENT INEQUALITIES

Transformation Applied to Inequality	Original Inequality	Equivalent Inequality
Add the same number to each side.	$x - 7 < 4$	$x <$ ___
Subtract the same number from each side.	$x + 3 \geq -1$	$x \geq$ ___
Multiply each side by the same positive number.	$\frac{1}{2}x > 10$	$x >$ ___
Divide each side by the same positive number.	$5x \leq 15$	$x \leq$ ___
Multiply each side by the same negative number and reverse the inequality.	$-x < 17$	x ___
Divide each side by the same negative number and reverse the inequality.	$-9x \geq 45$	x ___

Your Notes

Example 3 — Solve an inequality with a variable on both sides

Solve $4x + 5 > 9x - 10$. Then graph the solution.

$4x + 5 > 9x - 10$ Write original inequality.

_____ $+ 5 > -10$ Subtract _____ from each side.

$-5x > $ _____   Subtract ___ from each side.

$x < $ ___   Divide each side by _____ and _____ the inequality.

The solutions are real numbers _____ than ___.

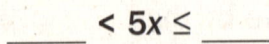

✔ Checkpoint Solve the inequality. Then graph the solution.

4. $x - 2 \leq 4x - 8$	5. $-7x + 6 > -1$

Example 4 — Solve an "and" compound inequality

Solve $-7 < 5x - 2 \leq 8$. Then graph the solution.

$-7 < 5x - 2 \leq 8$ Write original inequality.

$-7 + $ ___ $< 5x - 2 + $ ___ $\leq 8 + $ ___   Add 2 to each expression.

____ $< 5x \leq$ ____   Simplify.

____ $< x \leq$ ____   Divide each expression by ___.

The solutions are real numbers _____ than ____ and _____ than or equal to ___.

18 Lesson 1.6 • Algebra 2 Notetaking Guide   Copyright © McDougal Littell/Houghton Mifflin Company.

Your Notes

Example 5 — Solve an "or" compound inequality

Solve $4x - 7 \leq 5$ or $3x + 2 \geq 23$. Then graph the solution.

Solution

The solution of this inequality is a solution of either of its parts.

First Inequality		Second Inequality	
$4x - 7 \leq 5$	Write inequality.	$3x + 2 \geq 23$	Write inequality.
$4x \leq \underline{}$	Add ___ to each side.	$3x \geq \underline{}$	Subtract ___ from each side.
$x \leq \underline{}$	Divide each side by ___.	$x \geq \underline{}$	Divide each side by ___.

The solutions are all real numbers _____ than or equal to ___ or _____ than or equal to ___.

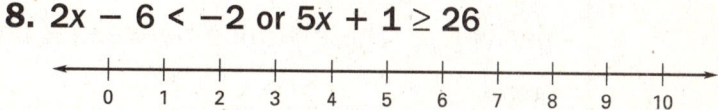

✓ **Checkpoint** Solve the inequality. Then graph the solution.

6. $-3 < 4x + 5 < 21$

7. $-9 < 2x - 3 \leq 1$

8. $2x - 6 < -2$ or $5x + 1 \geq 26$

Homework

1.7 Solve Absolute Value Equations and Inequalities

Goal • Solve absolute value equations and inequalities.

Your Notes

VOCABULARY

Absolute value

Extraneous solution

INTERPRETING ABSOLUTE VALUE EQUATIONS

Equation $|x| = |x - 0| = k$

Meaning The distance between x and 0 is ___.

Graph

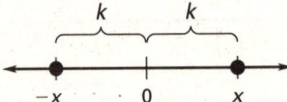

Solutions $x - 0 = -k$ or $x - 0 = k$

$x =$ ____ or $x =$ ____

Equation $|x - b| = k$

Meaning The distance between x and b is ___.

Graph

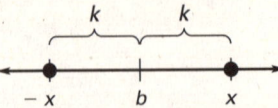

Solutions $x - b = -k$ or $x - b = k$

$x =$ _____ or $x =$ _____

Your Notes

> **Example 1** *Solve a simple absolute value equation*
>
> Solve $|x - 3| = 6$. Graph the solution.
>
> $|x - 3| = 6$ Write original equation.
>
> $x - 3 = \underline{}$ or $x - 3 = \underline{}$ Write equivalent equations.
>
> $x = \underline{}$ or $x = \underline{}$ Solve for *x*.
>
> $x = \underline{}$ or $x = \underline{}$ Simplify.
>
> The solutions are ____ and ___. These are the values of *x* that are ___ units away from ___ on a number line.
>
>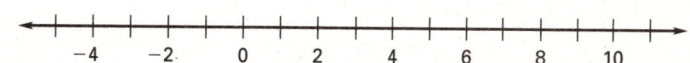

✔ **Checkpoint** Solve the equation. Then graph the solution.

1. $|x| = 5$

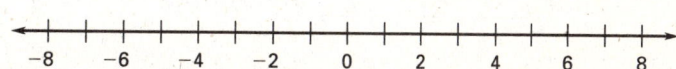

2. $|x - 5| = 2$

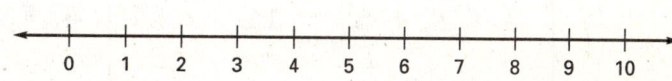

SOLVING AN ABSOLUTE VALUE EQUATION

Use these steps to solve an absolute value equation $|ax + b| = c$ where $c > 0$.

Step 1 Write two equations: $ax + b = \underline{}$ or $ax + b = \underline{}$.

Step 2 _____ each equation.

Step 3 **Check** each solution in the original _____ equation.

Your Notes

Example 2 *Solve an absolute value equation*

Solve $|4x + 10| = 6x$. Check for extraneous solutions.

$\|4x + 10\| = 6x$	Write original equation.
$4x + 10 = $ ___ or $4x + 10 = $ ___	Expression can equal ___ or ___.
$10 = $ ___ or $10 = $ ___	Subtract ___ from each side.
___ $= x$ or ___ $= x$	Solve for x.

Check the apparent solutions to see if either is extraneous.

CHECK

$|4x + 10| = 6x$ $|4x + 10| = 6x$

$|4(\_\_) + 10| \stackrel{?}{=} 6(\_\_)$ $|4(\_\_) + 10| \stackrel{?}{=} 6(\_\_)$

$|\_\_| \stackrel{?}{=} \_\_$ $|\_\_| \stackrel{?}{=} \_\_$

___ $=$ ___ ✓   ___ $\neq$ ___

The solution is ___. Reject ___ because it is an _____ solution.

> Always check your solutions in the original equation to make sure that they are not extraneous.

✔ **Checkpoint** Solve the equation. Check for extraneous solutions.

3. $\|2x + 5\| = 11$	4. $\|3x + 18\| = 6x$

ABSOLUTE VALUE INEQUALITIES

In the inequalities below, $c > 0$.

Inequality	Equivalent Form	Graph of Solution
$\|ax + b\|$ ___ c	$-c < ax + b < c$	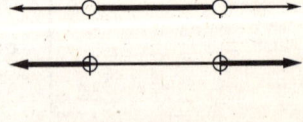
$\|ax + b\|$ ___ c	$ax + b < -c$ or $ax + b > c$	

> In the inequalities shown at the right, $\leq$ can replace $<$ and $\geq$ can replace $>$ and the graphs would have solid dots.

22 Lesson 1.7 • Algebra 2 Notetaking Guide

Your Notes

Example 3 *Solve an inequality of the form* $|ax + b| > c$

Solve $|2x + 5| > 3$. Then graph the solution.

The absolute value inequality is equivalent to
$2x + 5 <$ _____ or $2x + 5 >$ ___.

First Inequality		Second Inequality
$2x + 5 <$ _____	Write inequalities.	$2x + 5 >$ ___
$2x <$ _____	Subtract ___ from each side.	$2x >$ _____
$2x <$ _____	Divide each side by ___.	$x >$ _____

The solutions are all real numbers less than _____ or greater than _____.

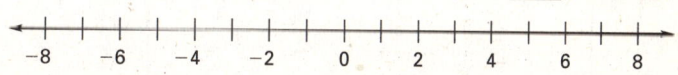

Example 4 *Solve an inequality of the form* $|ax + b| \le c$

Solve $|x - 1.5| \le 4.5$. Then graph the solution.

$x - 1.5 \le 4.5$ Write inequality.

_____ $\le x - 1.5 \le$ _____   Write equivalent compound inequality.

_____ $\le x \le$ _____   Add _____ to each expression.

The solution is between ___ and ___, inclusive.

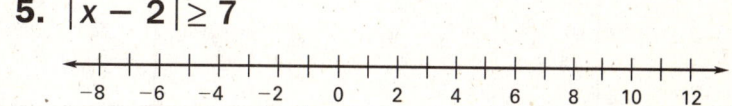

✓ **Checkpoint** Solve the inequality. Then graph the solution.

5. $|x - 2| \ge 7$

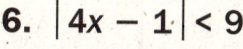

6. $|4x - 1| < 9$

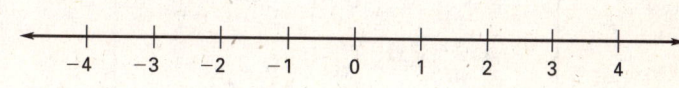

Homework

Words to Review

Give an example of the vocabulary word.

Opposite	Reciprocal
Power	Variable
Term	Coefficient
Identity	Equation
Linear equation	Solution
Equivalent Equations	Formula
Solve for a variable	Verbal model

Linear Inequality	Compound inequality
Equivalent inequalities	Absolute value
Extraneous solution	

Review your notes and Chapter 1 by using the Chapter Review on pages 61–64 of your textbook.

2.1 Represent Relations and Functions

Goal • Represent relations and graph linear functions.

Your Notes

VOCABULARY

Relation

Domain

Range

Function

Equation in two variables

Linear function

REPRESENTING RELATIONS

A relation can be represented in the following ways:

Ordered Pairs	Table		Graph	Mapping Diagram	
	x	y		Input	Output
(−2, 2)	−2	2		−2	2
(−2, −2)	−2	−2		0	2
(0, 1)	0	1		3	1
(3, 1)	3	1			

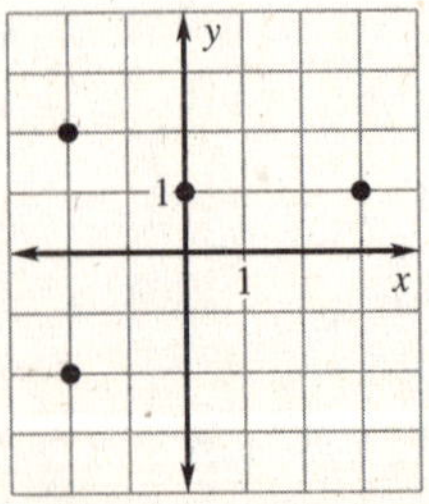

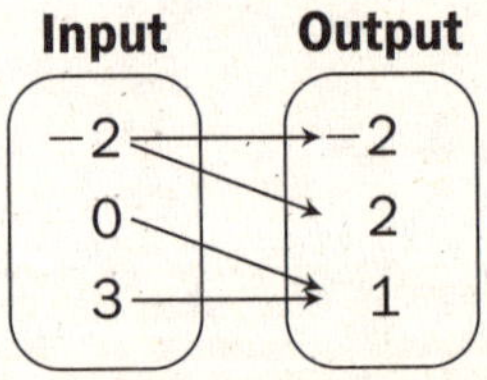

26 Lesson 2.1 • Algebra 2 Notetaking Guide

Your Notes

Example 1 — Identify functions

Tell whether each relation is a function. Explain.

a. 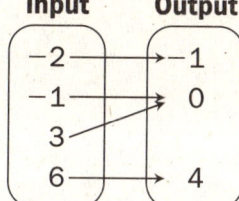   b.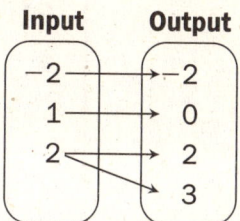

Solution

a. The relation _____ a function because each input is mapped onto _____ output.

b. The relation _____ a function because the input ___ is mapped onto ___ and ___.

✓ **Checkpoint** Complete the following exercise.

1. Is the relation given by the ordered pairs $(-5, 2)$, $(-3, -1)$, $(0, 0)$, $(0, 2)$ and $(0, 5)$ a function? Explain.

VERTICAL LINE TEST

A relation is a function if and only if no _____ line intersects the graph of the relation at more than _____.

Function   Not a function

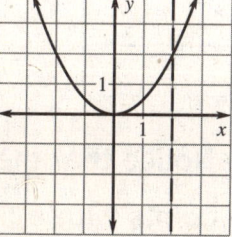   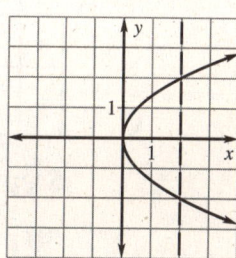

Your Notes

Example 2 — Use the vertical line test

Is the relation represented by the graph a function? Explain.

a. 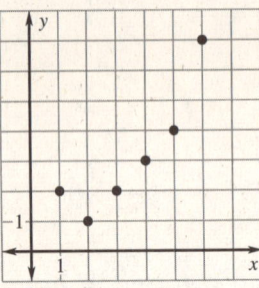   b.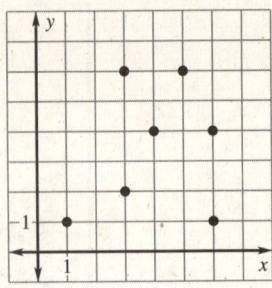

Solution

a. This graph _____ represent a function because no vertical line intersects the graph at more than _____.

b. This graph _____ represent a function because the vertical lines at $x =$ ___ and at $x =$ ___ intersect the graph at more than one point.

GRAPHING EQUATIONS IN TWO VARIABLES

To graph an equation in two variables, follow these steps:

Step 1 **Construct** a table of _____.

Step 2 **Plot** enough points from the table to recognize a _____.

Step 3 **Connect** the points with a _____ or _____.

Example 3 — Graph an equation in two variables

Graph the equation $y = -2x - 2$.

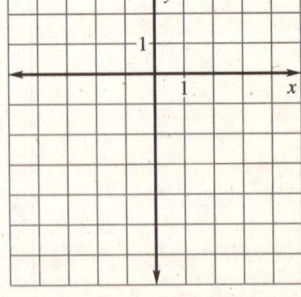

Solution

Step 1 **Construct** a table of values.

x	-2	-1	0	1	2
y	__	__	__	__	__

Step 2 **Plot** the points. Notice that they all lie on a _____.

Step 3 _____ the points with a line.

Your Notes

Example 4 — Classify and evaluate functions

Tell whether the function is linear. Then evaluate the function when $x = -3$.

a. $f(x) = 6x + 10$
b. $g(x) = 2x^2 + 4x - 1$

Solution

a. The function f is _____ because it has the form $f(x) = mx + b$.

$f(x) = 6x + 10$ Write function.

$f(\_\_\_) = 6(\_\_\_) + 10$ Substitute ___ for x.

$= \_\_\_$ Simplify.

b. The function g is _____ because it has an x^2-term.

$g(x) = 2x^2 + 4x - 1$ Write function.

$g(\_\_\_) = 2(\_\_\_)^2 + 4(\_\_\_) - 1$ Substitute ___ for x.

$= \_\_\_$ Simplify.

✓ Checkpoint Complete the following exercises.

2. Use the vertical line test to tell whether the relation is a function.

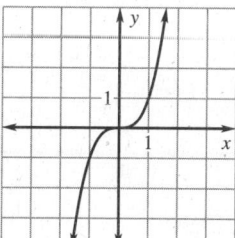

3. Graph the equation $y = 2x - 3$.

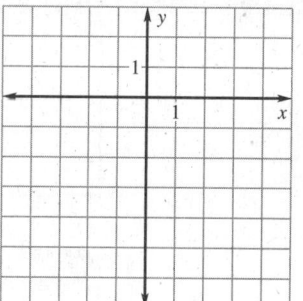

Tell whether the function is linear. Then evaluate the function when $x = -1$.

4. $f(x) = 2x^3 + 6 - x$

5. $g(x) = 4x + 9$

Homework

2.2 Find Slope and Rate of Change

Goal • Find slopes of lines and rates of change.

Your Notes

VOCABULARY

Slope

Parallel

Perpendicular

Rate of change

SLOPE OF A LINE

Words

The slope m of a nonvertical line is the ratio of _____ change (the rise) to _____ change (the run).

Algebra

$$m = \frac{y_2 - y_1}{x_2 - x_1} = \boxed{}$$

Graph

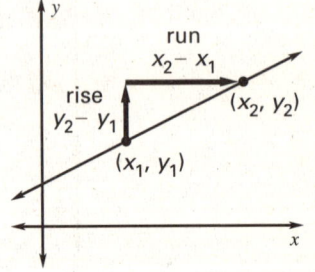

Example 1 Find slope

What is the slope of the line passing through the points (1, 3) and (6, 7)?

Let $(x_1, y_1) = (1, 3)$ and $(x_2, y_2) = (6, 7)$.

$$m = \frac{y_2 - y_1}{x_2 - x_1} = \boxed{} = \boxed{}$$

The slope of the line is ____.

> When calculating the slope, be sure to subtract the x- and y-coordinates in the correct order.

Your Notes

> A vertical line has "undefined slope" because for any two points, the slope formula's denominator becomes 0, and division by 0 is undefined.

CLASSIFICATION OF LINES BY SLOPE

The slope of a line indicates whether the line _____ from left to right, _____ from left to right, is _____, or is _____.

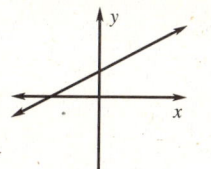 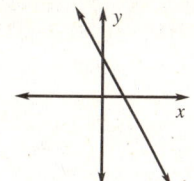 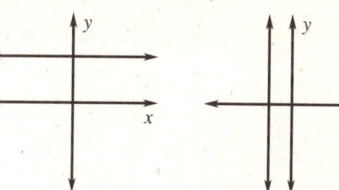

Positive slope   **Negative slope**   **Zero slope**   **Undefined slope**

Rises from left to right   Falls from left to right   Horizontal   Vertical

---

Example 2   *Classify lines using slope*

Without graphing, tell whether the line through the given points *rises, falls, is horizontal,* or is *vertical*.

a. (−6, −2), (1, 3)   b. (2, −1), (2, 2)

Solution

a. $m = \dfrac{\boxed{}}{\boxed{}} = \dfrac{\boxed{}}{\boxed{}}$ Because m ____ 0, the line _____.

b. $m = \dfrac{\boxed{}}{\boxed{}} = \dfrac{\boxed{}}{\boxed{}}$ Because m is _____, the line is _____.

✔ **Checkpoint** Complete the following exercises.

1. Find the slope of the line passing through the points (4, 2) and (7, 9).

2. Without graphing tell whether the line through the points (−3, 2) and (1, 4) *rises, falls, is horizontal,* or *is vertical*.

Your Notes

SLOPES OF PARALLEL AND PERPENDICULAR LINES

Consider two different nonvertical lines l_1 and l_2 with slopes m_1 and m_2.

Parallel lines The lines are parallel if and only if they have the _____ slope.

m_1 ___ m_2

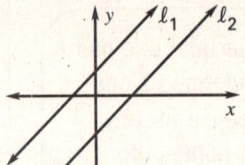

Perpendicular lines The lines are perpendicular if and only if their slopes are _____ of each other.

$m_1 = $ _____ , or $m_1 m_2 = $ _____

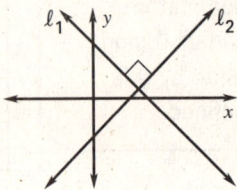

Example 3 *Classify parallel and perpendicular lines*

Tell whether the lines are *parallel* or *perpendicular*.

Line 1: through $(-3, -1)$ and $(2, 5)$
Line 2: through $(3, -4)$ and $(-3, 1)$

Find the slopes of the two lines.

$m_1 = \dfrac{\boxed{}}{\boxed{}} = \underline{} \qquad m_2 = \dfrac{\boxed{}}{\boxed{}} = \underline{}$

Because $m_1 m_2 = $ ___ (___) = ___ , m_1 and m_2 are negative _____ of each other. So, the lines are _____ .

Homework

✓ **Checkpoint** Tell whether the lines are *parallel*, *perpendicular*, or *neither*.

3. **Line 1:** through $(1, 0)$ and $(3, 4)$
   Line 2: through $(24, 6)$ and $(22, 5)$

2.3 Graph Equations of Lines

Goal • Graph linear equations in slope-intercept or standard form.

Your Notes

VOCABULARY

Parent function

y-intercept

Slope-intercept form

Standard form of a linear equation

x-intercept

PARENT FUNCTION FOR LINEAR FUNCTIONS

The parent function for the family of all linear functions is $y = $ ___. The graph of $y = x$ is shown.

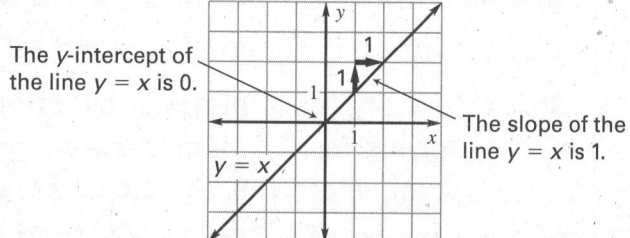

The y-intercept of the line $y = x$ is 0.

The slope of the line $y = x$ is 1.

In general, a _____ of a graph is the y-coordinate of a point where the graph intersects the y-axis.

Your Notes

USING SLOPE-INTERCEPT FORM TO GRAPH AN EQUATION

Step 1 Write the equation in _____ form by solving for y.

Step 2 _____ the y-intercept b and use it to plot the point (0, b) where the line crosses the ___-axis.

Step 3 Identify the _____ m and use it to plot a second point on the line.

Step 4 _____ a line through the two points.

Example 1   *Graph an equation in slope-intercept form*

Graph $y = -\frac{3}{2}x + 1$.

Step 1 The equation is already in slope-intercept form.

Step 2 The y-intercept is ___, so plot the point (___, ___) where the line crosses the _____.

Step 3 The slope is ___ or $\frac{\Box}{\Box}$, so plot a second point on the line by starting at (_____) and then moving down ___ units and right ___ units. The second point is (___, ____).

Step 4 Draw a line through the two points.

USING STANDARD FORM TO GRAPH AN EQUATION

Step 1 Write the equation in standard form.

Step 2 Identify the x-intercept by letting ___ = 0 and solving for ___. Use the x-intercept to plot the point where the line crosses the _____.

Step 3 Identify the y-intercept by letting ___ = 0 and solving for ___. Use the y-intercept to plot the point where the line crosses the _____.

Step 4 Draw a line through the two points.

Your Notes

Example 2 *Graph an equation in standard form*

Graph $2x + 3y = 12$.

Solution

Step 1 The equation is already in standard form.

Step 2

$2x + 3(\underline{}) = 12$ Let $y = \underline{}$.
$x = \underline{}$ Solve for x.

Plot the x-intercept at $(\underline{}, 0)$.

Step 3

$2(\underline{}) + 3y = 12$ Let $x = \underline{}$.
$y = \underline{}$ Solve for y.

Plot the y-intercept at $(0, \underline{})$.

Step 4 Draw a line through the two points.

HORIZONTAL AND VERTICAL LINES

Horizontal lines The graph of $y = c$ is the horizontal line through $(\underline{}, \underline{})$.

Vertical lines The graph of $x = c$ is the vertical line through $(\underline{}, \underline{})$.

Example 3 *Graph horizontal and vertical lines*

a. Graph $y = -1$.   b. Graph $x = 2$.

Solution

a. The graph of $y = -1$ is the _____ line that passes through the point $(0, \underline{})$. Notice that every point on the line has a y-coordinate of _____.

b. The graph of $x = 2$ is the _____ line that passes through the point $(\underline{}, 0)$. Notice that every point on the line has an x-coordinate of _____.

Your Notes

✓ **Checkpoint** Graph the equation.

1. $y = -2x + 2$

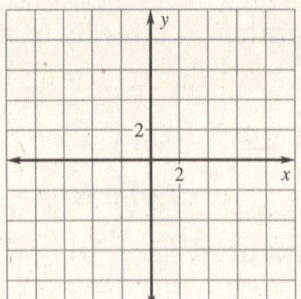

2. $y = \dfrac{4}{3}x - 4$

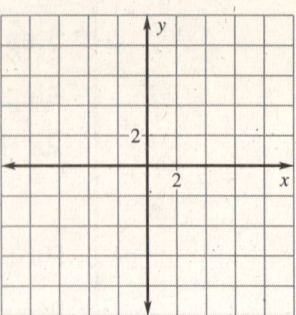

3. $4x + 2y = 8$

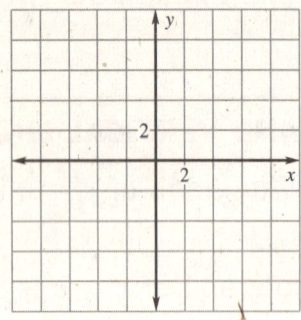

4. $-5x + 3y = 15$

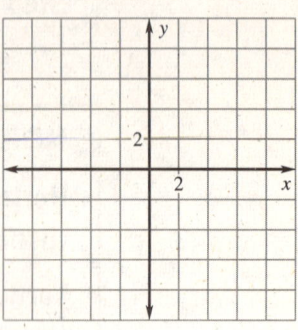

5. $y = 4$

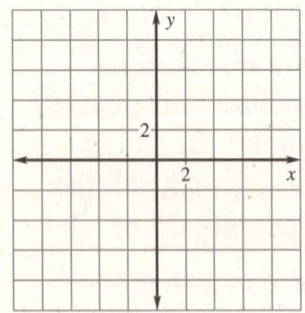

6. $x = -2$

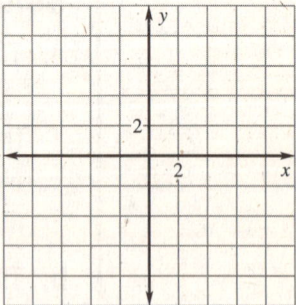

Homework

2.4 Write Equations of Lines

Goal • Write linear equations.

Your Notes

VOCABULARY

Point-slope form

WRITING AN EQUATION OF A LINE

Use slope-intercept form: Given slope m and y-intercept b, use the equation $y =$ _____.

Use point-slope form: Given slope m and a point (x_1, y_1), use the equation $y - y_1 =$ _____.

Use two points: Given points (x_1, y_1) and (x_2, y_2), first use the _____ formula to find m. Then use the _____ form with either given point.

Example 1 *Write an equation given the slope and y-intercept*

Write an equation of the line shown.

Solution

From the graph, you can see that the slope is $m =$ ____ and the y-intercept is $b =$ ___. Use the slope intercept form to write an equation of the line.

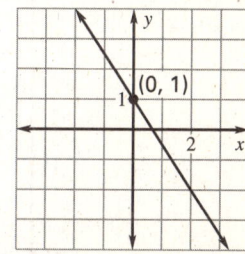

$y = mx + b$ Use slope-intercept form.

$y =$ ___ $x +$ ___   Substitute ___ for m and ___ for b.

Your Notes

Example 2 — Write an equation given the slope and a point

Write an equation of the line that passes through (2, 1) and has a slope of 2.

Solution

Because you know the slope and a point on the line, use the point-slope form to write an equation of the line. Let $(x_1, y_1) = (\underline{}, \underline{})$ and $m = \underline{}$.

$y - y_1 = m(x - x_1)$ Use point-slope form.

$y - \underline{} = \underline{}(x - \underline{})$ Substitute for m, x_1, and y_1.

$y - \underline{} = \underline{}x - \underline{}$ Distributive property

$y = \underline{}x - \underline{}$ Write in slope-intercept form.

Example 3 — Write equations of parallel or perpendicular lines

Write an equation of the line that passes through (−1, 1) and is (a) parallel to, and (b) perpendicular to, the line $y = -2x + 3$.

Solution

The given line has a slope of $m_1 = \underline{}$. A line that is parallel to it must have a slope of $m_2 = m_1 = \underline{}$. A line perpendicular to a line with slope $m_1 = \underline{}$ must have a slope of $m_2 = -\dfrac{1}{m_1} = \underline{}$. Use the point-slope form with $(x_1, y_1) = (\underline{}, \underline{})$ to write an equation of the line.

a. $y - y_1 = m_2(x - x_1)$

$y - \underline{} = \underline{}(x - \underline{})$

$y = \underline{}x - \underline{}$

b. $y - y_1 = m_2(x - x_1)$

$y - \underline{} = \underline{}(x - \underline{})$

$y = \underline{}x + \underline{}$

Your Notes

Example 4 — Write an equation given two points

Write an equation of the line through (3, 1) and (2, −3).

The line passes through $(x_1, y_1) = (3, 1)$ and $(x_2, y_2) = (2, -3)$. Find its slope.

$$m = \frac{y_2 - y_1}{x_2 - x_1} = \frac{\boxed{}}{\boxed{}} = \frac{\boxed{}}{\boxed{}} = \underline{}$$

Use the point-slope form with either given point to write an equation of the line.

$y - y_1 = m(x - x_1)$ Use point-slope form.

$\underline{} = \underline{}$ Substitute for m, x_1, and y_1.

$y = \underline{}$ Write in slope-intercept form.

✓ Checkpoint Write an equation of the line.

1. [graph showing line through (0, −3)]

2. Through (1, 5) with a slope of −2

3. Through (−2, 3) and (a) parallel and (b) perpendicular to $y = 4x - 6$

4. Through (6, 2) and (3, −2)

Homework

Lesson 2.4

2.5 Model Direct Variation

Goal • Write and graph direct variation equations.

Your Notes

VOCABULARY

Direct variation

Constant of variation

DIRECT VARIATION

Equation The equation $y =$ ____ represents direct variation between x and y, and y is said to _____ _____ with x. The nonzero constant a is called the constant of _____.

Graph The graph of a direct variation equation $y = ax$ is a _____ with slope a and y-intercept 0. The family of direct variation graphs consists of lines through the _____.

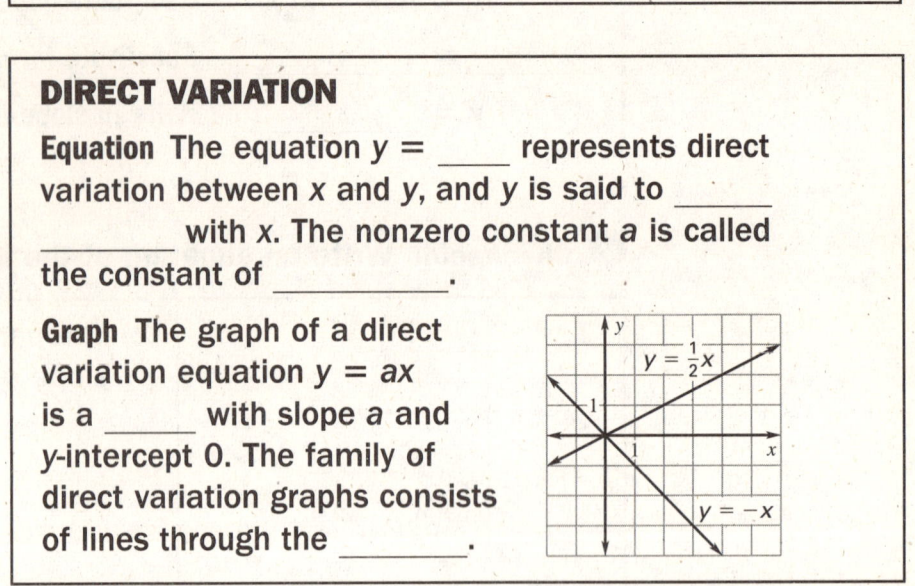

Example 1 *Write and graph a direct variation equation*

Write and graph a direct variation equation that has $(-3, 2)$ as a solution.

Solution

Use the given values of x and y to find the constant of variation.

$y = ax$ Write direct variation equation.

___ = a(___)   Substitute ___ for y and ___ for x.

___ = a   Solve for a.

The direct variation equation is $y =$ ___ x.

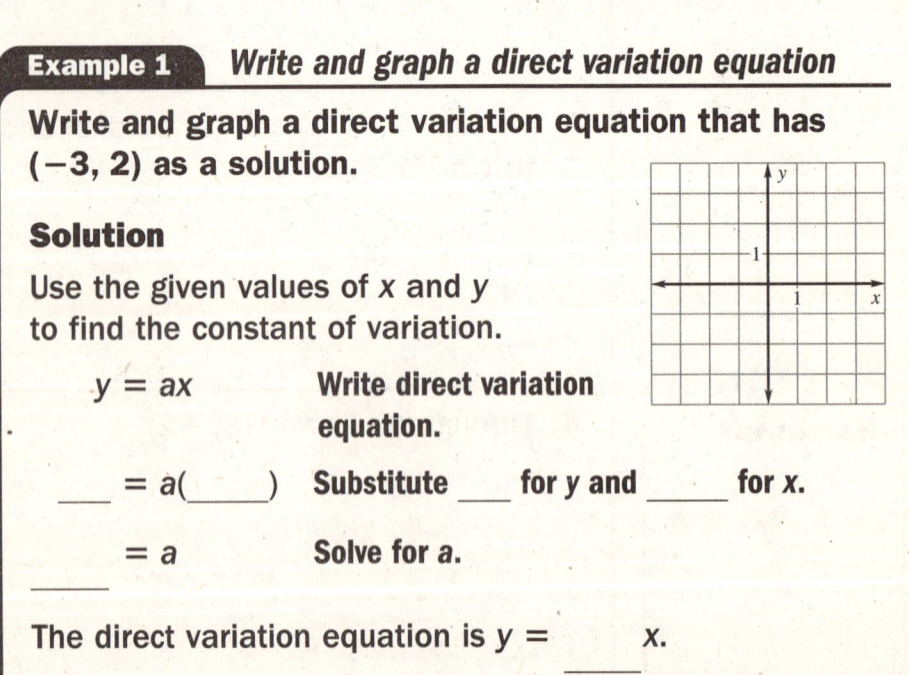

Your Notes

✓ **Checkpoint** Complete the following exercise.

1. Write and graph a direct variation equation that has the ordered pair (4, −2) as a solution.

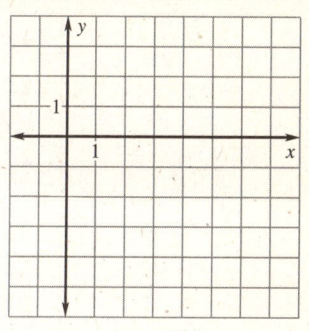

Example 2 *Write and apply a model for direct variation*

According to Hooke's law, the force that is needed to stretch a spring varies directly with the amount the spring is stretched.

a. If 64 pounds of force F stretches a spring a distance d of 8 inches, write an equation that relates F and d.

b. Predict the amount of force that is needed to stretch the spring to 14 inches.

Solution

a. Find the constant of variation.

$F = ad$ Write direct variation equation.

___ = a(___)   Substitute ___ for F and ___ for d.

___ = a   Solve for a.

An equation that relates F and d is $F =$ ___ d.

b. To stretch the spring $d = 14$ inches, the amount of force needed is $F =$ ___(___) = ___ pounds.

✓ **Checkpoint** Complete the following exercise.

2. In Example 2, suppose that the force being applied to the spring is 92 pounds. Predict how far the spring is being stretched.

Your Notes

Example 3 — Use ratios to identify direct variation

The table below gives sample cell phone bills, showing the total monthly cost and the number of minutes used that month. Tell whether total cost and the number of minutes show direct variation. If so, write an equation that relates the quantities.

Total cost, c (in dollars)	35	45	80	15	30
Minutes used, m	100	129	229	44	86

Solution

Find the ratio of the total cost c to the minutes used m for each month.

$$\frac{\boxed{}}{100} = \underline{} \qquad \frac{\boxed{}}{129} \approx \underline{} \qquad \frac{80}{\boxed{}} \approx 0.35$$

$$\frac{15}{\boxed{}} \approx 0.34 \qquad \frac{\boxed{}}{\boxed{}} \approx 0.35$$

Because the ratios are approximately equal, the data show direct variation.

An equation relating total cost to minutes used is $\frac{c}{m} =$ _____ or $c =$ _____ m.

✔ **Checkpoint** Complete the following exercise.

3. Tell whether the data in the table below shows direct variation. If so, write an expression relating x and y.

x	−1	1	3	5	7
y	−2	2	6	10	14

Homework

2.6 Draw Scatter Plots and Best Fitting Lines

Goal • Fit lines to data in scatter plots.

Your Notes

VOCABULARY

Scatter plot

Positive correlation

Negative correlation

Correlation coefficient

Best-fitting line

Example 1 Estimate correlation coefficients

For each scatter plot, describe the correlation shown and tell whether the correlation coefficient is closest to −1, −0.5, 0, 0.5, or 1.

a.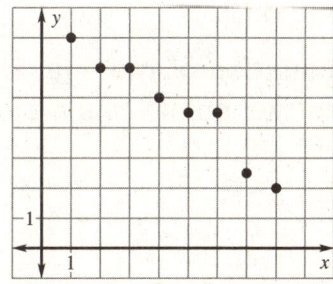

b.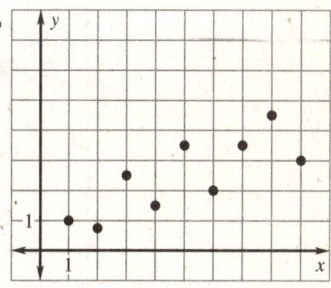

Solution

a. The scatter plot shows a _____ correlation. So, the best estimate given is $r =$ _____.

b. The scatter plot shows a _____ correlation. So, r is between ____ and ____ but not too close to either one. The best estimate given is $r =$ _____.

Your Notes

APPROXIMATING A BEST-FITTING LINE

Step 1 Draw a _____ of the data.

Step 2 Sketch the _____ that appears to follow most closely the trend given by the data points. There should be about as many points _____ the line as _____ it.

Step 3 Choose _____ on the line, and estimate the coordinates of each point.

Step 4 Write an _____ of the line that passes through the two points from Step 3.

Example 2 *Approximating a best-fitting line*

The table below gives the number of people y who atended each of the first seven football games x of the season. Approximate the best-fitting line for the data.

x	1	2	3	4	5	6	7
y	722	763	772	826	815	857	897

> Be sure that about the same number of points lie above your line of fit as below it.

1. **Draw** a _____.
2. **Sketch** the best-fit line.
3. **Choose** two points on the line. For the scatter plot shown, you might choose (1, _____) and (2, _____).

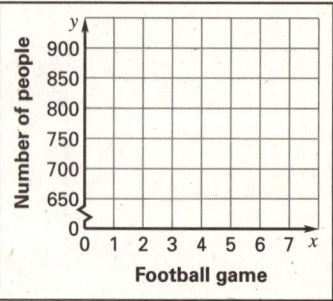

4. **Write** an equation of the line. The line that passes through the two points has a slope of:

$$m = \frac{\boxed{}}{\boxed{}} = \underline{}$$

Use the point-slope form to write the equation.

$y - y_1 = m(x - x_1)$ Point-slope form

$y - \underline{} = \underline{}$ Substitute for m, x_1, and y_1.

$y = \underline{}$ Simplify.

An approximation of the best-fitting line is $y = \underline{}$.

Your Notes

Example 3 *Use a line of fit to make predictions*

Use the equation of the line of best fit from Example 2 to predict the number of people that will attend the tenth football game.

Because you are predicting the tenth game, substitute _____ for x in the equation from Example 2.

y = _____ = _____ = _____

You can predict that _____ people will attend the tenth football game.

✓ **Checkpoint** Complete the following exercises.

For each scatter plot (a) tell whether the data has *positive correlation, negative correlation,* or *no correlation,* and (b) tell whether the correlation coefficient is closest to −1, −0.5, 0, 0.5, or 1.

1.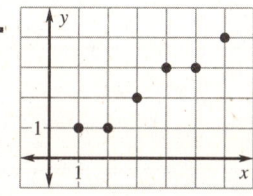

2.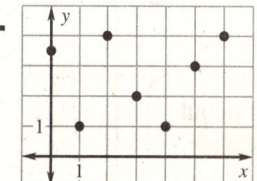

3. The table gives the average class score y on each chapter test for the first six chapters x of the textbook.

x	1	2	3	4	5	6
y	84	83	86	88	87	90

a. Approximate the best-fitting line for the data.

b. Use your equation from part (a) to predict the test score for the 9th test that the class will take.

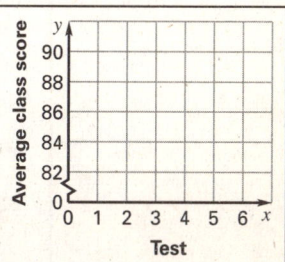

Homework

2.7 Use Absolute Value Functions and Transformations

Goal • Graph and write absolute value functions.

Your Notes

VOCABULARY

Absolute value function

Vertex of an absolute value graph

Transformation

Translation

Reflection

PARENT FUNCTION FOR ABSOLUTE VALUE FUNCTIONS

The parent function for the family of all absolute value functions is $y = |x|$. The graph of $y = |x|$ is _____ and is _____ about the y-axis. So, for every point (x, y) on the graph, the point $(-x, y)$ is also on the graph.

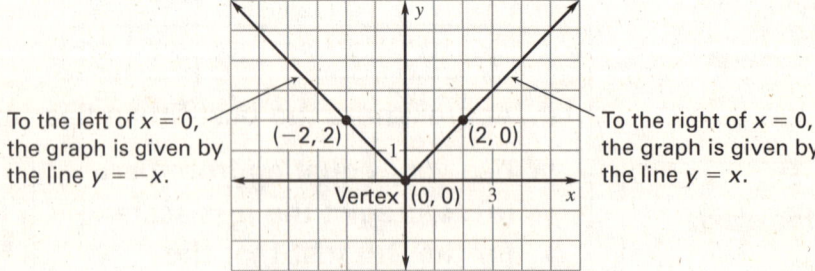

To the left of $x = 0$, the graph is given by the line $y = -x$.

$(-2, 2)$ $(2, 0)$

To the right of $x = 0$, the graph is given by the line $y = x$.

Vertex $(0, 0)$

The highest or lowest point on the graph of an absolute value function is called the _____ _____. The vertex of the graph $y = |x|$ is (___, ___).

Lesson 2.7 • Algebra 2 Notetaking Guide

Your Notes

TRANSFORMATIONS OF GENERAL GRAPHS

For $|a| > 1$, the graph is vertically _____ and $y = a|x|$ is _____ than the graph of $y = |x|$.

For $|a| < 1$, the graph is vertically _____ and $y = a|x|$ is _____ than the graph of $y = |x|$.

Example 1 *Graph functions of the form $y = a|x|$*

Graph (a) $y = \frac{1}{3}x$ and (b) $y = -2|x|$. Compare each graph with the graph of $y = |x|$.

a. The graph of $y = \frac{1}{3}|x|$ is the graph of $y = |x|$ vertically _____ by a factor of ___.
   The graph has a vertex (___, ___) and passes through (___, ___) and (___, ___).

b. The graph of $y = -2|x|$ is the graph of $y = |x|$ vertically _____ by a factor of ___ and then _____ in the x-axis. The graph has a vertex of (___, ___) and passes through (___, ___) and (___, ___).

✓ **Checkpoint** Graph the function. Compare the graph with $y = |x|$.

1. $y = 3|x|$

Your Notes

To identify the vertex, rewrite the given function as $y = -3|x - (-2)| + (-1)$. So, $h = -2$ and $k = -1$.

Example 2 *Graph a function of the form* $y = a|x - h| + k$

Graph $y = -3|x + 2| - 1$. Compare the graph with the graph of $y = |x|$.

Solution

1. Identify and plot the vertex, $(h, k) = (\underline{}, \underline{})$.

2. Plot another point on the graph such as $(\underline{}, \underline{})$. Use symmetry to pot a third point, $(\underline{}, \underline{})$.

3. Connect the points with a _____ graph.

4. Compare with $y = |x|$. The graph of $y = -3|x + 2| - 1$ is the graph of $y = |x|$ first stretched _____ by a factor of ___, then reflected in the _____, and finally translated _____ units and _____ unit.

Example 3 *Write an absolute value equation*

Write an equation of the graph shown.

Solution

The vertex of the graph is $(\underline{}, \underline{})$. So, the equation has the form $y = a|x - \underline{}| + \underline{}$. Substitute the coordinates of the point $(\underline{}, \underline{})$ into the equation and solve for a.

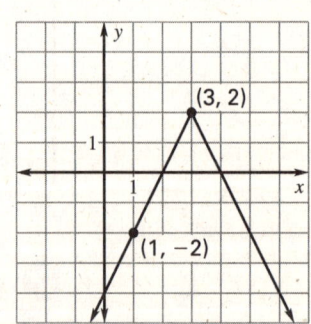

$\underline{} = a|\underline{}| + \underline{}$ Substitute for x and for y.

$\underline{} = a$ Solve for a.

An equation for the graph is $y = $ _____.

Your Notes

✓ **Checkpoint** Complete the following exercises.

2. Graph the function $y = -\frac{1}{2}|x - 1| - 2$. Compare the graph with the graph of $y = |x|$.

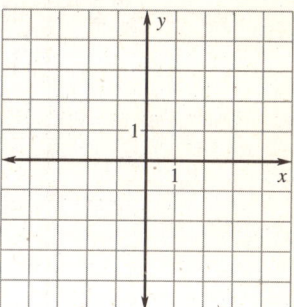

3. Write an equation of the graph shown.

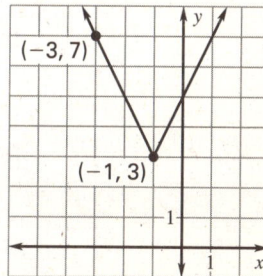

TRANSFORMATIONS OF GENERAL GRAPHS

The graph of $y = a \cdot f(x - h) + k$ can be obtained from the graph of $y = f(x)$ by performing these steps:

Step 1 **Stretch** or shrink the graph of $y = f(x)$ by a factor of $|a|$ if $|a| \neq 1$. If $|a| > 1$, _____ the graph. If $|a| < 1$, _____ the graph.

Step 2 **Reflect** the resulting graph from Step 1 in the x-axis if _____.

Step 3 **Translate** the resulting graph from Step 2 _____ h units and _____ k units.

Your Notes

Example 4   Apply transformations to a graph

The graph of a function $y = f(x)$ is shown. Sketch the graph of the given function.

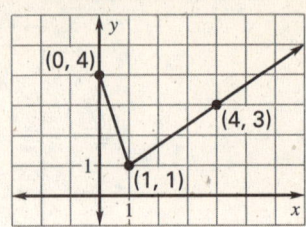

a. $y = \dfrac{1}{2} \cdot f(x)$

b. $y = -f(x - 1) + 2$

Solution

a. The graph of $y = \dfrac{1}{2} \cdot f(x)$ is the graph of $y = f(x)$ shrunk _____ by a factor of ___ .

To draw the graph, multiply the y-coordinate of each labeled point on the graph of $y = f(x)$ by ___ and connect their images.

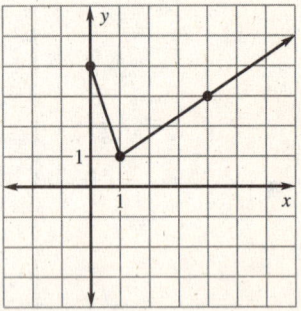

b. The graph of $y = -f(x - 1) + 2$ is the graph of $y = f(x)$ _____ in the x-axis, then translated _____ unit and _____ units. To draw the graph, first reflect the labeled points and connect their images. Then translate and connect these points to form the final image.

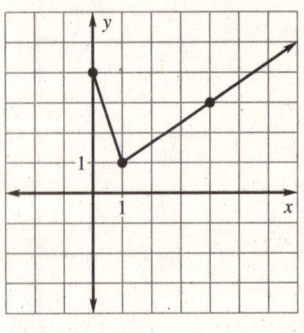

✓ **Checkpoint** Use the graph of $y = f(x)$ in Example 4 to graph the given function.

4. $y = -\dfrac{1}{4} \cdot f(x)$

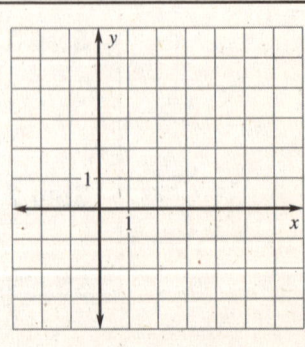

Homework

2.8 Graph Linear Inequalities in Two Variables

Goal • Graph linear inequalities in two variables.

Your Notes

VOCABULARY

Linear inequality in two variables

Solution of a linear inequality

Graph of a linear inequality

Half-plane

Example 1 *Checking solutions of inequalities*

Check whether the ordered pairs (a) (3, 2) and (b) (−1, 4) are solutions of $4x + 2y > 6$.

Ordered Pair	Substitute	Conclusion
a. (3, 2)	4(___) + 2(___) = _____	(3, 2) ___ a solution.
b. (−1, 4)	4(___) + 2(___) = _____	(−1, 4) _____ a solution.

✓ Checkpoint Check whether the ordered pair is a solution of $2x - y \leq 8$.

1. (6, 2)	2. (3, −1)

Lesson 2.8 • Algebra 2 Notetaking Guide 51

Your Notes

GRAPHING A LINEAR INEQUALITY

To graph a linear inequality in two variables, follow these steps:

Step 1 **Graph** the boundary line for the inequality. Use a _____ line for < or > and a _____ line for ≤ or ≥.

Step 2 **Test** a point _____ the boundary line to determine whether it is a solution of the inequality. If it ____ a solution shade the half-plane containing the point. If it _____ a solution, shade the other half-plane.

Example 2 *Graph a linear inequality with one variable*

Graph $y < -1$ in a coordinate plane.

Solution

1. **Graph** the boundary line $y = -1$. Use a _____ line because the inequality symbol is <.

2. **Test** the point (0, 0). Because (0, 0) _____ a solution of the inequality, shade the half-plane that _____ contain (0, 0).

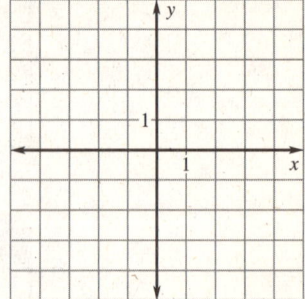

Example 3 *Graph a linear inequality with two variables*

Graph $3x - 2y < -6$ in a coordinate plane.

Solution

1. **Graph** the boundary line $3x - 2y = -6$. Use a _____ line because the inequality symbol is <.

2. **Test** the point (0, 0). Because (0, 0) _____ a solution of the inequality, shade the half-plane that _____ contain (0, 0).

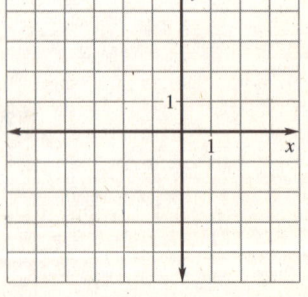

It is often convenient to use (0, 0) as a test point. However, if (0, 0) lies on a boundary line, you must choose a different test point.

Your Notes

Example 4 *Graph an absolute value inequality*

Graph $y > -3|x - 1| + 2$ in a coordinate plane.

1. **Graph** the equation of the boundary, $y = -3|x - 1| + 2$. Use a _____ line because the inequality symbol is >.

2. **Test** the point (0, 0). Because (0, 0) ____ a solution of the inequality, shade the portion of the coordinate plane _____ the absolute value graph.

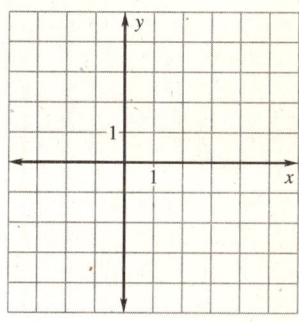

✓ **Checkpoint** Graph the inequality in a coordinate plane.

3. $x < -2$

4. $y \leq -x + 2$

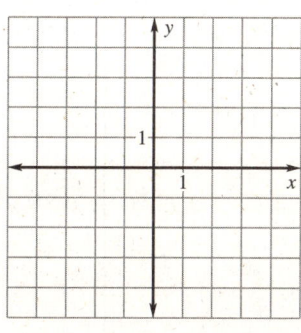

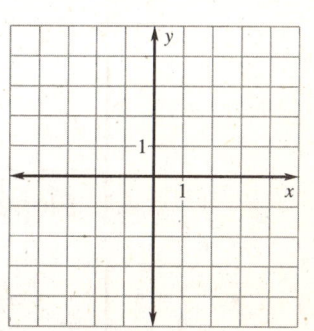

5. $9x + 3y > 9$

6. $y \geq 2|x + 2| - 1$

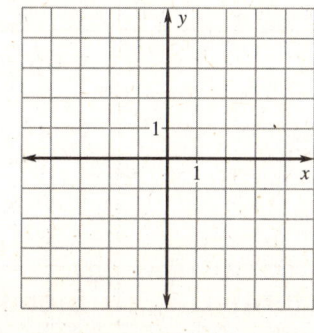

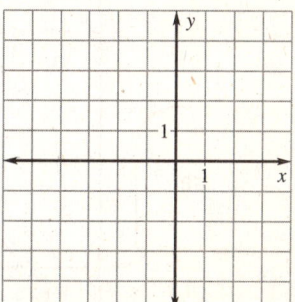

Homework

Words to Review

Give an example of the vocabulary word.

Relation	Domain
Range	Function
Equation in two variables	Linear function
Slope	Parallel
Perpendicular	Rate of change
Parent function	y-intercept
Slope-intercept form	Standard form of a linear equation

x-intercept	Point-slope form
Direct Variation	Constant of variation
Scatter plot	Positive correlation
Negative correlation	Correlation coefficient
Best-fitting line	Absolute value function

Vertex of an absolute value graph	Transformation

Translation	Reflection

Linear inequality in two variables	Solution of a linear inequality

Graph of linear inequality	Half-plane

Review your notes and Chapter 2 by using the Chapter Review on pages 141–144 of your textbook.

3.1 Solve Linear Systems by Graphing

Goal • Solve systems of linear equations.

Your Notes

VOCABULARY

System of two linear equations

Solution of a system

Consistent

Inconsistent

Independent

Dependent

Example 1 *Solve a system graphically*

Graph the system and estimate the solution. Then check the solution algebraically.

$4x + 2y = 4$ **Equation 1**
$2x - 3y = 10$ **Equation 2**

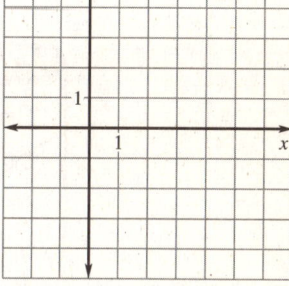

Solution

Graph both equations. The lines appear to intersect at (___, ___). Check this algebraically as follows:

Equation 1	Equation 2
$4x + 2y = 4$	$2x - 3y = 10$
$4(\_\_) + 2(\_\_) \stackrel{?}{=} 4$	$2(\_\_) - 3(\_\_) \stackrel{?}{=} 10$
$\_\_ = 4 \checkmark$	$\_\_ = 10 \checkmark$

> Remember to check the visual solution in *both* equations.

Your Notes

✓ **Checkpoint** Graph the linear system and estimate the solution. Then check the solution algebraically.

1. $4x + y = -2$
    $-6x - 3y = 12$

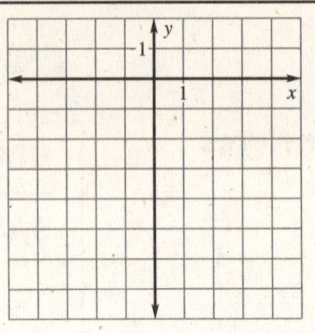

NUMBER OF SOLUTIONS OF A LINEAR SYSTEM

Exactly one solution	Infinitely many solutions	No solutions

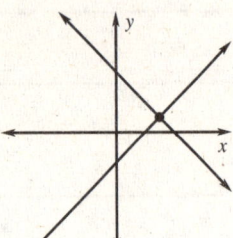 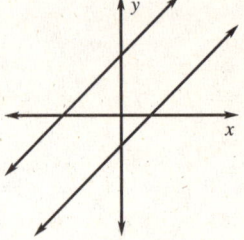

Lines intersect at _____ consistent and _____

Lines _____; consistent and _____

Lines are _____;

Example 2 *Solve a system with many solutions*

Solve the system. Then classify the system as *consistent and independent*, *consistent and dependent*, or *inconsistent*.

$-2x + y = 4$ Equation 1
$4x - 2y = -8$ Equation 2

The graphs of the equations are _____. So, each point on the line is a solution, and the system has _____ solutions. Therefore, the system is _____.

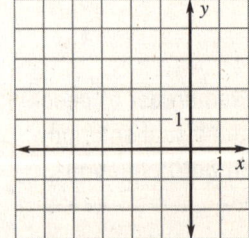

Your Notes

Example 3 Solve a system with no solution

Solve the system. Then classify the system as *consistent and independent*, *consistent and dependent*, or *inconsistent*.

$-2x + 4y = 8$ Equation 1
$-2x + 4y = -4$ Equation 2

Solution

The graphs of the equations are two _____. Therefore, the system is _____.

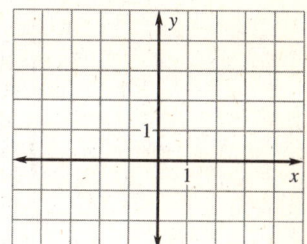

✓ **Checkpoint** Solve the system. Then classify the system as *consistent and independent*, *consistent and dependent*, or *inconsistent*.

2. $3x - 2y = -6$
    $-5x + 4y = 8$

    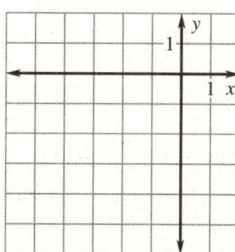

3. $-x - 2y = -5$
    $-2x - 4y = -10$

    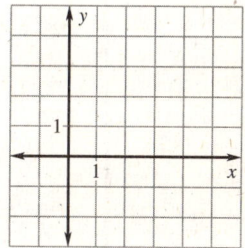

4. $6x - 3y = 12$
    $6x - 3y = -6$

    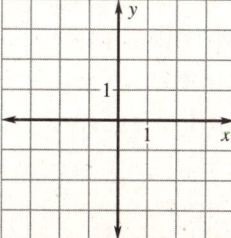

5. $x + y = 2$
    $4x - 3y = 1$

    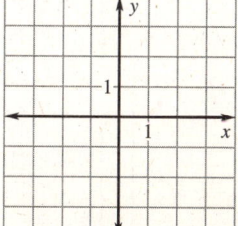

Lesson 3.1 • Algebra 2 Notetaking Guide

Your Notes

Example 4 Writing and using a linear system

Ice Cream Shop At an ice cream shop, one customer pays $9 for 2 sundaes and 2 milkshakes. A second customer pays $13 for 2 sundaes and 4 milkshakes. How much do each sundae and milkshake cost?

Verbal model

$$\boxed{\begin{array}{c}\text{Total}\\\text{cost}\\\text{(dollars)}\end{array}} = \boxed{\begin{array}{c}\text{Number}\\\text{of}\\\text{sundaes}\end{array}} \cdot \boxed{\begin{array}{c}\text{Cost per}\\\text{sundae}\\\text{(dollars/}\\\text{sundae)}\end{array}} + \boxed{\begin{array}{c}\text{Number}\\\text{of}\\\text{shakes}\end{array}} \cdot \boxed{\begin{array}{c}\text{Cost per}\\\text{shake}\\\text{(dollars/}\\\text{shake)}\end{array}}$$

___ = ___ · x + ___ · y   Equation 1 (Customer 1)

___ = ___ · x + ___ · y   Equation 2 (Customer 2)

Graph the equations

___x + ___y = ___ and
___x + ___y = ___.

The lines appear to intersect at about the point (___, ___).

Check this algebraically.

___(___) + ___(___) = ___ + ___ = 9 ✓ Equation 1 checks.

___(___) + ___(___) = ___ + ___ = 13 ✓ Equation 2 checks.

The solution is (___, ___). So, each sundae costs $___ and each milkshake costs $___.

✓ **Checkpoint** Complete the following exercise.

6. In Example 4, how much do each sundae and milkshake cost if the first customer pays $7 and the second customer pays $10?

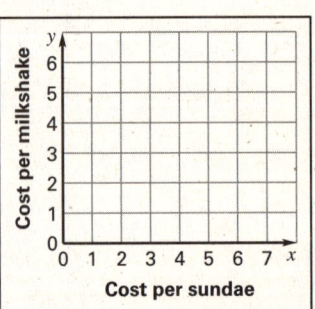

Homework

3.2 Solve Linear Systems Algebraically

Goal • Solve linear systems algebraically.

Your Notes

VOCABULARY

Substitution method

Elimination method

THE SUBSTITUTION METHOD

Step 1 Solve one of the equations for one of its variables.

Step 2 Substitute the expression from _____ into the other equation and solve for the other variable.

Step 3 Substitute the value from _____ into the revised equation from Step 1 and solve.

Example 1 *Use the substitution method*

Solve the system using the substitution method.

$x + 2y = -2$ Equation 1
$3x + 4y = 6$ Equation 2

1. **Solve** Equation 1 for x.

   $x =$ _____   Revised Equation 1.

2. **Substitute** into Equation 2 and solve for y.

   $3(\underline{\quad\quad}) + 4y = 6$ Substitute for x.

   $y =$ ____   Solve for y.

3. **Substitute** into revised Equation 1 and solve for x.

   $x =$ _____   Write revised Equation 1.

   $x =$ _____   Substitute −6 for y.

   $x =$ ____   Simplify.

   The solution is (____, ____).

Your Notes

THE ELIMINATION METHOD

Step 1 Multiply one or both of the equations by a _____ to obtain coefficients that differ only in _____ for one of its variables.

Step 2 Add the revised equations from _____. Combining like terms will _____ one of the variables. Solve for the remaining variable.

Step 3 Substitute the value obtained in _____ into either of the original equations and solve for the other variable.

Example 2 *Use the elimination method*

Solve the system using the elimination method.

$2x + 5y = 14$ **Equation 1**

$4x + 2y = -4$ **Equation 2**

1. **Multiply** Equation 1 by _____ so that the coefficients of x differ only in sign.

   $2x + 5y = 14$ × _____   _____

   $4x + 2y = -4$ _____

2. **Add** the revised equations and solve for y.   _____

        $y = $ ___

3. **Substitute** the value of y into one of the original equations. Solve for x.

   $2x + 5y = 14$ Write Equation 1.

   $2x + 5(\_\_) = 14$ Substitute for y.

   $2x + \_\_\_ = 14$ Simplify.

   $x = \_\_\_$ Solve for x.

The solution is (____, ___).

CHECK You can check the solution algebraically using the method shown in Example 1. You can also use a graphing calculator to check the solution.

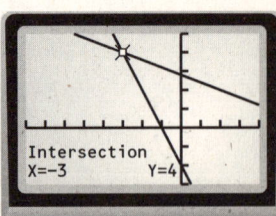

Lesson 3.2 • Algebra 2 Notetaking Guide

Your Notes

✓ **Checkpoint** Complete the following exercises.

1. Solve the linear system using the substitution method.

   $2x + y = -2$
   $5x + 3y = -8$

2. Solve the linear system using the elimination method.

   $3x + 8y = -5$
   $-2x + 2y = 18$

Example 3 *Use the elimination method*

Solve the linear system using the elimination method.

$3x - 4y = -37$ **Equation 1**
$-5x + 3y = 14$ **Equation 2**

Solution

Multiply Equation 1 by ___ and Equation 2 by ___ so that the coefficients of x only differ in sign.

$3x - 4y = -37$ × ___   _____
$-5x + 3y = 14$ × ___   _____

Add the revised equations and solve for y.

$y = $ ___

Substitute the value of y into one of the original equations and solve for x.

$3x - 4y = -37$ Write equation 1.
$3x - 4(\_\_\_) = -37$ Substitute for y.
$x = $ ___   Solve for x.

The solution is (___, ___). Check the solution algebraically or graphically.

Your Notes

Example 4 — Solve linear systems with many or no solutions

Solve the linear system.

a. $x - 3y = 7$
    $2x - 6y = 12$

b. $2x - 6y = 12$
    $-5x + 15y = -30$

Solution

a. Because the coefficient of x in the first equation is ___, use the substitution method. Solve the first equation for x.

   $x - 3y = 7$

   $x =$ _____

   Substitute the expression for x into the second equation.

   $2x - 6y = 12$ Write second equation.

   $2(\underline{}) - 6y = 12$ Substitute for x.

   ___ = ___   Simplify.

   Because the statement ___ = ___ is _____, there _____.

b. Because no coefficient is _____, use the elimination method. Multiply the first equation by ___ and the second equation by ___.

   $2x - 6y = 12$ × ___   _____
   $-5x + 15y = -30$ × ___   _____

   Add the revised equations.   _____

   Because the equation ___ = ___ is _____, there _____.

✓ Checkpoint Solve the linear system.

3. $2x - y = 6$
    $8x - 4y = 13$

4. $2x + 3y = 7$
    $5x + 7y = 15$

Homework

3.3 Graph Systems of Linear Inequalities

Goal • Graph systems of linear inequalities

Your Notes

VOCABULARY

System of linear inequalities

Solution of a system of linear inequalities

Graph of a system of linear inequalities

GRAPHING A SYSTEM OF LINEAR INEQUALITIES

To graph a system of linear inequalities, follow these steps:

Step 1 Graph each inequality in the system. You may want to use colored pencils to distinguish the different _____.

Step 2 Identify the region that is _____ to all the graphs of the inequalities. This region is the graph of the system. If you used colored pencils, the graph of the system is the region that has been shaded with _____ color.

Example 1 Graph a system of two inequalities

Graph the system.

$y < 2x + 1$ Inequality 1
$y \leq -x - 3$ Inequality 2

Graph each inequality in the system. Use different shades for each half-plane. **Identify** the region that is _____ to both graphs.

> The graph of the system is the intersection of the shaded regions.

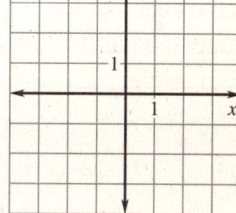

Lesson 3.3 • Algebra 2 Notetaking Guide 65

Your Notes

The shaded regions _____ intersect.

Example 2 Graph a system with no solution

Graph the system. $y \le -\dfrac{3}{4}x + 1$ Inequality 1

$3x + 4y > 16$ Inequality 2

Graph each inequality in the system. Use different shades for each half-plane. **Identify** the region that is common to both graphs. There is no region shaded _____. So, the system has _____.

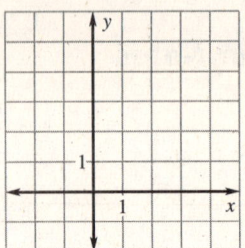

✓ **Checkpoint** Graph the system of inequalities.

1. $y > 2x - 3$
   $y \le -\dfrac{1}{2}x + 2$

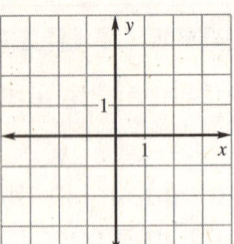

2. $-x + 3y > -6$
   $y \le \dfrac{1}{3}x + 1$

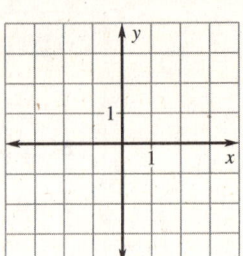

Example 3 Graph a system with an absolute value inequality

Graph the system. $y \le 4$ Inequality 1

$y > |x - 2| + 1$ Inequality 2

The graph of the system is the intersection of the shaded regions.

Graph each inequality in the system. Use different shades for each region. **Identify** the region that is _____ to both graphs.

66 Lesson 3.3 • Algebra 2 Notetaking Guide

Your Notes

Example 4 *Solve a multi-step problem*

Pizzas You are selling pizzas to raise money for a school field trip. Cheese pizzas cost $8 and pepperoni pizzas cost $9. You need to sell at least two of each pizza type, and you want to sell at least $150 worth of pizzas.

a. Write and graph a system of linear inequalities that describes the information given above.

b. You sell 12 cheese pizzas and 10 pepperoni pizzas. Did you reach your sales goal?

Solution

a. Let x be the number of cheese pizzas sold and let y be the number of pepperoni pizzas sold. From the given information, you can write the following system of inequalities.

$x \geq$ ___   Must sell at least ___ cheese pizzas.

$y \geq$ ___   Must sell at least ___ pepperoni pizzas.

_____   Total sales must be at least $____.

Graph the system of inequalities.

b. From the graph, you can see see that (12, 10) ___ in the solution region. By selling 12 cheese pizzas and 10 pepperoni pizzas you ___ reach your sales goal.

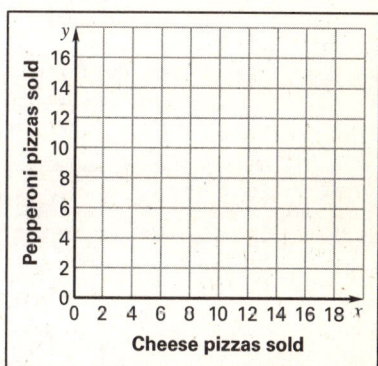

✓ **Checkpoint** Graph the system.

3. $y > x - 1$

   $y \leq \frac{1}{2}|x + 2|$

   $x \geq -2$

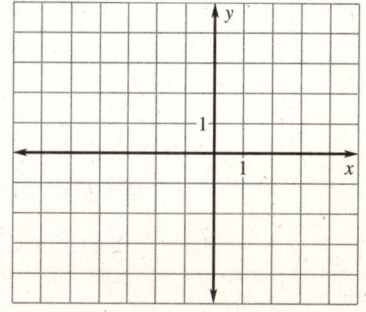

Homework

3.4 Solve Systems of Linear Equations in Three Variables

Goal • Solve systems of equations in three variables.

Your Notes

VOCABULARY

Linear equation in three variables

System of three linear equations

Solution of a system of three linear equations

Ordered triple

THE ELIMINATION METHOD FOR A THREE-VARIABLE SYSTEM

Step 1 Rewrite the linear system in three variables as a linear system in _____ variables by using the elimination method.

Step 2 Solve the new linear system for both of its variables.

Step 3 Substitute the values found in _____ into one of the original equations and solve for the remaining variable.

If you obtain a _____ equation, such as 0 = 1, in any of the steps, then the system has _____.

If you do not obtain a false equation, but obtain an _____ such as 0 = 0, then the system has _____.

Your Notes

Example 1   *Use the elimination method*

Solve the system. $3x - 2y + 4z = 20$ **Equation 1**
$-x + 5y + 12z = 73$ **Equation 2**
$x + 3y - 2z = 1$ **Equation 3**

1. **Rewrite** the system as a linear system in two variables.

   $3x - 2y + 4z = 20$ Add _____ times the third equation to the first.
   _____
   _____   New Equation 1

   $-x + 5y + 12z = 73$ Add the third equation to the second.
   $x + 3y - 2z = 1$
   _____   New Equation 2

2. **Solve** the new linear system for both of its variables.

   _____   Add _____ times new Equation 2 to new Equation 1.
   _____
   _____

   $y = $ ___   Solve for y.

   $z = $ ___   Substitute y in new Equation 1 or 2 and solve for z.

3. **Substitute** y and z into an original equation and solve.

   $x + 3y - 2z = 1$ Equation 3
   $x + $ _____ $= 1$ Substitute for y and z.
   $x = $ ___   Solve for x.

The solution is the ordered triple (___, ___, ___). Check the solution in each of the original equations.

✓ **Checkpoint** Solve the linear system.

1. $4x - 3y + 5z = -19$
   $3x + -y - 8z = -21$
   $-2x + y + 3z = 13$

Your Notes

Example 2 Solve a three-variable system with no solution

Solve the system. $2x + 4y + 10z = 14$ Equation 1
$x + 2y + 5z = -4$ Equation 2
$3x - 4y - 3z = 15$ Equation 3

$2x + 4y + 10z = 14$ Add _____ times the second
_____   equation to the first.
_____   New Equation 1

Because you obtain a _____, you can conclude that the original system has _____.

Example 3 Solve a three-variable system with many solutions

Solve the system. $2x - 2y + 4z = 6$ Equation 1
$4x + 2y + 8z = 12$ Equation 2
$4x - 2y + 8z = 12$ Equation 3

1. **Rewrite** the system as a linear system in two variables.

   $2x - 2y + 4z = 6$ Add the first equation
   $4x + 2y + 8z = 12$ to the second.
   _____   New Equation 1

   $4x + 2y + 8z = 12$ Add the second equation
   $4x - 2y + 8z = 12$ to the third.
   _____   New Equation 2

2. **Solve** the new linear system for both of its variables.

   _____   Add ___ times new Equation 1
   _____   and _____ times new
   _____   Equation 2.

   Because you obtain the identity ___ = ___, the system has _____.

3. **Describe** the solution. One way to do this is to divide new Equation 1 by 6 to get _____ or $x =$ _____. Substituting this into original Equation 1 produces $y =$ ___. So, any ordered triple of the form (_____, ___, ___) is a solution of the system.

Your Notes

Example 4 — Solve a system using substitution

Solve the system.
$$2x + y + z = 8 \quad \text{Equation 1}$$
$$-x + 3y - 2z = 3 \quad \text{Equation 2}$$
$$y = x + z \quad \text{Equation 3}$$

1. **Rewrite** the system as a linear system in two variables by substituting $x + z$ for y in Equations 1 and 2.

$2x + y + z = 8$	Write Equation 1.
$2x + (\underline{\quad}) + z = 8$	Substitute for y.
$\underline{\quad} = \underline{\quad}$	New Equation 1.
$-x + 3y - 2z = 3$	Write Equation 2.
$-x + 3(\underline{\quad}) - 2z = 3$	Substitute for y.
$\underline{\quad} = \underline{\quad}$	New Equation 2.

2. **Solve** the new linear system in two variables.

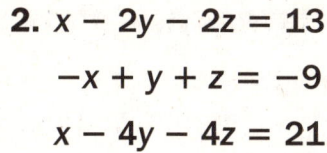

	Add new Equation 1 and -2 times new Equation 2.
$x = \underline{\quad}$	Solve for x.
$z = \underline{\quad}$	Substitute into new Equation 1 or new Equation 2 to find z.
$y = \underline{\quad}$	Substitute into an original equation to find y.

The solution is (___, ___, ___).

✓ Checkpoint Solve the linear system.

2. $x - 2y - 2z = 13$
$-x + y + z = -9$
$x - 4y - 4z = 21$

3. $2x - 2y + z = 7$
$4x - 4y + 2z = 17$
$3x + 2y - 6z = -2$

Homework

3.5 Perform Basic Matrix Operations

Goal • Perform operations with matrices.

Your Notes

VOCABULARY

Matrix

Dimensions

Elements

Equal matrices

Scalar

Scalar multiplication

ADDING AND SUBTRACTING MATRICES

To add or subtract two matrices, simply add or subtract _____ elements. You can add or subtract matrices only if they have the same _____.

Adding Matrices
$$\begin{bmatrix} a & b \\ c & d \end{bmatrix} + \begin{bmatrix} e & f \\ g & h \end{bmatrix} = \begin{bmatrix} a+e & b+f \\ c+g & d+h \end{bmatrix}$$

Subtracting Matrices
$$\begin{bmatrix} a & b \\ c & d \end{bmatrix} - \begin{bmatrix} e & f \\ g & h \end{bmatrix} = \begin{bmatrix} a-e & b-f \\ c-g & d-h \end{bmatrix}$$

Your Notes

Example 1 — Add and subtract matrices

Perform the indicated operation, if possible.

a. $\begin{bmatrix} 6 & -2 \\ 1 & 3 \end{bmatrix} - \begin{bmatrix} 3 \\ 2 \end{bmatrix}$

b. $\begin{bmatrix} -2 & 1 \\ 0 & 3 \\ 7 & 6 \end{bmatrix} + \begin{bmatrix} 1 & -4 \\ -2 & 9 \\ 1 & 5 \end{bmatrix}$

Solution

a. The dimensions of $\begin{bmatrix} 6 & -2 \\ 1 & 3 \end{bmatrix}$ are _____ and the dimensions of $\begin{bmatrix} 3 \\ 2 \end{bmatrix}$ are _____. So, you _____ subtract the matrices.

b. The dimensions are _____. So, add the matrices.

$\begin{bmatrix} -2 & 1 \\ 0 & 3 \\ 7 & 6 \end{bmatrix} + \begin{bmatrix} 1 & -4 \\ -2 & 9 \\ 1 & 5 \end{bmatrix} = \begin{bmatrix} & \\ & \\ & \end{bmatrix}$

$= \begin{bmatrix} \end{bmatrix}$

Example 2 — Multiply a matrix by a scalar

Perform the indicated operation, if possible.

a. $3 \begin{bmatrix} 0 & 2 & -7 \\ -1 & 6 & 4 \end{bmatrix} = \begin{bmatrix} \end{bmatrix}$

$= \begin{bmatrix} \end{bmatrix}$

b. $-2 \begin{bmatrix} 1 & 0 \\ 3 & -5 \end{bmatrix} = \begin{bmatrix} \end{bmatrix} = \begin{bmatrix} \end{bmatrix}$

✓ **Checkpoint** Perform the indicated operation, if possible.

1. $\begin{bmatrix} -6 & 2 \\ -1 & -5 \end{bmatrix} - \begin{bmatrix} 3 & 0 \\ 7 & -1 \end{bmatrix}$

2. $-3 \begin{bmatrix} -1 & 3 & -2 & 4 \\ 2 & 9 & -6 & 0 \end{bmatrix}$

Your Notes

PROPERTIES OF MATRIX OPERATIONS

Let A, B, and C be matrices with the same dimensions, and let k be a scalar.

Associative Property of Addition
$(A + B) + C =$ _____

Commutative Property of Addition $A + B =$ _____

Distributive Property of Addition $k(A + B) =$ _____

Distributive Property of Subtraction $k(A - B) =$ _____

Example 3   *Solve a multi-step problem*

Pet Stores Two pet stores sell both dogs and cats. Sales from each store for last month and this month are shown below.

Last Month: Store 1 sold 42 dogs, 33 cats.
Store 2 sold 56 dogs, 21 cats.

This Month: Store 1 sold 36 dogs, 51 cats.
Store 2 sold 48 dogs, 37 cats.

Organize the data into matrices, then write and interpret a matrix giving the average monthly sales for the two month period.

Organize the data into two 2 × 2 matrices.

```
        Last month(A)              This month(B)
         dogs cats                  dogs cats
Store 1 [        ]         Store 1 [        ]
Store 2 [_____]         Store 2 [_____]
```

Write a matrix for the average monthly sales by adding A and B and then multiplying the result by $\frac{1}{2}$.

$\frac{1}{2}(A + B) = \frac{1}{2}\left(\begin{bmatrix} \end{bmatrix} + \begin{bmatrix} \end{bmatrix}\right)$

$= \frac{1}{2}\begin{bmatrix} \end{bmatrix} = \begin{bmatrix} \end{bmatrix}$

Store 1 sold an average of ____ dogs and ____ cats, while Store 2 sold an average of ____ dogs and ____ cats.

Your Notes

Example 4 — Solve a matrix equation

Solve the matrix equation for x and y.

$$4\left(\begin{bmatrix} 3x & 1 \\ 0 & 6 \end{bmatrix} + \begin{bmatrix} 1 & -3 \\ 2 & -2y \end{bmatrix}\right) = \begin{bmatrix} -8 & -8 \\ 8 & 0 \end{bmatrix}$$

Solution

Simplify the left side of the equation.

$4\left(\begin{bmatrix} 3x & 1 \\ 0 & 6 \end{bmatrix} + \begin{bmatrix} 1 & -3 \\ 2 & -2y \end{bmatrix}\right) = \begin{bmatrix} -8 & -8 \\ 8 & 0 \end{bmatrix}$ Write original equation.

$4\left(\begin{bmatrix} \underline{} \end{bmatrix}\right) = \begin{bmatrix} -8 & -8 \\ 8 & 0 \end{bmatrix}$ Add matrices inside parentheses.

$\begin{bmatrix} \underline{} \end{bmatrix} = \begin{bmatrix} -8 & -8 \\ 8 & 0 \end{bmatrix}$ Perform scalar multiplication.

Equate corresponding elements and solve the two resulting equations.

$\underline{} = -8$ $\underline{} = 0$

$x = \underline{}$ $y = \underline{}$

✓ **Checkpoint** Complete the following exercises.

3. Solve the matrix equation for x and y.

$$-2\left(\begin{bmatrix} 3 & -2x \\ 1 & 7 \end{bmatrix} - \begin{bmatrix} 1 & -6 \\ -5y & 4 \end{bmatrix}\right) = \begin{bmatrix} -4 & 12 \\ 8 & -6 \end{bmatrix}$$

Homework

3.6 Multiply Matrices

Goal • Multiply matrices.

Your Notes

Example 1 — Describe matrix products

State whether the product AB is defined. If so, give the dimensions of AB.

a. A: 2 × 3, B: 4 × 3   b. A: 3 × 3, B: 3 × 2

a. Because the number of _____ in A (three) _____ the number of _____ in B (four), the product AB _____ defined.

b. Because A is a 3 × 3 matrix and B is a 3 × 2 matrix, the product AB ____ defined and is a _____ matrix.

MULTIPLYING MATRICES

Words To find the element in the *i*th row and *j*th column of the product matrix AB, multiply each element in the _____ by the corresponding element in the _____, then add the products.

Algebra
$$\overset{A}{\begin{bmatrix} a & b \\ c & d \end{bmatrix}} \cdot \overset{B}{\begin{bmatrix} e & f \\ g & h \end{bmatrix}} = \overset{AB}{\begin{bmatrix} ae+bg & af+bh \\ ce+dg & cf+dh \end{bmatrix}}$$

Example 2 — Find the product of two matrices

Find AB if $A = \begin{bmatrix} 1 & -2 \\ 5 & -4 \end{bmatrix}$ and $B = \begin{bmatrix} 3 & -6 \\ 7 & -1 \end{bmatrix}$.

Because A is a 2 × 2 matrix and B is a 2 × 2 matrix, the product AB ____ defined and is a _____ matrix.

$$AB = \begin{bmatrix} 1 & -2 \\ 5 & -4 \end{bmatrix} \begin{bmatrix} 3 & -6 \\ 7 & -1 \end{bmatrix}$$

$$= \begin{bmatrix} 1(\_\_) + (-2)(\_\_) & 1(\_\_) + (-2)(\_\_) \\ 5(\_\_) + (-4)(\_\_) & 5(\_\_) + (-4)(\_\_) \end{bmatrix}$$

$$= \begin{bmatrix} & \\ & \end{bmatrix}$$

Your Notes

✓ **Checkpoint** Given A and B, give the dimensions of AB. Then find AB.

1. $A = \begin{bmatrix} 6 & 2 \\ -1 & 3 \\ 0 & -4 \end{bmatrix}$, $B = \begin{bmatrix} -1 & 2 \\ 5 & -2 \end{bmatrix}$

2. $A = \begin{bmatrix} 4 & -6 \\ 7 & 3 \end{bmatrix}$, $B = \begin{bmatrix} 9 \\ 2 \end{bmatrix}$

Example 3 *Use matrix operations*

If $A = \begin{bmatrix} 4 & -3 \\ -1 & 2 \end{bmatrix}$, $B = \begin{bmatrix} 1 & 7 \\ -4 & -2 \end{bmatrix}$, and $C = \begin{bmatrix} 3 & -5 & -2 \\ 1 & 0 & 6 \end{bmatrix}$, evaluate each expression.

a. $(A + B)C$
b. $AC + BC$

Solution

a. $(A + B)C = \left(\begin{bmatrix} 4 & -3 \\ -1 & 2 \end{bmatrix} + \begin{bmatrix} 1 & 7 \\ -4 & -2 \end{bmatrix} \right) \begin{bmatrix} 3 & -5 & -2 \\ 1 & 0 & 6 \end{bmatrix}$

$= \underline{} \begin{bmatrix} 3 & -5 & -2 \\ 1 & 0 & 6 \end{bmatrix} = \underline{}$

b. $AC + BC = \begin{bmatrix} 4 & -3 \\ -1 & 2 \end{bmatrix} \begin{bmatrix} 3 & -5 & -2 \\ 1 & 0 & 6 \end{bmatrix}$
$+ \begin{bmatrix} 1 & 7 \\ -4 & -2 \end{bmatrix} \begin{bmatrix} 3 & -5 & -2 \\ 1 & 0 & 6 \end{bmatrix}$

$= \underline{} + \underline{}$

$= \underline{}$

Your Notes

PROPERTIES OF MATRIX MULTIPLICATION

Let A, B, and C be matrices and let k be a scalar.

Associative Property of Matrix Multiplication	$A(BC) = $ _____
Left Distributive Property	$A(B + C) = $ _____
Right Distributive Property	$(A + B)C = $ _____
Associative Property of Scalar Multiplication	$k(AB) = $ _____ = _____

Example 4   *Use matrices to calculate total cost*

The school stores from the middle school and the high school each submit an inventory list for the year. Each sweatshirt costs $15, each T-shirt costs $9, and each pennant costs $5. Use matrix multiplication to find the total cost of the inventory for each school store.

Middle School: 61 sweatshirts, 63 T-shirts, and 74 pennants

High School: 58 sweatshirts, 71 T-shirts, and 92 pennants

Write the inventory and the cost in matrix form.

```
              Inventory                      Cost
                                           Dollars
       Sweatshirt T-shirt Pennant     Sweatshirt  [ __ ]
Middle [  __       __      __  ]      T-shirt     [ __ ]
High   [  __       __      __  ]      Pennant     [ __ ]
```

> Remember to set up the matrices so that the columns of the inventory matrix match the rows of the cost matrix.

Find the total cost of inventory for each school store by multiplying the inventory matrix by the cost matrix.

$$\begin{bmatrix} 61 & 63 & 74 \\ 58 & 71 & 92 \end{bmatrix} \begin{bmatrix} 15 \\ 9 \\ 5 \end{bmatrix} = \underline{}$$

$$= \underline{}$$

Label the product matrix:

                                        Total Cost
                                          Dollars

Middle School
High School
[__]

The total cost for the Middle School store is $_____, and the total cost for the High School store is $_____.

Your Notes

✓ **Checkpoint** Complete the following exercises.

3. If $A = \begin{bmatrix} -2 & 1 \\ 3 & -2 \\ 0 & 4 \end{bmatrix}$, $B = \begin{bmatrix} -2 & -4 \\ 5 & 1 \end{bmatrix}$, and $C = \begin{bmatrix} -3 \\ 2 \end{bmatrix}$, find $A(BC)$.

4. In Example 4, suppose that a sweatshirt costs $17, a T-shirt costs $11, and a pennant costs $7. Calculate the total cost of inventory for each school store.

Homework

3.7 Evaluate Determininants and Apply Cramer's Rule

Goal • Evaluate determinants of matrices.

Your Notes

VOCABULARY

Determinant

Cramer's Rule

Coefficient matrix

THE DETERMINANT OF A MATRIX

Determinant of a 2 × 2 matrix

$$\det \begin{bmatrix} a & b \\ c & d \end{bmatrix} = \begin{vmatrix} a & b \\ c & d \end{vmatrix} = \underline{} - \underline{}$$

Determinant of a 3 × 3 matrix

$$\det \begin{bmatrix} a & b & c \\ d & e & f \\ g & h & i \end{bmatrix} =$$

$$\begin{vmatrix} a & b & c & a & b \\ d & e & f & d & e \\ g & h & i & g & h \end{vmatrix} = (aei + bfg + cdh) - (gec + hfa + idb)$$

Your Notes

Example 1 Evaluate determinants

Evaluate the determinant of the matrix.

a. $\begin{bmatrix} 4 & -3 \\ 5 & 2 \end{bmatrix}$ b. $\begin{bmatrix} 1 & 1 & 2 \\ -1 & 3 & 4 \\ 0 & 2 & 6 \end{bmatrix}$

Solution

a. $\begin{vmatrix} 4 & -3 \\ 5 & 2 \end{vmatrix} = 4(\_\_) - 5(\_\_) = _____ = \_\_$

b. $\begin{vmatrix} 1 & 1 & 2 \\ -1 & 3 & 4 \\ 0 & 2 & 6 \end{vmatrix}$ = (_____ −

= _____ = __

AREA OF A TRIANGLE

The area of a triangle with vertices
(x_1, y_1), (x_2, y_2), and (x_3, y_3) is given by

Area = $\pm \, \underline{} \begin{vmatrix} x_1 & y_1 & 1 \\ x_2 & y_2 & 1 \\ x_3 & y_3 & 1 \end{vmatrix}$

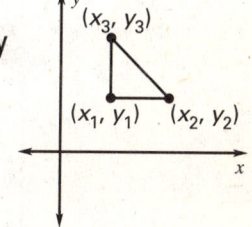

where the symbol ± indicates that the appropriate sign should be chosen to yield a _____ value.

Example 2 The area of a triangle

Find the area of the triangle shown.

Area = $\pm \dfrac{1}{2} \begin{vmatrix} \_\_ & \_\_ & 1 \\ \_\_ & \_\_ & 1 \\ \_\_ & \_\_ & 1 \end{vmatrix}$

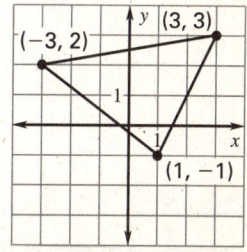

= $\pm \dfrac{1}{2}[\underline{}]$ = ___

Your Notes

✓ **Checkpoint** Complete the following exercises.

1. Evaluate the determinant of $\begin{bmatrix} 2 & -4 \\ 3 & 7 \end{bmatrix}$.	2. Find the area of a triangle with vertices (1, 4), (3, 1), and (−1, 0).

CRAMER'S RULE FOR A 2 × 2 SYSTEM

Let A be the coefficient matrix of this linear system:

$ax + by = e$
$cx + dy = f$

If det $A \neq$ ____, then the system has _____ solution.

$$x = \frac{\begin{vmatrix} e & b \\ f & d \end{vmatrix}}{\det A} \quad \text{and} \quad y = \frac{\begin{vmatrix} a & e \\ c & d \end{vmatrix}}{\det A}$$

Example 3 Use Cramer's rule for a 2 × 2 system

Use Cramer's Rule to solve this system:

$3x + 2y = -4$
$2x - 7y = -11$

Evaluate the determinant of the _____ matrix.

$\begin{vmatrix} \underline{\quad} & \underline{\quad} \\ \underline{\quad} & \underline{\quad} \end{vmatrix} = \underline{\quad\quad\quad} = \underline{\quad}$

Apply Cramer's rule because the determinant is not ___.

$x = \dfrac{\begin{vmatrix} \underline{\quad} & \underline{\quad} \\ \underline{\quad} & \underline{\quad} \end{vmatrix}}{\underline{\quad\quad}} = \dfrac{\underline{\quad\quad}}{\underline{\quad\quad}} = \underline{\quad}$

$y = \dfrac{\begin{vmatrix} \underline{\quad} & \underline{\quad} \\ \underline{\quad} & \underline{\quad} \end{vmatrix}}{\underline{\quad\quad}} = \dfrac{\underline{\quad\quad}}{\underline{\quad\quad}} = \underline{\quad}$

Remember to check your solution in each of the original equations.

The solution is (____, ____).

Your Notes

CRAMER'S RULE FOR A 3 × 3 SYSTEM

Let A be the coefficient matrix of the linear system:

$ax + by + cz = j$
$dx + ey + fz = k$
$gx + hy + iz = \ell$

If det A ≠ ___, then the system has _____ solution.

$$x = \frac{\begin{vmatrix} j & b & c \\ k & e & f \\ \ell & h & i \end{vmatrix}}{\det A}, \quad y = \frac{\begin{vmatrix} a & j & c \\ d & k & f \\ g & \ell & i \end{vmatrix}}{\det A}, \quad z = \frac{\begin{vmatrix} a & b & j \\ d & e & k \\ g & h & \ell \end{vmatrix}}{\det A}$$

Example 4 — Use Cramer's rule for a 3 × 3 system

Use Cramer's rule to solve this system:

$3x + 4y - z = 9$
$-2x - 3y + 4z = -14$
$4x - y + z = -18$

Evaluate the determinant of the _____ matrix.

$$\begin{vmatrix} \_\_ & \_\_ & \_\_ \\ \_\_ & \_\_ & \_\_ \\ \_\_ & \_\_ & \_\_ \end{vmatrix} = \underline{\qquad\qquad}$$

$= \_\_\_$

Apply Cramer's rule because the determinant is not ___.

$x = \dfrac{\qquad}{\qquad} = \dfrac{\quad}{\quad} = \_\_\_$

$y = \dfrac{\qquad}{\qquad} = \dfrac{\quad}{\quad} = \_\_\_$

$z = \dfrac{\qquad}{\qquad} = \dfrac{\quad}{\quad} = \_\_\_$

Your Notes

✓ **Checkpoint** Use Cramer's rule to solve the system.

3. $3x + y = 4$
   $5x + 4y = -5$

4. $2x - 3y - 2z = -10$
   $-x + 2y + 3z = 14$
   $4x + y + 2z = -4$

Homework

3.8 Use Inverse Matrices to Solve Linear Systems

Goal • Solve linear systems using inverse matrices.

Your Notes

VOCABULARY

Identity matrix

Inverse matrices

Matrix of variables

Matrix of constants

THE INVERSE OF A 2 × 2 MATRIX

The inverse of the matrix $A = \begin{bmatrix} a & b \\ c & d \end{bmatrix}$ is

$A^{-1} = \dfrac{1}{\boxed{}} \begin{bmatrix} d & -b \\ -c & a \end{bmatrix} = \dfrac{1}{\boxed{}} \begin{bmatrix} d & -b \\ -c & a \end{bmatrix}$

provided $\underline{} \neq 0$.

Example 1 Find the inverse of a 2 × 2 matrix

Find the inverse of $A = \begin{bmatrix} 3 & -2 \\ 4 & -4 \end{bmatrix}$.

$A^{-1} = \dfrac{1}{\boxed{}} \begin{bmatrix} \end{bmatrix}$

$= \underline{} \begin{bmatrix} \end{bmatrix} = \begin{bmatrix} \end{bmatrix}$

> You can check the inverse by showing that $AA^{-1} = I = A^{-1}A$.

Your Notes

Example 2 — Solve a matrix equation

Solve the matrix equation $AX = B$ for the 2×2 matrix X.

$$\overbrace{\begin{bmatrix} -3 & -1 \\ 4 & 1 \end{bmatrix}}^{A} X = \overbrace{\begin{bmatrix} 9 & 4 \\ -12 & -3 \end{bmatrix}}^{B}$$

Begin by finding the inverse of A.

$$A^{-1} = \frac{}{\underline{\hspace{1cm}}} \begin{bmatrix} \underline{\hspace{1cm}} \end{bmatrix} = \begin{bmatrix} \underline{\hspace{1cm}} \end{bmatrix}$$

To solve the equation for X, multiply both sides of the equation by A^{-1} on the left.

$$\begin{bmatrix} \underline{\hspace{1cm}} \end{bmatrix} \begin{bmatrix} -3 & -1 \\ 4 & 1 \end{bmatrix} X$$

$$= \begin{bmatrix} \underline{\hspace{1cm}} \end{bmatrix} \begin{bmatrix} 9 & 4 \\ -12 & -3 \end{bmatrix} \qquad A^{-1}AX = A^{-1}B$$

$$\begin{bmatrix} \underline{\hspace{1cm}} \end{bmatrix} X = \begin{bmatrix} \underline{\hspace{1cm}} \end{bmatrix} \qquad IX = A^{-1}B$$

$$X = \begin{bmatrix} \underline{\hspace{1cm}} \end{bmatrix} \qquad X = A^{-1}B$$

Example 3 — Find the inverse of a 3×3 matrix

Use a graphing calculator to find the inverse of A. Then use the calculator to verify your result.

$$A = \begin{bmatrix} 3 & 2 & -1 \\ 7 & 5 & 0 \\ 5 & 3 & -2 \end{bmatrix}$$

Solution

Enter the matrix A into a graphing calculator and calculate A^{-1}. Then compute _____ and _____ to verify that you obtain the _____ identity matrix.

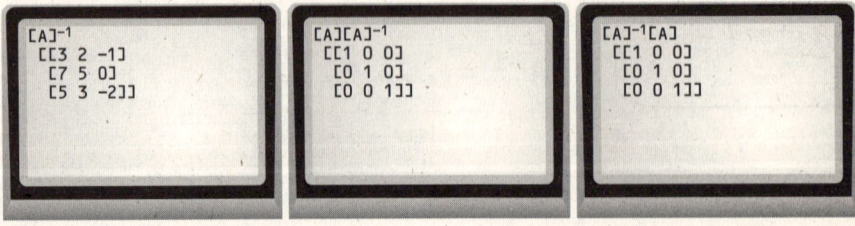

Your Notes

USING AN INVERSE MATRIX TO SOLVE A LINEAR SYSTEM

Step 1 Write the system as a matrix equation $AX = B$. The matrix A is the _____ matrix, X is the matrix of _____, and B is the matrix of _____.

Step 2 Find the inverse of matrix A.

Step 3 Multiply each side of $AX = B$ by A^{-1} on the _____ to find the solution $X = A^{-1}B$.

Example 4 *Solve a linear system*

Use an inverse matrix to solve the linear system.

$2x + 3y = 15$ **Equation 1**
$x - 2y = -17$ **Equation 2**

Solution

If A does not have an inverse, then the system has either no solution or infinitely many solutions.

1. Write the linear system as a matrix equation $AX = B$.

$$\begin{matrix} A & X & B \end{matrix}$$
$$[\quad\quad]\begin{bmatrix} x \\ y \end{bmatrix} = [\quad]$$

2. Find the inverse of matrix A.

$$A^{-1} = \underline{\quad\quad}\begin{bmatrix} -2 & -3 \\ -1 & 2 \end{bmatrix} = \begin{bmatrix} \quad \\ \quad \end{bmatrix}$$

3. Multiply the matrix of constants by A^{-1} on the left.

$$X = A^{-1}B = [\quad\quad][\quad] = [\quad] = \begin{bmatrix} x \\ y \end{bmatrix}$$

The solution of the system is (____, ____).

Your Notes

✓ **Checkpoint** Complete the following exercises.

1. Find the inverse of the matrix. $\begin{bmatrix} 6 & 4 \\ 4 & 3 \end{bmatrix}$	2. Solve the matrix equation. $\begin{bmatrix} -7 & 3 \\ -5 & 2 \end{bmatrix} X = \begin{bmatrix} -6 & 9 \\ -7 & 5 \end{bmatrix}$
3. Use a calculator to find the inverse of the matrix. Check the result. $\begin{bmatrix} -1 & 2 & 0 \\ 3 & -6 & 1 \\ -2 & 0 & 4 \end{bmatrix}$	4. Use an inverse matrix to solve the linear system. $3x + 2y = 8$ $-2x - 5y = 2$

Homework

Words to Review

Give an example of the vocabulary word.

System of two linear equations	Solution of a system
Consistent	Inconsistent
Independent	Dependent
Substitution Method	Elimination Method
System of linear inequalities	Solution of a system of linear inequalities.

Graph of a system of linear inequalities	Linear equation in three variables
System of three linear equations	Solution of a system of three linear equations
Ordered Triple	Matrix
Dimensions of a matrix	Elements of a matrix
Equal matrices	Scalar

Scalar Multiplication	Determinant
Cramer's Rule	Coefficient matrix
Identity matrix	Inverse matrices
Matrix of variables	Matrix of constants

Review your notes and Chapter 3 by using the Chapter Review on pages 222–226 of your textbook.

4.1 Graph Quadratic Functions in Standard Form

Goal • Graph quadratic functions.

Your Notes

VOCABULARY

Quadratic function

Parabola

Vertex

Axis of symmetry

Minimum and maximum value

PARENT FUNCTION FOR QUADRATIC FUNCTIONS

The parent function for the family of all quadratic functions is $f(x) =$ _____. The graph is shown below.

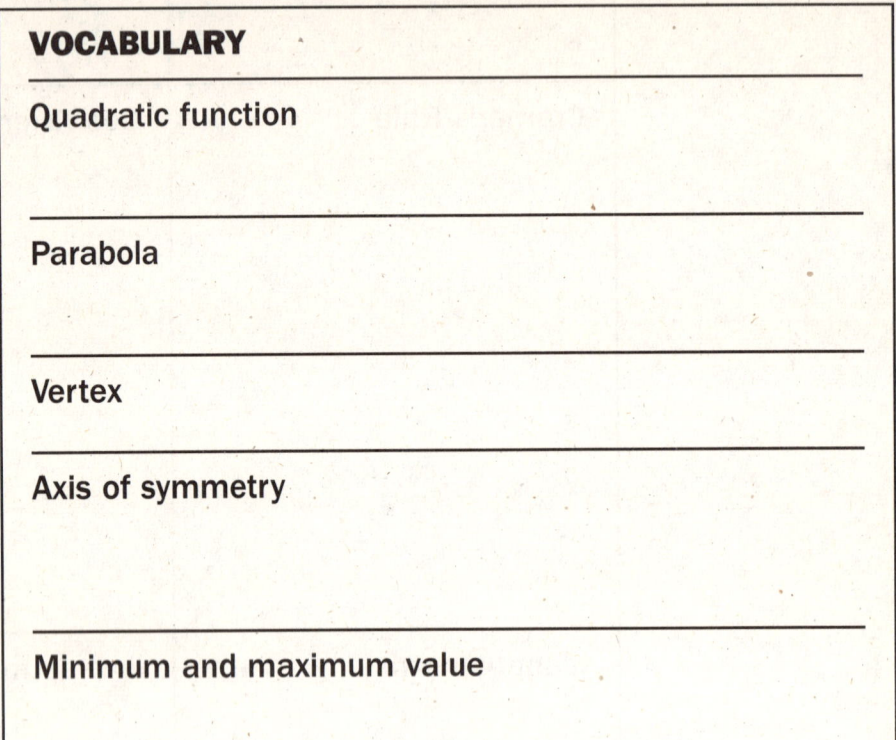

The axis of symmetry divides the parabola into mirror images and passes through the vertex.

The lowest or highest point on a parabola is the vertex. The vertex for $f(x) = x^2$ is $(0, 0)$.

For $f(x) = ax^2$, and for any quadratic function $g(x) = ax^2 + bx + c$ where $b = 0$, the vertex lies on the _____ and the axis of symmetry is $x =$ ____.

Your Notes

Choose values of x on both sides of the axis of symmetry $x = 0$.

Example 1 — Graph a function of the form $y = ax^2 + c$

Graph $y = -2x^2 + 2$. Compare the graph with the graph of $y = x^2$.

Solution

1. **Make** a table of values for $y = -2x^2 + 2$.

x	-2	-1	0	1	2
y	___	___	___	___	___

2. **Plot** the points from the table.

3. **Draw** a smooth _____ through the points.

4. **Compare** the graphs of $y = -2x^2 + 2$ and $y = x^2$. Both graphs have the same _____. However, the graph of $y = -2x^2 + 2$ opens _____ and is _____ than the graph of $y = x^2$. Also, its vertex is ___ units higher.

PROPERTIES OF THE GRAPH OF $y = ax^2 + bx + c$

Characteristics of the graph of $y = ax^2 + bx + c$:

- The graph opens up if a ___ 0 and opens down if a ___ 0.

- The graph is narrower than the graph of $y = x^2$ if $|a|$ ___ 1 and wider if $|a|$ ___ 1.

- The axis of symmetry is $x = $ _____ and the vertex has x-coordinate _____.

- The y-intercept is ___. So, the point (0, ___) is on the parabola.

Your Notes

Example 2 *Graph a function of the form* $y = ax^2 + bx + c$

Graph $y = -x^2 + 4x - 3$.

Solution

1. **Identify** the coefficients of the function. The coefficients are $a =$ _____, $b =$ _____, and $c =$ _____. Because a ___ 0, the parabola opens _____.

> Be sure to include the negative sign before the fraction when calculating the *x*-coordinate of the vertex.

2. **Find** the vertex. First, calculate the *x*-coordinate.

   $x = -\dfrac{b}{2a} =$ _____ = ___

   Then find the *y*-coordinate.

   $y =$ _____ = ___

   The vertex is (___ , ___). Plot this point.

3. **Draw** the axis of symmetry $x =$ ___.

4. **Identify** the *y*-intercept *c*, which is _____.
   Plot the point (0, ____). Then reflect this point in the axis of symmetry to plot another point (4, ____).

5. **Evaluate** the function for another value of *x*, such as $x = 1$.

   $y =$ _____ = ___

   Plot the point (1, ___) and its reflection (3, ___) in the axis of symmetry.

6. **Draw** a parabola through the plotted points.

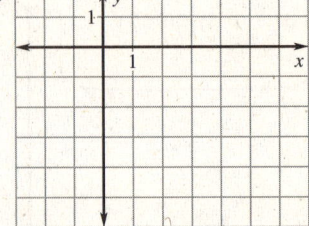

MINIMUM AND MAXIMUM VALUES

Words For $y = ax^2 + bx + c$, the vertex's *y*-coordinate is the minimum value of the function if a ___ 0 and the maximum value if a ___ 0.

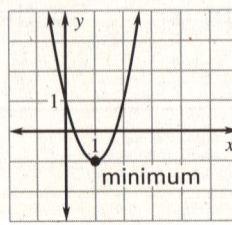

a is positive

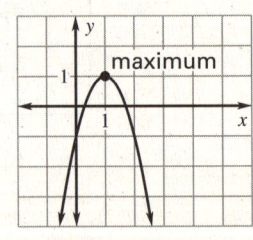

a is negative.

Your Notes

Example 3 — Find the minimum or maximum value

Tell whether the function $y = -3x^2 + 12x - 6$ has a *minimum value* or a *maximum value*. Then find the minimum or maximum value.

Solution

Because a ___ 0, the function has a _____ value. To find it, calculate the coordinates of the vertex.

$x = -\dfrac{b}{2a} = $ _____ $ = $ ___

$y = $ _____ $ = $ ___

The maximum value is $y = $ ___.

✓ **Checkpoint** Complete the following exercises.

Graph the function.

1. $y = -x^2$

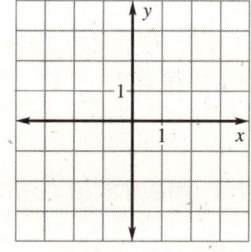

2. $y = \dfrac{1}{3}x^2 + 3$

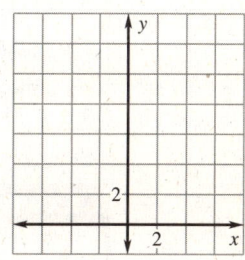

3. Graph the function. Label the vertex and axis of symmetry.

   $y = x^2 - 4x + 2$

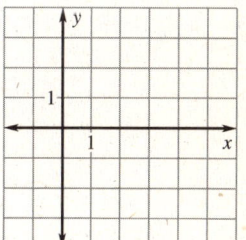

4. Find the minimum value of $y = 2x^2 - 6x + 6$.

Homework

4.2 Graph Quadratic Functions in Vertex or Intercept Form

Goal • Graph quadratic functions in vertex form or intercept form.

Your Notes

VOCABULARY

Vertex form

Intercept form

GRAPH OF VERTEX FORM $y = a(x - h)^2 + k$

The graph of $y = a(x - h)^2 + k$ is the parabola $y = ax^2$ translated _____ h units and _____ k units.

- The vertex is (___, ___).
- The axis of symmetry is $x =$ ___.
- The graph opens up if a ___ 0 and down if a ___ 0.

Example 1 *Graph a quadratic function in vertex form*

Graph $y = \frac{1}{2}(x + 1)^2 - 2$.

1. **Identify** the constants $a =$ ___, $h =$ ___ and $k =$ ___. Because $a > 0$, the parabola opens ___.

2. **Plot** the vertex $(h, k) =$ (___, ___) and draw the axis of symmetry at $x =$ ___.

3. **Evaluate** the function for two values of x.
   $x = 1$: $y = 0$
   $x = 3$: $y = 6$

   Plot the points (1, ___) and (3, ___) and their reflections in the axis of symmetry.

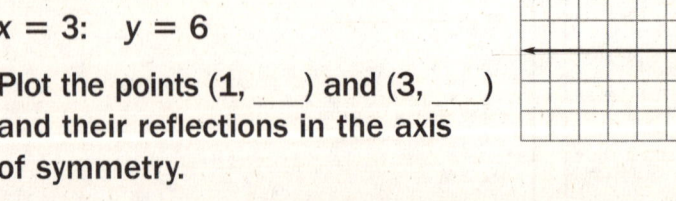

4. **Draw** a parabola through the plotted points.

Your Notes

GRAPH OF INTERCEPT FORM $y = a(x - p)(x - q)$

Characteristics of the graph $y = a(x - p)(x - q)$:

- The x-intercepts are ___ and ___.
- The axis of symmetry is halfway between (___, 0) and (___, 0). It has equation $x = \dfrac{\boxed{}}{2}$.
- The graph opens up if a ___ 0 and opens down if a ___ 0.

Example 2 *Graph a quadratic function in intercept form*

Graph $y = -2(x - 1)(x - 5)$.

1. **Identify** the x-intercepts. Because $p = $ ___ and $q = $ ___, the x-intercepts occur at the points (___, 0) and (___, 0).

2. **Find** the coordinates of the vertex.

$$x = \frac{p+q}{2} = \frac{\boxed{}}{2} = \underline{}$$

$y = $ _____ = ___

So, the vertex is (___, ___).

3. **Draw** a parabola through the vertex and the points where the x-intercepts occur.

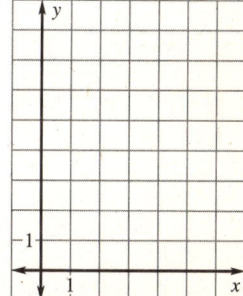

✓ **Checkpoint** Complete the following exercises.

1. Graph the function. Label the vertex and the axis of symmetry.

   $y = -(x - 3)^2 + 4$

   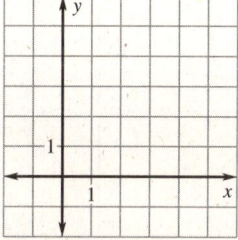

2. Graph the function. Label the vertex, axis of symmetry, and the x-intercepts.

   $y = (x - 4)(x + 2)$

Lesson 4.2 • Algebra 2 Notetaking Guide

Your Notes

FOIL METHOD

Words To multiply two expressions that each contain two terms, add the products of the _____ terms, the _____ terms, the _____ terms, and the _____ terms.

Example   F   O   I   L
$(x + 4)(x + 7) = x^2 + 7x + 4x + 28 = x^2 + 11x + 28$

Example 3 *Change from intercept form to standard form*

Write $y = 3(x + 2)(x - 5)$ in standard form.

$y = 3(x + 2)(x - 5)$ Original function

$= 3\underline{\hspace{3cm}}$ Multiply using FOIL.

$= 3\underline{\hspace{2cm}}$ Combine like terms.

$= \underline{\hspace{2cm}}$ Distributive property

Example 4 *Change from vertex form to standard form*

Write $f(x) = -5(x + 2)^2 + 8$ in standard form.

$f(x) = -5(x + 2)^2 + 8$ Original function

$= -5(\underline{\hspace{1cm}})(\underline{\hspace{1cm}}) + 8$ Rewrite $(x + 2)^2$.

$= -5(\underline{\hspace{2cm}}) + 8$ Multiply using FOIL.

$= -5(\underline{\hspace{2cm}}) + 8$ Combine like terms.

$= \underline{\hspace{2cm}} + 8$ Distributive property

$= \underline{\hspace{2cm}}$ Combine like terms.

✓ **Checkpoint** Write the quadratic function in standard form.

Homework

3. $y = 4(x - 3)^2 - 10$

4. $y = -3(x - 7)(x + 6)$

4.3 Solve $x^2 + bx + c = 0$ by Factoring

Goal • Solve quadratic equations.

Your Notes

VOCABULARY

Monomial

Binomial

Trinomial

Quadratic equation

Root of an equation

Zero of a function

Example 1 *Factor trinomials of the form $x^2 + bx + c$*

Factor the expression $x^2 + 7x - 8$.

Solution

You want $x^2 + 7x - 8 = (x + m)(x + n)$ where $mn = $ ____ and $m + n = $ ___.

Factors of −8 (m, n)	−1, ___	1, ___
Sum of factors (m + n)	___	___

Factors of −8 (m, n)	−2, ___	2, ___
Sum of factors (m + n)	___	___

Notice that $m = $ ____ and $n = $ ___. So, $x^2 + 7x - 8 = ($ _____ $)($ _____ $)$.

Your Notes

SPECIAL FACTORING PATTERNS

Pattern Name

Difference of Two Squares
$$a^2 - b^2 = (\underline{})(\underline{})$$
$$x^2 - 4 = (x + 2)(x - 2)$$

Perfect Square Trinomial
$$a^2 + 2ab + b^2 = (\underline{})^2$$
$$x^2 + 6x + 9 = (x + 3)^2$$

Perfect Square Trinomial
$$a^2 - 2ab + b^2 = (\underline{})^2$$
$$x^2 - 4x + 4 = (x - 2)^2$$

Example 2 *Factor with special patterns*

Factor the expression.

a. $x^2 - 25 = x^2 - \underline{}$ Difference of two squares
   $= (\underline{})(\underline{})$

b. $m^2 - 22m + 121$ Perfect square trinomial
   $= m^2 - 2(m)(\underline{}) + \underline{}^2$
   $= (\underline{})^2$

✓ **Checkpoint** Factor the expression. If it cannot be factored, say so.

1. $x^2 + 7x + 12$

2. $x^2 - 81$

ZERO PRODUCT PROPERTY

Words   If the _____ of two expressions is zero, then _____ or _____ of the expressions equals zero.

Algebra   If A and B are expressions and $AB = \underline{}$, then $A = \underline{}$ or $B = \underline{}$.

Example   If $(x + 5)(x + 2) = 0$, then $x + 5 = 0$ or $x + 2 = 0$. That is, $x = \underline{}$ or $x = \underline{}$.

Your Notes

Example 3 — Find the roots of an equation

Find the roots of the equation $x^2 - 2x - 15 = 0$.

Solution

$x^2 - 2x - 15 = 0$	Original equation
(_____)(_____) = 0	Factor.
_____ = 0 or _____ = 0	Zero product property
$x =$ ___ or $x =$ ___	Solve for x.

The roots are ___ and ___.

Example 4 — Find the zeros of a quadratic function

Find the zeros of the function $y = x^2 + 5x - 6$ by rewriting the function in intercept form.

Solution

$y = x^2 + 5x - 6$	Write original equation.
$=$ (_____)(_____)	Factor.

The zeros of the function are ___ and ___.

CHECK Graph $y = x^2 + 5x - 6$. The graph passes through (___, 0) and (___, 0).

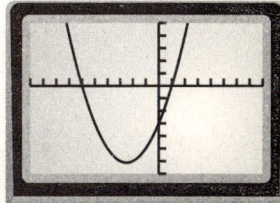

✓ **Checkpoint** Complete the following exercises.

3. Find the roots of the equation $x^2 - 3x + 2 = 0$.

4. Find the zeros of the function $y = x^2 + 3x - 40$ by rewriting the function in intercept form.

Homework

4.4 Solve $ax^2 + bx + c = 0$ by Factoring

Goal • Use factoring to solve equations of the form $ax^2 + bx + c = 0$.

Your Notes

Example 1 Factor $ax^2 + bx + c$ where $c > 0$

Factor $2x^2 + 9x + 7$.

You want $2x^2 + 9x + 7 = (kx + m)(\ell x + n)$ where k and ℓ are factors of ____ and m and n are factors of ____. Because mn ____ 0, m and n have the same sign. So, m and n must both be _____ because the coefficient of x, 9, is _____.

k, ℓ	m, n	$(kx + m)(\ell x + n)$	$ax^2 + bx + c$
2, 1	1, ___	(_____)(_____)	_____
2, 1	7, ___	(_____)(_____)	_____

The correct factorization is

$2x^2 + 9x + 7 = ($ _____ $)($ _____ $)$.

Example 2 Factor $ax^2 + bx + c$ where $c < 0$

Factor $3x^2 - x - 2$.

You want $3x^2 - x - 2 = (kx + m)(\ell x + n)$ where k and ℓ are factors of ____ and m and n are factors of ____. Because mn ____ 0, m and n have the _____ signs.

k, ℓ	m, n	$(kx + m)(\ell x + n)$	$ax^2 + bx + c$
3, 1	−1, ___	(_____)(_____)	_____
3, 1	2, ___	(_____)(_____)	_____
3, 1	1, ___	(_____)(_____)	_____
3, 1	−2, ___	(_____)(_____)	_____

The correct factorization is

$3x^2 - x - 2 = ($ _____ $)($ _____ $)$.

Your Notes

✓ **Checkpoint** Factor the experssion. If it cannot be factored, say so.

1. $3x^2 + 7x - 20$	2. $5x^2 - 13x + 6$

Example 3 *Factor with special patterns*

Factor the expression.

a. $16x^2 - 36 = (\underline{})^2 - \underline{}^2$ Difference of two squares
$= (\underline{})(\underline{})$

b. $9y^2 + 42y + 49$ Perfect square trinomial
$= (\underline{})^2 + 2(\underline{})(\underline{}) + \underline{}^2$
$= (\underline{})^2$

c. $25t^2 - 110t + 121$ Perfect square trinomial
$= (\underline{})^2 - 2(\underline{})(\underline{}) + \underline{}^2$
$= (\underline{})^2$

✓ **Checkpoint** Factor the expression.

3. $16y^2 - 40y + 25$	4. $4x^2 - 81$

Example 4 *Factor out monomials first*

Factor the expression.

a. $4x^2 - 4 = 4(\underline{}) = 4(\underline{})(\underline{})$
b. $-3y^2 - 18y = -3y(\underline{})$
c. $-4m^2 - 10m + 24 = -2(\underline{})$
$= -2(\underline{})(\underline{})$
d. $5z^2 - 25z + 40 = 5(\underline{})$

Lesson 4.4 • Algebra 2 Notetaking Guide

Your Notes

✓ **Checkpoint** Factor the expression.

5. $36x^2 - 16$	6. $15p^2 + 24p - 63$

Example 5 — Solve quadratic equations

a.
$2x^2 - x - 21 = 0$ — Original equation
$(\_\_\_\_)(\_\_\_\_) = 0$ — Factor.
$\_\_\_\_ = 0$ or $\_\_\_\_ = 0$ — Zero product property
$x = \_\_\_$ or $x = \_\_\_$ — Solve for x.

b.
$4r^2 - 18r + 24 = 6r - 12$ — Original equation
$_____ = 0$ — Standard form
$_____ = 0$ — Divide each side by $\_\_\_$.
$_____ = 0$ — Factor.
$_____ = 0$ — Zero product property
$r = \_\_\_$ — Solve for r.

✓ **Checkpoint** Solve the equation.

7. $2x^2 + 4x - 30 = 0$	8. $z^2 + 13z + 12 = 5z - 4$

Homework

4.5 Solve Quadratic Equations by Finding Square Roots

Goal • Solve quadratic equations by finding square roots.

Your Notes

VOCABULARY

Square root

Radical

Radicand

Rationalizing the denominator

Conjugates

PROPERTIES OF SQUARE ROOTS ($a > 0$, $b > 0$)

		Example
Product Property	$\sqrt{ab} = \underline{} \cdot \underline{}$	$\sqrt{18} = \sqrt{9} \cdot \sqrt{2} = 3\sqrt{2}$
Quotient Property	$\sqrt{\dfrac{a}{b}} = \dfrac{\boxed{}}{\boxed{}}$	$\sqrt{\dfrac{2}{25}} = \dfrac{\sqrt{2}}{\sqrt{25}} = \dfrac{\sqrt{2}}{5}$

Example 1 Use properties of square roots

a. $\sqrt{24} = \underline{} \cdot \underline{} = \underline{}$

b. $\sqrt{5} \cdot \sqrt{18} = \underline{} = \underline{} \cdot \underline{} = \underline{}$

c. $\sqrt{\dfrac{9}{64}} = \dfrac{\boxed{}}{\boxed{}} = \underline{}$

Your Notes

Example 2 Rationalize denominators of fractions

Simplify (a) $\sqrt{\dfrac{7}{3}}$ and (b) $\dfrac{4}{5+\sqrt{3}}$.

a. $\sqrt{\dfrac{7}{3}} = \dfrac{\boxed{}}{\boxed{}} \cdot \dfrac{\boxed{}}{\boxed{}} = \underline{}$

b. $\dfrac{4}{5+\sqrt{3}} = \dfrac{4}{5+\sqrt{3}} \cdot \dfrac{\boxed{}}{\boxed{}}$

$= \dfrac{\boxed{}}{\boxed{}}$

$= \underline{}$

✓ **Checkpoint** Simplify the expression.

1. $\sqrt{5} \cdot \sqrt{10}$	2. $\sqrt{\dfrac{9}{11}}$

Example 3 Solve a quadratic equation

Solve $\dfrac{1}{4}(y-6)^2 = 8$.

$\dfrac{1}{4}(y-6)^2 = 8$ Original equation

$\underline{} = \underline{}$ Multiply each side by ___.

$\underline{} = \underline{}$ Take square roots of each side.

$y = \underline{}$ Add ___ to each side.

$y = \underline{}$ Simplify.

The solutions are _____ and _____.

Your Notes

Example 4 — Model a dropped object with a quadratic function

Water Balloon A water balloon is dropped from a window 59 feet above the sidewalk. How long does it take for the water balloon to hit the sidewalk?

Solution.

$h = -16t^2 + h_0$ — Write height function.

___ $= -16t^2 +$ ___ — Substitute ___ for h and ___ for h_0.

___ $= -16t^2$ — Subtract ___ from each side.

___ $= t^2$ — Divide each side by ___.

___ $= t$ — Take square roots of each side.

___ $\approx t$ — Use a calculator.

Reject the negative solution, ___, because time must be positive. The water balloon will fall for about ___ seconds before it hits the ground.

✓ **Checkpoint** Complete the following exercises.

3. Solve the equation $2x^2 - 16 = 34$.

4. In Example 4, suppose that the water balloon is dropped from a height of 27 feet. How long does it take for the balloon to hit the sidewalk?

Homework

4.6 Perform Operations with Complex Numbers

Goal • Perform operations with complex numbers.

Your Notes

VOCABULARY

Imaginary unit i

Complex number

Imaginary number

Complex conjugates

Complex plane

Absolute value of a complex number

THE SQUARE ROOT OF A NEGATIVE NUMBER

Property

1. If r is a positive real number, then $\sqrt{-r} = i\sqrt{r}$.

2. By Property (1), it follows that $(i\sqrt{r})^2 = -r$.

Example

$\sqrt{-3} = $ _____

$(i\sqrt{3})^2 = i^2 \cdot 3$
$= $ _____

Your Notes

Example 1 *Solve a quadratic equation*

$2x^2 + 15 = -35$ Original equation

_____   Subtract ____ from each side.

_____   Divide each side by ___.

_____   Take square roots of each side.

_____   Write in terms of *i*.

_____   Simplify radical.

The solutions are ____ and ____.

✔ **Checkpoint** Solve the equation.

1. $3x^2 + 13 = -23$

SUMS AND DIFFERENCES OF COMPLEX NUMBERS

To add (or subtract) two complex numbers, add (or subtract) their _____ parts and their _____ parts _____.

Sum of complex numbers:
$(a + bi) + (c + di) = (a + c) + (b + d)i$

Difference of complex numbers:
$(a + bi) - (c + di) = (a - c) + (b - d)i$

Example 2 *Add and subtract complex numbers*

Write as a complex number in standard form.

a. $(6 + 3i) - (4 - i)$

   = (_____) + (_____)i Complex subtraction

   = _____   Standard form

b. $(2 + 5i) + (7 - 2i)$

   = (_____) + (_____)i Complex addition

   = _____   Standard form

Your Notes

Example 3 *Multiply complex numbers*

Write the expression $(2 + i)(-5 + 2i)$ as a complex number in standard form.

$(2 + i)(-5 + 2i)$

= _____ Multiply using FOIL.

= _____ Simplify and use $i^2 = -1$.

= _____ Simplify.

= _____ Write in standard form.

Example 4 *Divide complex numbers*

Write the quotient $\dfrac{6 + 4i}{2 + i}$ in standard form.

$\dfrac{6 + 4i}{2 + i} = \dfrac{6 + 4i}{2 + i} \cdot$ _____ Multiply numerator and denominator by _____, the complex conjugate of $2 + i$.

= _____ Multiply using FOIL.

= _____ Simplify.

= _____ Write in standard form.

✓ **Checkpoint** Write the expression as a complex number in standard form.

2. $(12 - 2i) - (16 + 3i)$	3. $-4i(9 + 5i)$
4. $\dfrac{8 - 4i}{3 + i}$	5. $(4 + 4i) + (-6 + 3i)$

Your Notes

Example 5 — Plot complex numbers

Plot the complex numbers in the same complex plane.

a. $4 + 3i$ b. $-5 - 4i$

Solution

a. To plot $4 + 3i$, start at the origin, move _____, and then move _____.

b. To plot $-5 - 4i$, start at the origin, move _____, and then move _____.

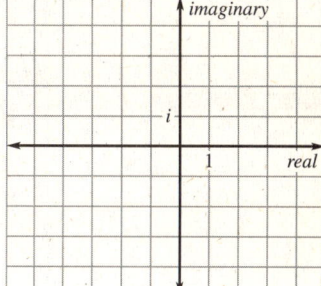

ABSOLUTE VALUE OF A COMPLEX NUMBER

The absolute value of a complex number $z = a + bi$, denoted $|z|$, is a _____ real number defined as $|z| = \sqrt{a^2 + b^2}$. This is the distance of z from the _____ in the complex plane.

Example 6 — Find absolute values of complex numbers

Find the absolute value of (a) $6 - 8i$ and (b) $-6i$.

a. $|6 - 8i| = \sqrt{\underline{}} = \sqrt{\underline{}} = \underline{}$

b. $|-6i| = \sqrt{\underline{}} = \sqrt{\underline{}} = \underline{}$

✓ **Checkpoint** Plot the complex numbers in the same complex plane. Then find the absolute value.

6. $-4i$

7. $2 + 3i$

8. $-3 + i$

Homework

4.7 Complete the Square

Goal • Solve quadratic equations by completing the square.

Your Notes

VOCABULARY

Completing the square

COMPLETING THE SQUARE

Words To complete the square for the expression $x^2 + bx$, add $\left(\underline{}\right)^2$.

Algebra $x^2 + bx + \left(\underline{}\right)^2 = \left(x + \dfrac{b}{2}\right)\left(x + \dfrac{b}{2}\right)$

$\phantom{x^2 + bx + \left(\underline{}\right)^2} = \left(\underline{}\right)^2$

Example 1 *Make a perfect square trinomial*

Find the value of c that makes $x^2 + 12x + c$ a perfect square trinomial. Then write the expression as the square of a binomial.

Solution

1. **Find** half the coefficient of x. $\dfrac{\boxed{}}{2} = \underline{}$

2. **Square** the result of Step 1. $\underline{} = \underline{}$

3. **Replace** c with the result of Step 2. $\underline{}$

The trinomial $x^2 + 12x + c$ is a perfect square when $c = \underline{}$. Then

$\underline{} = (\underline{})(\underline{}) = (\underline{})^2$.

Your Notes

✓ **Checkpoint** Find the value of c that makes the expression a perfect square trinomial. Then write the expression as the square of a binomial.

1. $x^2 - 24x + c$	2. $x^2 + 10x + c$

Example 2 *Solve $ax^2 + bx + c = 0$ when $a = 1$*

Solve $x^2 - 10x + 13 = 0$ by completing the square.

Solution

$x^2 - 10x + 13 = 0$ Write original equation.

_____ = ____   Write left side in the form $x^2 + bx$.

_____ = _____   Complete the square.

_____ = ____   Write left side as a binomial squared.

_____ = _____   Take square roots of each side.

$x =$ _____   Solve for x.

$x =$ _____   Simplify.

The solutions are _____ and _____.

Lesson 4.7 • Algebra 2 Notetaking Guide

Your Notes

Example 3 — Solve $ax^2 + bx + c = 0$ when $a \neq 1$

Solve $3x^2 - 12x + 27 = 0$ by completing the square.

Solution

$3x^2 - 12x + 27 = 0$	Write original equation.
$\underline{x^2 - 4x + 9} = \underline{0}$	Divide each side by the coefficient of x^2.
$\underline{x^2 - 4x} = \underline{-9}$	Write left side in the form $x^2 + bx$.
$\underline{x^2 - 4x + 4} = \underline{-9 + 4}$	Complete the square.
$\underline{(x-2)^2} = \underline{-5}$	Write left side as binomial squared.
$\underline{x - 2} = \underline{\pm\sqrt{-5}}$	Take square roots of each side.
$x = \underline{2 \pm i\sqrt{5}}$	Write in terms of the imaginary unit i.

The solutions are $\underline{2 + i\sqrt{5}}$ and $\underline{2 - i\sqrt{5}}$.

✓ **Checkpoint** Solve the equations by completing the square.

3. $x^2 - 8x + 7 = 0$	4. $2x^2 - 20x + 24 = 0$

Lesson 4.7 • Algebra 2 Notetaking Guide

Your Notes

Example 4 — Write a quadratic function in vertex form

Write $y = x^2 + 14x + 44$ in vertex form. Then identify the vertex.

Solution

$y = x^2 + 14x + 44$ Write original function.

$y + \underline{} = (x^2 + 14x + \underline{}) + 44$ Complete the square.

$y + \underline{} = (\underline{})^2 + 44$ Write as a binomial squared.

$y = \underline{}$ Solve for y.

The vertex form of the function is $y = \underline{}$.
The vertex is (___ , ___).

✓ **Checkpoint** Write the quadratic function in vertex form. Then identify the vertex.

5. $y = x^2 - 12x + 22$	6. $y = x^2 + 16x + 53$

Homework

4.8 Use the Quadratic Formula and the Discriminant

Goal • Solve quadratic equations using the quadratic formula.

Your Notes

VOCABULARY

Quadratic formula

Discriminant

THE QUADRATIC FORMULA

Let a, b, and c be real numbers such that $a \neq 0$. The solutions of the quadratic equation $ax^2 + bx + c$ are:

$$x = \frac{\_\_\_ \pm \sqrt{\_\_\_ - 4\_\_\_}}{2\_\_\_}$$

Example 1 Solve an equation with two real solutions

Solve $x^2 + 7x = 6$.

$x^2 + 7x = 6$	Original equation
$x^2 + 7x \_\_\_\_\_ = 0$	Standard form
$x = \dfrac{\_\_\_ \pm \sqrt{\_\_\_ - 4\_\_\_}}{2\_\_\_}$	Quadratic formula
$x = \dfrac{\_\_\_ \pm \sqrt{\_\_\_ - 4\_\_\_}}{2\_\_\_}$	$a = \_\_\_$, $b = \_\_\_$, $c = \_\_\_$
$x = \_\_\_\_\_$	Simplify.

The solutions are $x = \_\_\_\_\_ \approx \_\_\_\_\_$ and $x = \_\_\_\_\_ \approx \_\_\_\_\_$.

Your Notes

Example 2 — Solve an equation with one real solution

Solve $2x^2 - 8x + 8 = 0$.

Solution

$2x^2 - 8x + 8 = 0$ Original equation

$x = \dfrac{\_\_\_ \pm \sqrt{\_\_\_ - 4\_\_\_\_}}{2\_\_\_}$ $a = \_\_$, $b = \_\_\_$, $c = \_\_$

$x = \_\_\_\_\_$ Simplify.

$x = \_\_\_$ Simplify.

The solution is $\_\_\_$.

Example 3 — Solve an equation with imaginary solutions

Solve $-x^2 + 2x = 5$.

Solution

$-x^2 + 2x = 5$ Original equation

$-x^2 + 2x \_\_\_\_ = 0$ Standard form

$x = \dfrac{\_\_\_ \pm \sqrt{\_\_\_ - 4\_\_\_\_}}{2\_\_\_}$ $a = \_\_\_$, $b = \_\_$, $c = \_\_\_$

$x = _____$ Simplify.

$x = \_\_\_\_\_$ Rewrite using the imaginary unit i.

$x = \_\_\_\_\_$ Simplify.

The solutions are $_____$ and $_____$.

Your Notes

✓ Checkpoint Use the quadratic formula to solve the equation.

1. $2x^2 + 12x = -16$	2. $4x^2 - 13x = 7x - 25$
3. $3x^2 - 6x + 6 = 0$	4. $x^2 - 3x + 3 = 0$

USING THE DISCRIMINANT OF $ax^2 + bx + c = 0$

When $b^2 - 4ac > 0$, the equation has _____ _____. The graph has ____ x-intercepts.

When $b^2 - 4ac = 0$, the equation has _____ _____. The graph has ____ x-intercept.

When $b^2 - 4ac < 0$, the equation has _____ _____. The graph has ____ x-intercepts.

Your Notes

Example 4 *Use the discriminant*

Find the discriminant of the quadratic equation and give the number and type of solutions of the equation.

a. $x^2 + 6x + 5 = 0$

b. $x^2 + 6x + 9 = 0$

c. $x^2 + 6x + 13 = 0$

Discriminant	Solution(s)
$b^2 - 4ac$	$x = \dfrac{-b \pm \sqrt{b^2 - 4ac}}{2a}$
a. _____	_____
b. _____	_____
c. _____	_____

✓ **Checkpoint** Find the discriminant of the quadratic equation and give the number and type of solutions of the equation.

5. $x^2 - 8x + 17 = 0$	6. $x^2 + 4x + 3 = 0$
7. $-x^2 + 2x - 1 = 0$	8. $x^2 + 6x + 4 = 0$

Homework

4.9 Graph and Solve Quadratic Inequalities

Goal • Graph and solve quadratic inequalities.

Your Notes

VOCABULARY

Quadratic inequality in two variables

_____

Quadratic inequality in one variable

GRAPHING A QUADRATIC INEQUALITY IN TWO VARIABLES

To graph a quadratic inequality, follow these steps:

Step 1 Graph the parabola with equation

$y = ax^2 + bx + c$.

Make the parabola _____ for inequalities with < or > and _____ for inequalities with ≤ or ≥.

Step 2 Test a point (x, y) _____ the parabola to determine whether the point is a solution of the inequality.

Step 3 Shade the region _____ the parabola if the point from Step 2 is a solution. Shade the region _____ the parabola if it is not a solution.

Your Notes

Example 1 — Graph a quadratic inequality

Graph $y \le -x^2 + 2x + 3$.

1. **Graph** $y = -x^2 + 2x + 3$. The inequality symbol is $\le$, so make the parabola _____.

2. **Test** the point (0, 0).

   _____

   _____

   So, (0, 0) _____.

3. **Shade** the region _____ the parabola.

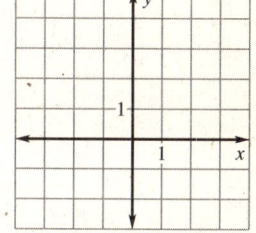

✓ Checkpoint Graph $y > x^2 - 2$.

1.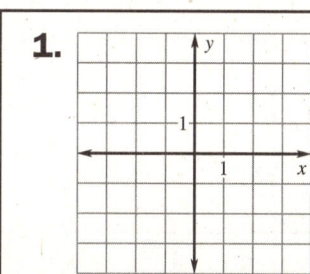

Example 2 — Graph a system of quadratic inequalities

Graph the system of quadratic inequalities.

$y > x^2 - 2$ **Inequality 1**
$y \le -x^2 - 3x + 4$ **Inequality 2**

Solution

1. Graph $y > x^2 - 2$. The graph is the region _____ (but not including) the parabola $y =$ _____.

2. Graph $y \le -x^2 - 3x + 4$. The graph is the region _____ and including the parabola $y =$ _____.

3. Identify the region where the two graphs overlap. This region is the graph of the system.

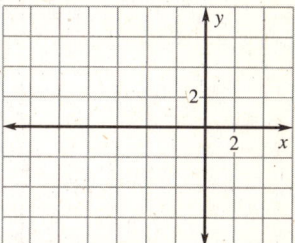

Your Notes

✓ **Checkpoint** Graph the system.

2. $y < -x^2 + 3$
   $y \geq 2x^2 + 3x - 2$

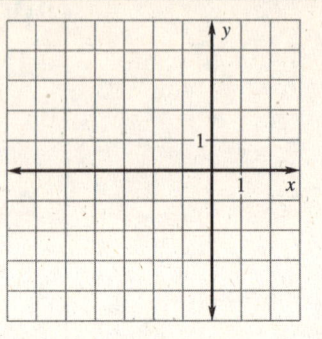

Example 3 *Solve a quadratic inequality using a table*

Solve $x^2 + 3x \leq 4$.

Rewrite the inequality as $x^2 + 3x - 4 \leq 0$. Then make a table of values.

x	−5	−4	−3	−2	−1
$x^2 + 3x - 4$	___	___	___	___	___

x	0	1	2
$x^2 + 3x - 4$	___	___	___

Notice that $x^2 + 3x - 4 \leq 0$ when the values of x are between ____ and ___, inclusive.

The solution of the inequality is _____.

✓ **Checkpoint** Complete the following exercise.

3. Solve the quadratic inequality $x^2 + 2x \leq 3$ using a table.

Your Notes

> **Example 4** *Solve a quadratic inequality by graphing*
>
> Solve $-3x^2 - 5x + 3 \leq 0$.
>
> The solution consists of the x-values for which the graph of $y = -3x^2 - 5x + 3$ lies _____ the x-axis. Find the graph's x-intercepts by letting $y = 0$ and using _____ to solve for x.
>
> $0 = -3x^2 - 5x + 3$
>
> $x =$ _____
>
> $x =$ _____
>
> $x \approx$ _____ or $x \approx$ _____
>
> Sketch a parabola that opens _____ and has _____ and _____ as x-intercepts. The graph lies _____ the x-axis to the left of (and including) $x =$ _____ and to the right of (and including) $x =$ _____.
>
> The solution is approximately _____.

✓ **Checkpoint** Complete the following exercise.

4. Solve the quadratic inequality $2x^2 + 3x \geq 5$ by graphing.

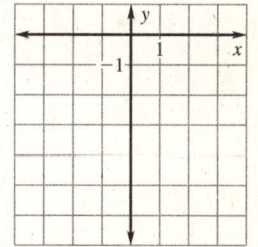

Lesson 4.9 • Algebra 2 Notetaking Guide

Your Notes

Example 5 *Solve a quadratic inequality algebraically*

Solve $x^2 + x \geq 12$.

First, write and solve the equation obtained by replacing $\geq$ with ____.

_____ Write corresponding equation.

_____ Write in standard form.

_____ Factor.

_____ Zero product property.

The numbers _____ are the critical x-values of the inequality $x^2 + x \geq 12$. Plot _____ on a number line, using _____ dots. The critical x-values partition the number line into three intervals. Test an x-value in each interval to see if it satisfies the inequality.

←——+——+——+——+——+——+——+——+——+——+——→

Test $x = $ ____: Test $x = $ ____:

_____   _____

Test $x = $ ____:

_____

The solution is _____.

✓ **Checkpoint** Solve the inequality algebraically.

5. $-2x^2 + 12x \leq 16$

Homework

4.10 Write Quadratic Functions and Models

Goal • Write quadratic functions and models.

Your Notes

VOCABULARY

Best-fitting quadratic model

Example 1 *Write a quadratic function in vertex form*

Use the vertex form because the vertex is given.

Write a quadratic equation for the parabola shown.

$y = a(x - h)^2 + k$

$y = a(x\_\_\_\_)^2 \_\_\_\_$ Substitute.

Use the other given point, (__, __), to find a.

$\_\_ = a(\_\_\_\_)^2 \_\_\_\_$ Substitute for x and y.

$_____$ Solve for a.

A quadratic function for the parabola is _____.

Example 2 *Write a quadratic function in intercept form*

Use the intercept form because the x-intercepts are given.

Write a quadratic equation for the parabola shown.

$y = a(x - p)(x - q)$

$y = a(x\_\_\_\_)(x\_\_\_\_)$ Substitute.

Use the other given point, (___, ___), to find a.

$\_\_\_\_ = a(\_\_\_\_\_)(\_\_\_\_\_)$ Substitute for x and y.

$\_\_\_ = a$ Solve for a.

A quadratic function for the parabola is _____.

Lesson 4.10 • Algebra 2 Notetaking Guide

Your Notes

✓ **Checkpoint** Write a quadratic function whose graph has the given characteristics.

1. x-intercepts: −2, 1 point on graph: (−1, −4)	2. vertex: (2, 1) point on graph: (0, 4)

Example 3 *Write a quadratic function in standard form*

Write a quadratic function in standard form for the parabola that passes through the points (−2, −6), (0, 6) and (2, 2).

Substitute the coordinates of each point into $y = ax^2 + bx + c$ to obtain a system of three linear equations.

____ = a(____)² + b(____) + c   Substitute for *x* and *y*.
____ = _____   Equation 1

____ = a(____)² + b(____) + c   Substitute for *x* and *y*.
____ = ____   Equation 2

____ = a(____)² + b(____) + c   Substitute for *x* and *y*.
____ = _____   Equation 3

Rewrite the system as a system of two equations.

> Substitute 6 for *c* in Equation 1.

_____ = ____   Substitute for *c*.
_____ = ____   Revised Equation 1

> Substitute 6 for *c* in Equation 3.

_____ = ____   Substitute for *c*.
_____ = ____   Revised Equation 3

Solve the system consisting of revised Equations 1 and 3.

_____   Revised Equation 1
_____   Revised Equation 3
_____   Add Equations.
a = ____   Solve for *a*.

So _____ = ____, which means *b* = ____.

A quadratic function for the parabola is
_____.

Your Notes

Example 4 *Solve a multi-step problem*

Baseball The table shows the height of a baseball hit, with x representing the time (in seconds) and y representing the baseball's height (in feet). Use a graphing calculator to find the best-fitting model for the data.

Time, x	0	2	4	6	8
Height, y	3	28	40	37	26

Solution

Enter the data into two lists of a graphing calculator.

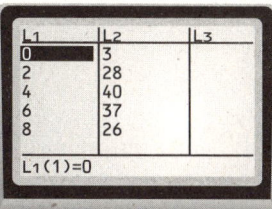

Make a scatter plot of the data.

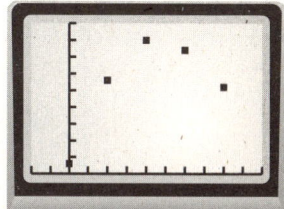

Use the quadratic regression model feature to find the best-fitting quadratic model for the data.

QuadReg

$y = ax^2 + bx + c$

a = _____

b = _____

c = _____

The best fitting quadratic model is

_____ .

Check how well the model fits the data by graphing the model and the data in the same viewing window.

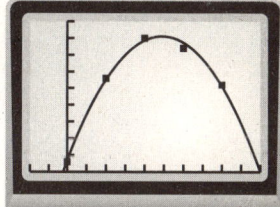

Your Notes

✓ **Checkpoint** Complete the exercises below.

3. Write a quadratic function in standard form for the parabola that passes through $(-1, -5)$, $(2, 1)$ and $(3, -1)$.

4. Use a graphing calculator to find the best-fitting model for the data in the table.

Time, x	0	2	4	6	8
Height, y	4	23	30	25	7

Homework

Words to Review

Give an example of the vocabulary word.

Quadratic function	Parabola
Vertex	Axis of symmetry
Minimum value	Maximum value
Vertex form	Intercept form
Monomial	Binomial
Trinomial	Quadratic equation

Root of an equation	Zero of a function
Square root	Radical
Radicand	Rationalizing the denominator
Conjugates	Imaginary unit *i*
Complex number	Imaginary number
Complex conjugates	Complex plane

Absolute value of a complex number	Completing the square
Quadratic formula	Discriminant
Quadratic inequality in two variables	Quadratic inequality in one variable
Bext-fitting quadratic model	

Review your notes and Chapter 4 by using the Chapter Review on pages 318–322 of your textbook.

5.1 Use Properties of Exponents

Goal • Simplify expressions involving powers.

Your Notes

VOCABULARY

Scientific notation

PROPERTIES OF EXPONENTS

Let a and b be real numbers and let m and n be integers.

Product of Powers Property $a^m \cdot a^n = a\underline{}$

Power of a Power Property $(a^m)^n = a\underline{}$

Power of a Product Property $(ab)^m = a\underline{}b\underline{}$

Negative Exponent Property $a^{-m} = \dfrac{}{\underline{}}$, $a \neq 0$

Zero Exponent Property $a^0 = \underline{}$, $a \neq 0$

Quotient of Powers Property $\dfrac{a^m}{a^n} = a\underline{}$, $a \neq 0$

Power of a Quotient Property $\left(\dfrac{a}{b}\right)^m = \dfrac{}{\underline{}}$, $b \neq 0$

Example 1   Evaluate numerical expressions

a. $(6^2)^3 = 6\underline{} = 6\underline{} = \underline{}$

b. $\dfrac{4^5}{4^3} = 4\underline{} = 4\underline{} = \underline{}$

c. $7^{-4} = \dfrac{}{\underline{}} = \dfrac{}{\underline{}}$

132   Lesson 5.1 • Algebra 2 Notetaking Guide

Your Notes

Example 2 *Use scientific notation in real life*

Iceland Iceland covers about 1.03×10^5 square kilometers and has approximately 2.94×10^5 people. About how many people are there per square kilometer?

Solution

$\dfrac{\text{Population}}{\text{Land area}} =$ _____   Divide population by land area.

$=$ _____   Quotient of powers property

$\approx$ _____   Use a calculator.

$=$ _____   Zero exponent property

There are about ___ people per square kilometer.

Example 3 *Simplify expressions*

a. $\dfrac{(x^5 y^2)^3}{x^{15} y^8} = \dfrac{\boxed{}}{x^{15} y^8}$ Power of a product property

$= \dfrac{\boxed{}}{x^{15} y^8}$ Power of a power property

$=$ _____   Quotient of powers property

$=$ ___   Simplify exponents.

$=$ ___   Zero exponent property

$=$ ___   Negative exponent property

b. $\left(\dfrac{a^{-4}}{b^2}\right)^2 = \dfrac{\boxed{}}{\boxed{}}$ Power of a quotient property

$= \dfrac{\boxed{}}{\boxed{}}$ Power of a power property

$= \dfrac{\boxed{}}{\boxed{}}$ Negative exponent property

Your Notes

✔ **Checkpoint** Evaluate or simplify each expression.

1. $\left(\dfrac{8^5}{8^2}\right)^{-1}$	2. $(4 \times 10^3)(7 \times 10^{-2})$
3. $(x^2 y^{-6})^7$	4. $\left(\dfrac{-2a^2 b}{a^5 b}\right)^3$

Example 4 *Compare real-life volumes*

Beach Ball The radius of a beach ball is about 5.6 times greater than the radius of a baseball. How many times as great as the baseball's volume is the beach ball's volume?

Solution

Let r represent the radius of the baseball.

$\dfrac{\text{Beach ball's volume}}{\text{Baseball's volume}} = \dfrac{\frac{4}{3}\pi(\boxed{})^3}{\frac{4}{3}\pi r^3}$ The volume of a sphere is $\frac{4}{3}\pi r^3$.

$= \dfrac{\frac{4}{3}\pi \boxed{}}{\frac{4}{3}\pi r^3}$ Power of a product property

$= \underline{}$ Quotient of powers

$= \underline{}$ Zero exponent property

$\approx \underline{}$ Approximate power.

The beach ball's volume is about _____ times as great as the baseball's volume.

Homework

5.2 Evaluate and Graph Polynomial Functions

Goal • Evaluate and graph other polynomial functions.

Your Notes

VOCABULARY

Polynomial

Polynomial function

Synthetic substitution

End behavior

Example 1 Identify polynomial functions

Decide whether the function is a polynomial function. If so, write it in standard form and state its degree, type, and leading coefficient.

a. $f(x) = 3x^3 + 4x^{2.5} - 6x^2$ b. $f(x) = x^2 + 3.7x + 9x^4$

Solution

a. The function _____ a polynomial function because the term _____ has an exponent that is _____ _____.

b. The function ___ a polynomial function written as _____ in its standard form. It has degree ___ (_____) and a leading coefficient of ___.

Your Notes

✓ **Checkpoint** State the degree, type, and leading coefficient of the function.

1. $f(x) = -2x^3 + 2x^2 - 3x^4 + 5$

Example 2 *Evaluate by synthetic substitution*

Use synthetic substitution to evaluate $f(x) = 2x^4 + 3x^3 - 6x^2 + 3$ when $x = 2$.

Write the coefficients of $f(x)$ in order of _____ exponents. Write the value of x to the left. Bring down the leading coefficient. Multiply the leading coefficient by ___ and write the product under the second coefficient. _____. Multiply the previous sum by ___ and write the product under the second coefficient. Add. Repeat for all of the remaining coefficients.

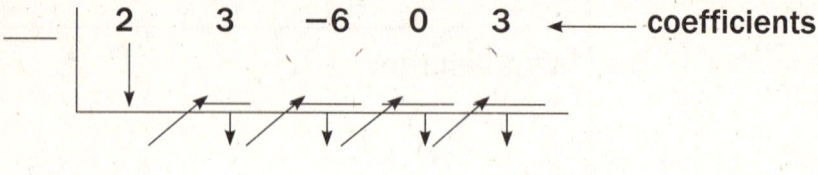
coefficients

$f(2) = $ ____

END BEHAVIOR OF POLYNOMIAL FUNCTIONS

For the graph of
$f(x) = a_n x^n + a_{n-1} x^{n-1} + \cdots + a_1 x + a_0$:

- If $a_n > 0$ and n is odd, then $f(x) \to$ ____ as $x \to -\infty$ and $f(x) \to$ ____ as $x \to +\infty$.

- If $a_n < 0$ and n is odd, then $f(x) \to$ ____ as $x \to -\infty$ and $f(x) \to$ ____ as $x \to +\infty$.

- If $a_n > 0$ and n is even, then $f(x) \to$ ____ as $x \to -\infty$ and $f(x) \to$ ____ as $x \to +\infty$.

- If $a_n < 0$ and n is even, then $f(x) \to$ ____ as $x \to -\infty$ and $f(x) \to$ ____ as $x \to +\infty$.

Your Notes

Example 3 Graph polynomial functions

Graph $f(x) = -x^3 + 2x^2 + 2x - 1$.

Solution

Make a table of values and plot the corresponding points. Connect the points with a smooth curve and check the end behavior.

x	−3	−2	−1	0	1	2	3
f(x)	___	___	___	___	___	___	___

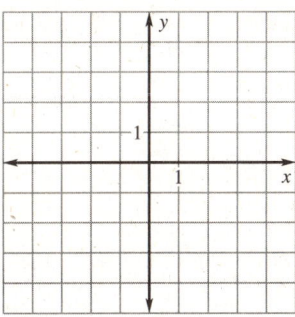

The degree is _____ and the leading coefficient is _____, so $f(x) \to$ _____ as $x \to -\infty$ and $f(x) \to$ _____ as $x \to +\infty$.

Checkpoint Complete the following exercises using the function $f(x) = -x^4 + 3x^3 + x^2 - 4x - 1$.

2. Evaluate $f(x)$ for $x = -2$ using synthetic substitution.

3. Graph $f(x)$.

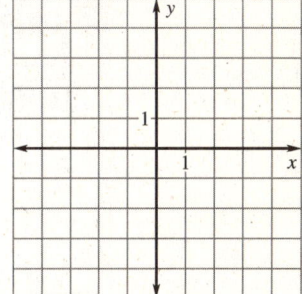

Homework

5.3 Add, Subtract, and Multiply Polynomials

Goal • Add, subtract, and multiply polynomials.

Your Notes

Example 1 Add polynomials vertically and horizontally

a. $3x^3 - 2x^2 + 4x - 6$
   $+\ x^3 - 5x^2\ \ \ \ \ \ \ + 3$
   _____

b. $(2y^3 + 7y^2 - 6y) + (-4y^2 + 3y - 9)$

   = _____

   = _____

Example 2 Subtract polynomials vertically and horizontally

a.
   $\ \ \ \ 7x^3 - 6x^2 - 3x + 7$ $\ \ \ \ \ \ \ \ 7x^3 - 6x^2 - 3x + 7$
   $-(6x^3 + 3x^3 - 7x + 5)$ ⟶ _____

   _____

b. $(8x^2 - 5x + 11) - (12x^2 - 9x - 3)$

   $= 8x^2 - 5x + 11$ _____

   = _____

✓ **Checkpoint** Find the sum or difference.

1. $(8t + 6 - 5t^2) - (2t^3 - 3t^2 + 7)$

2. $(4p^2 - 6p - 6) + (8p^2 - 7p + 4)$

Your Notes

Example 3 — Multiply polynomials vertically and horizontally

a.
$$3x^2 - x + 4$$
$$\times \quad x + 2$$

_____   Multiply $3x^2 - x + 4$ by 2.

_____   Multiply $3x^2 - x + 4$ by x.

_____   Combine like terms.

b. $(x - 3)(x^2 + 2x - 5)$

$= (x - 3)\_\_\_ + (x - 3)\_\_\_ - (x - 3)\_\_\_$

$= _____$

$= _____$

Example 4 — Multiply three binomials

Multiply $(x - 3)(x + 7)(x + 1)$ in a horizontal format.

$(x - 3)(x + 7)(x + 1)$

$= (_____)(x + 1)$

$= (_____)(x) + (_____)(1)$

$= _____$

$= _____$

SPECIAL PRODUCT PATTERNS

Sum and Difference   **Example**

$(a + b)(b - a) = a^2 - b^2$ $(x + 2)(x - 2) = _____$

Square of a Binomial

$(a + b)^2 = a^2 + 2ab + b^2$ $(y + 4)^2$
                                      $= _____$

$(a - b)^2 = a^2 - 2ab + b^2$ $(3p^2 - 2)^2$
                                      $= _____$

Cube of a Binomial

$(a + b)^3 = a^3 + 3a^2b$ $(x + 1)^3$
$\quad + 3ab^2 + b^3$ $= _____$

$(a - b)^3 = a^3 - 3a^2b$ $(r - 3)^3$
$\quad + 3ab^2 - b^3$ $= _____$

Your Notes

Example 5 *Use special product patterns*

a. $(7m - 3)(7m + 3) = (\underline{})^2 - \underline{}^2$
   $= \underline{}$

b. $(4t^3 + 6)^2 = (\underline{})^2 + 6(\underline{})(\underline{}) + \underline{}^2$
   $= \underline{}$

c. $(xy - 4)^3 = (\underline{})^3 - 3(\underline{})^2(\underline{})$
   $ + 3(\underline{})(\underline{})^2 - \underline{}^3$
   $= \underline{}$

Checkpoint Find the product.

3. $(x - 2)(6x^2 + 3x - 5)$

4. $(x + 3)(x - 6)(x + 5)$

5. $(6q - 3r)^2$

6. $(2m + 5)^3$

Homework

5.4 Factor and Solve Polynomial Equations

Goal • Factor and solve other polynomial equations.

Your Notes

VOCABULARY

Prime polynomial

Factored completely

Factor by grouping

Quadratic form

FACTORING POLYNOMIALS

Definition A polynomial with two or more terms is a prime polynomial if it _____ be written as a product of polynomials of lesser degree using only integer coefficients and constants and if the only common factors of its terms are ____ and ___.

Example $16x^2 - 4x + 8$ _____ a prime polynomial because ___ is a common factor of all its terms.

Definition A polynomial is factored completely if it is written as a monomial or the product of a monomial and one or more _____ polynomials.

Example $(x + 2)(x^2 - 5x + 6)$ is not factored completely because $x^2 - 5x + 6 =$ _____.

Your Notes

SPECIAL FACTORING PATTERNS

Sum of Two Cubes

$a^3 + b^3 = (a + b)(a^2 - ab + b^2)$

Example

$x^3 + 8 = (x + 2)(\underline{})$

Difference of Two Cubes

$a^3 - b^3 = (a - b)(a^2 + ab + b^2)$

Example

$8x^3 - 1 = (2x - 1)(\underline{})$

Example 1 *Factor the sum or difference of two cubes*

Factor the polynomial completely.

a. $z^3 - 125 = z^3 - \underline{}$ Difference of two cubes

           $= (z - \underline{})(\underline{})$

b. $81y^4 + 192y = 3y(\underline{})$ Factor common monomial.

                $= 3y[\underline{} + \underline{}]$ Sum of two cubes

                $= 3y(\underline{})(\underline{})$

✓ **Checkpoint** Factor the polynomial completely.

1. $8x^3 + 64$

Example 2 *Factor by grouping*

Factor the polynomial $x^3 - 2x^2 - 9x + 18$ completely.

$x^3 - 2x^2 - 9x + 18$

$= x^2(\underline{}) - 9(\underline{})$ Factor by grouping.

$= \underline{}$ Distributive property

$= \underline{}$ Difference of two squares

142 Lesson 5.4 • Algebra 2 Notetaking Guide

Your Notes

Example 3 *Factor polynomials in quadratic form*

Factor completely: (a) $16x^4 - 256$ and (b) $3y^7 - 15y^5 + 18y^3$.

a. $16x^4 - 256 = (\underline{})^2 - \underline{}^2$

$ = \underline{}$

$ = \underline{}$

b. $3y^7 - 15y^5 + 18y^3 = 3y^3(\underline{})$

$ = \underline{}$

✓ **Checkpoint** Factor each polynomial completely.

2. $x^3 + 2x^2 - 25x - 50$	3. $x^4 - 14x^2 + 45$

Example 4 *Solve a polynomial equation*

What are the real-number solutions of the equation $x^4 + 9 = 10x^2$?

$x^4 + 9 = 10x^2$ Write original equation.

$\underline{} = 0$ Write in standard form.

$\underline{} = 0$ Factor trinomial.

$\underline{} = 0$ Difference of two squares

$x = \underline{}, x = \underline{}, x = \underline{}, x = \underline{}$ Zero product property

The solutions are $\underline{}$.

Homework

✓ **Checkpoint** Find the real-number solutions.

4. $2x^5 + 24x = 14x^3$

5.5 Apply the Remainder and Factor Theorems

Goal • Use theorems to factor polynomials.

Your Notes

VOCABULARY

Polynomial long division

_____

Synthetic division

Example 1 Use polynomial long division

Divide $4x^4 + 5x^2 - 9x + 18$ by $x^2 + 2x + 4$.

Write polynomial division in the same format you use when dividing numbers. Include a "0" as the coefficient of x^3. At each stage, divide the term with the highest power in what is left of the dividend by the first term of the divisor. This gives the next term of the quotient.

$$x^2 + 2x + 4 \overline{\smash{)}\, 4x^4 + 0x^3 + 5x^2 - 9x + 18}$$

> You can check the result of a division problem by multiplying the quotient by the divisor and adding the remainder. The result should be the dividend.

Write the result:

$$\frac{4x^4 + 5x^2 - 9x + 18}{x^2 + 2x + 4} = \underline{\hspace{3cm}}$$

Your Notes

> **REMAINDER THEOREM**
>
> If a polynomial $f(x)$ is divided by $x - k$, then the remainder is $r =$ _____.

Example 2 *Use synthetic division*

Divide $f(x) = x^3 + 4x^2 - 5x + 3$ by $x + 2$.

Solution

$$-2 \ | \ 1 \quad\quad 4 \quad\quad -5 \quad\quad 3$$

$$\frac{x^3 + 4x^2 - 5x + 3}{x + 2} = \underline{\hspace{2cm}}$$

> **FACTOR THEOREM**
>
> A polynomial $f(x)$ has a factor $x - k$ if and only if $f(k) =$ ___.

Example 3 *Factor a polynomial*

Factor $2x^3 - 11x^2 + 3x + 36$ completely given that $x - 3$ is a factor.

Solution

Because $x - 3$ is a factor of $f(x)$, you know that $f(3) =$ ___. Use synthetic division to find the other factors.

$$\underline{\quad} \ | \ 2 \quad\quad -11 \quad\quad 3 \quad\quad 36$$

Use the result to write $f(x)$ as a product of two factors and then factor completely.

$f(x) = 2x^3 - 11x + 3x + 36$
$\quad\quad = (\underline{\quad\quad})(\underline{\quad\quad\quad\quad})$
$\quad\quad = (\underline{\quad\quad})(\underline{\quad\quad})(\underline{\quad\quad})$

Your Notes

Example 4 Find zeros of a polynomial function

One zero of $f(x) = x^3 + 4x^2 - 15x - 18$ is $x = -1$. Find the other zeros.

Solution

Because $f(-1) = 0$, _____ is a factor of f. Use synthetic division to find the other factors.

$$\underline{} \; \big| \;\; 1 \quad\quad 4 \quad\quad -15 \quad\quad -18$$

Use the result to write f as a product of two factors and then factor completely.

$f(x) = x^3 + 4x^2 - 15x - 18$

$= (\underline{})(\underline{})$

$= (\underline{})(\underline{})(\underline{})$

The zeros are _____.

✓ **Checkpoint** Complete the following exercises.

1. Use long division to divide $x^3 - 6x^2 + 9$ by $x - 4$.

2. Use synthetic division to divide $2x^3 + 4x^2 - 3x - 6$ by $x + 3$.

3. Factor $f(x) = 3x^3 + 8x^2 + 3x - 2$ given that $x + 2$ is a factor.

4. A zero of $f(x) = x^3 - 4x^2 - 11x + 30$ is $x = 2$. Find the other zeros.

Homework

5.6 Find Rational Zeros

Goal • Find all real zeros of a polynomial function.

Your Notes

THE RATIONAL ZERO THEOREM

If $f(x) = a_nx^n + \cdots + a_1x + a_0$ has _____ coefficients, then every rational zero of f has the following form:

$$\frac{p}{q} = \frac{\text{factor of constant term }\square}{\text{factor of leading coefficient }\square}$$

Example 1 Find zeros when the leading coefficient is 1

Find all real zeros of $f(x) = x^3 - 4x^2 - 7x + 10$.

1. **List** the possible rational zeros. The leading coefficient is ___ and the constant term is ___. So, the possible rational zeros are: $x =$ ___ ___ ___ ___

2. **Test** these zeros using synthetic division. Test $x =$ ___:

   ___ | 1   −4   −7   10
       | ___   ___   ___
       ___ ___ ___ ___ ⟶ ___ is a zero.

3. **Factor** the trinomial and use the factor theorem.

   $f(x) = ($_____$)($_____$)$.

   $= $ _____.

   The zeros of f are _____.

✓ **Checkpoint** Find all real zeros of the function.

1. $f(x) = x^3 + 3x^2 - 10x - 24$

Your Notes

Example 2 *Find zeros when the leading coefficient is not 1*

Find all real zeros of $f(x) = 8x^4 + 2x^3 - 21x^2 - 7x + 3$.

1. **List** the possible rational zeros of f:

   _____

2. **Choose** reasonable values using the function's graph.

   $x =$ _____

3. **Check** the chosen values using synthetic division.

   $-\frac{3}{2}$ | 8   2   −21   −7   3

   _____ _____ _____ _____

   ___ _____ _____ _____ _____   _____ is a zero.

4. **Factor** out a binomial.

   $f(x) =$ _____   Write as a product of factors.

   $=$ _____   Factor out ___.

   $=$ _____   Multiply by ___.

5. **Repeat** the steps above for $g(x) =$ _____.
   Any zero of g will also be a zero of f. Synthetic division shows that ___ is a zero and yields the quotient _____. Factoring a 4 out of the quotient yields $f(x) =$ _____.

6. **Find** the remaining zeros by solving _____ = 0.

   $x =$ _____   Use quadratic formula.

   $x =$ _____   Simplify.

The real zeros of f are _____.

Your Notes

Example 3 *Solve a multi-step problem*

Sandbox You are building a wooden square sandbox for a local playground. You want the volume of the box to be 16 cubic feet. You want the height of the box to be x feet and the length of each side of the square base to be $x + 3$ feet. What are the dimensions?

Solution

The volume is $V = Bh$ where $B =$ base area and $h =$ height.

$$\boxed{\text{Volume (cubic feet)}} = \boxed{\text{Area of base (square feet)}} \cdot \boxed{\text{Height (feet)}}$$

$$16 = (x + 3)^2 \cdot x$$

$16 =$ _____ Write the equation.

$16 =$ _____ Multiply.

$0 =$ _____ Subtract ____ from each side.

Find the possible rational solutions:

_____

Test the possible solutions. Only positive x-values make sense.

1 | __ __ __ __
  | __ __ __
   __ __ __ __

Check for other solutions. The other possible rational solutions _____ solutions, so $x =$ ___ is the solution.

The height of the sandbox should be ___ foot and each side of the base should be ___ + 3 = ___ feet.

Homework

✓ **Checkpoint** Find all real zeros of the function.

2. $f(x) = 9x^4 + 12x^3 - 26x^2 - 11x + 6$

5.7 Apply the Fundamental Theorem of Algebra

Goal • Classify the zeros of polynomial functions.

Your Notes

VOCABULARY

Repeated Solution

THE FUNDAMENTAL THEOREM OF ALGEBRA

Theorem: If $f(x)$ is a polynomial of degree n where n ___ 0, then the equation $f(x) = 0$ has at least ___ solution in the set of complex numbers.

Corollary: If $f(x)$ is a polynomial of degree n, then the equation $f(x) = 0$ has exactly ___ solutions provided each solution repeated twice is counted as ___ solutions, each solution repeated three times is counted as ___ solutions and so on.

Example 1 *Find the number of solutions or zeros*

Find the number of solutions or zeros for each equation or function.

a. Because $x^3 - 3x^2 + 9x - 27 = 0$ is a _____ degree polynomial equation, it has _____ solutions.

b. Because $f(x) = x^4 + 6x^3 - 32x$ is a _____ degree polynomial function, it has _____ zeros.

✔ **Checkpoint** Complete the following exercise.

1. State the number of zeros of
   $f(x) = x^3 - 2x^2 - 9x + 18$.

Your Notes

> **Example 2** *Find the zeros of a polynomial function*
>
> Find all zeros of $f(x) = x^5 - 5x^4 - 9x^3 - 5x^2 - 8x + 12$.
>
> **Solution**
>
> 1. **Find** the rational zeros of f. Because f is a fifth-degree function, it has _____ zeros. The possible rational zeros are _____. Using synthetic division, you can determine that ___ is a zero repeated twice and _____ is also a zero.
>
> 2. **Write** $f(x)$ in factored form. Dividing f by its known factors gives a quotient of _____. So,
>
> $f(x) =$ _____
>
> 3. **Find** the complex zeros of f. Use the quadratic formula to factor the trinomial into linear factors.
>
> $f(x) =$ _____
>
> The zeros of f are _____

✓ **Checkpoint** Find all zeros of the polynomial function.

> 2. $f(x) = x^4 - 7x^3 + 13x^2 + x - 20$

COMPLEX CONJUGATES THEOREM

If f is a polynomial function with _____ coefficients, and _____ is an imaginary zero of f, then _____ is also a zero of f.

IRRATIONAL CONJUGATES THEOREM

Suppose f is a polynomial function with _____ coefficients, and a and b are rational numbers such that $\sqrt{b}$ is irrational. If _____ is a zero of f, then _____ is also a zero of f.

Your Notes

Example 3 — Use zeros to write a polynomial function

Write a polynomial function f of least degree that has real coefficients, a leading coefficient of 1, and -2 and $3 + i$ as zeros.

Because the coefficients are real and $3 + i$ is a zero, _____ must also be a zero. Use the three zeros and the factor theorem to write $f(x)$ as a product of three factors.

$f(x) = ($ _____ $)[x - ($ _____ $)][x - ($ _____ $)]$ Factored form

$ = ($ _____ $)[$ _____ $][$ _____ $]$ Regroup terms.

$ =$ _____ Multiply.

$ =$ _____ Expand, use $i^2 = -1$.

$ =$ _____ Simplify.

$ =$ _____ Multiply.

$ =$ _____ Combine like terms.

> You can check this result by evaluating $f(x)$ at each of its three zeros.

✓ **Checkpoint** Complete the following exercise.

3. Write a polynomial of least degree that has rational coefficients, a leading coefficient of 1, and 4 and $1 + \sqrt{6}$ as zeros.

DESCARTES' RULE OF SIGNS

Let $f(x) = a_n x^n + a_{n-1} x^{n-1} + \cdots + a_2 x^2 + a_1 x + a_0$ be a polynomial function with real coefficients.

- The number of _____ real zeros of f is equal to the number of changes in sign of the coefficients of _____ or is less than this by an _____ number.

- The number of _____ real zeros of f is equal to the number of changes in sign of the coefficients of _____ or is less than this by an _____ number.

Your Notes

Example 4 — Use Descartes' rule of signs

Determine the possible numbers of positive real zeros, negative real zeros, and imaginary zeros for
$f(x) = 2x^5 - 7x^4 + 12x^3 + 2x^2 + 4x + 6$.

Solution

$f(x) = 2x^5 - 7x^4 + 12x^3 + 2x^2 + 4x + 6$

The coefficients in $f(x)$ have ___ sign changes, so f has _____ positive real zero(s).

$f(-x) = 2(-x)^5 - 7(-x)^4 + 12(-x)^3 + 2(-x)^2 + 4(-x) + 6$

$f(x) = $ _____

The coefficients in $f(-x)$ have ___ sign changes, so f has _____ negative real zero(s).

Positive real zeros	Negative real zeros	Imaginary zeros	Total zeros
___	___	___	___
___	___	___	___
___	___	___	___
___	___	___	___

✓ **Checkpoint** Complete the following exercise.

4. Determine the possible numbers of positive real zeros, negative real zeros, and imaginary zeros for $f(x) = 3x^5 - 4x^4 + x^3 + 6x^2 + 7x - 8$.

Homework

5.8 Analyze Graphs of Polynomial Functions

Goal • Use intercepts to graph polynomial functions.

Your Notes

VOCABULARY

Local maximum

Local minimum

ZEROS, FACTORS, SOLUTIONS, AND INTERCEPTS

Let $f(x) = a_n x^n + a_{n-1} x^{n-1} + \cdots + a_1 x + a_0$ be a polynomial function. If k is a real number, then the following statements are equivalent.

Zero: ___ is a zero of the polynomial function f.

Factor: _____ is a factor of the polynomial $f(x)$.

Solution: ___ is a solution of the polynomial equation $f(x) = 0$.

x-intercept: ___ is an x-intercept of the graph of the polynomial function f. The graph of f contains (___, 0).

Your Notes

Example 1 *Use x-intercepts to graph a polynomial function*

Graph the function
$f(x) = \frac{1}{4}(x + 1)^2(x - 4)$.

1. **Use** the intercepts. Because ____ and ____ are zeros of f, plot (____, ____) and (____, ____).

2. **Plot** points between and beyond the x-intercepts.

x	−2	0	1	2	3	5
y						

3. **Determine** the end behavior. Because f has _____ factors of the form $x - k$, and a constant factor of ____, it is a _____ function with a _____ leading coefficient. So, $f(x) \to$ ____ as $x \to -\infty$ and $f(x) \to$ ____ as $x \to +\infty$.

4. **Draw** the graph so that it passes through the plotted points and has the appropriate end behavior.

✓ **Checkpoint** Complete the following exercise.

1. Graph the function
$f(x) = 2(x - 2)(x + 1)(x - 1)$.

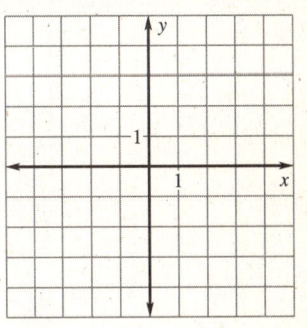

TURNING POINTS OF POLYNOMIAL FUNCTIONS

The graph of every polynomial function of degree n has at most _____ turning points. Moreover, if a polynomial function has n distinct real zeros, then its graph has exactly _____ turning points.

Your Notes

Example 2 Find turning points

Graph the function. Identify the x-intercepts and the points where the local maximums and local minimums occur.

a. $f(x) = x^3 - 4x^2 + 6$

b. $f(x) = -x^4 + 3x^3 + x^2 - 4x$

a. Use a graphing calculator to graph the function. Notice that the graph of f has _____ x-intercepts and _____ turning points. Use the graphing calculator's *zero*, *maximum*, and *minimum* features to approximate the coordinates of the points.

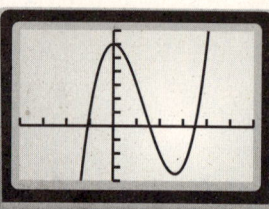

The x-intercepts of the graph are _____ _____. The function has a local maximum at (___, ___) and a local minimum at (___, ___).

b. Use a graphing calculator to graph the function. Notice that the graph has _____ x-intercepts and _____ turning points. Use the graphing calculator's *zero*, *maximum*, and *minimum* features to approximate the coordinates of the points.

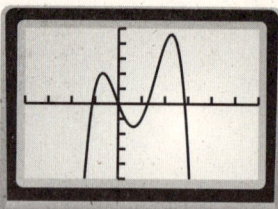

The x-intercepts of the graph are _____ _____. The function has local maximums at (___, ___) and (___, ___). The function has a local minimum at (___, ___).

✓ **Checkpoint** Complete the following exercise.

Homework

2. Use a graphing calculator to identify the x-intercepts, local maximums, and local minimums of the graph of $f(x) = x^4 + x^3 - 5x^2 + 4$.

5.9 Write Polynomial Functions and Models

Goal • Write higher-degree polynomial functions.

Your Notes

VOCABULARY

Finite differences

Example 1   Write a cubic function

Write the cubic function whose graph is shown.

Solution

1. Use the three given x-intercepts to write the function in intercept form.

   $f(x) = a$ _____

2. Find a by substituting the coordinates of the fourth point.

   ____ = a(_____)(_____)(_____)

   ____ = ____ a

   a = ____

The function is $f(x) =$ _____.

CHECK Check the end behavior for f. The degree of f is ____ and a ____ 0. So, $f(x) \to$ ____ as $x \to -\infty$ and $f(x) \to$ ____ as $x \to +\infty$, which matches the graph.

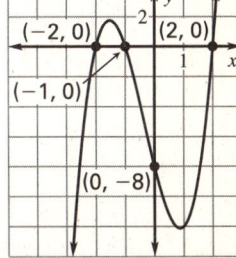

Checkpoint Complete the following exercise.

1. Write the cubic function of the graph shown.

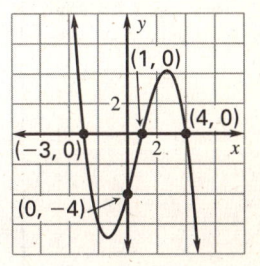

Your Notes

Example 2 *Finding finite differences*

An equation for a polynomial function is $f(n) = n^3 + 2n^2 - 4n + 3$. Show that this function has constant third-order differences.

Solution

Write the first several function values. Find the first-order differences by subtracting consecutive function values. Then find the second-order differences by subtracting consecutive _____ differences. Finally, find the third-order differences by subtracting consecutive _____ differences.

$f(1)$ $f(2)$ $f(3)$ $f(4)$ $f(5)$ $f(6)$ Function values for equally-spaced *n*-values

First-order differences

Second-order differences

Thrid-order differences

Each third-order difference is ___, so the third-order differences are constant.

✔ **Checkpoint** Complete the following exercise.

2. Show that $f(n) = n^2 - 5n + 4$ has constant second-order differences.

PROPERTIES OF FINITE DIFFERENCES

1. If a polynomial function $f(x)$ has degree *n*, then the *n*th-order differences of function values for equally-spaced *x*-values are _____.

2. Conversely, if the *n*th-order differences of equally spaced data are _____, then the data can be represented by a polynomial function of degree *n*.

Example 3 Model with finite differences

The values of a polynomial function for five consecutive whole numbers are given below. Write a polynomial function for $f(n)$.

$f(1) = 3$ $f(2) = 8$ $f(3) = 14$ $f(4) = 21$ $f(5) = 29$

Solution

Begin by finding the finite differences.

$f(1)$ $f(2)$ $f(3)$ $f(4)$ $f(5)$ Function values for equally spaced n-values

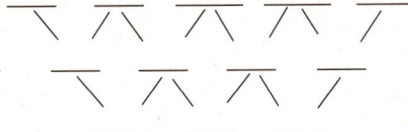

First-order differences

Second-order differences

Because the _____ differences are constant, you know that the numbers can be represented by a _____ function which has the form
$f(n) =$ _____.

Substitute the first three values into the function to obtain a system of linear equations in _____ variables.

_____ → _____

_____ → _____

_____ → _____

The solution to the linear system is

$a =$ ___, $b =$ ___, and $c =$ ___.

So, the polynomial function is $f(n) =$ _____.

✓ Checkpoint Complete the following exercise.

3. Values of a polynomial function for six consecutive numbers are given. Write a polynomial function for $f(n)$.

   $f(1) = 1, f(2) = 4, f(3) = 13, f(4) = 34,$
   $f(5) = 73, f(6) = 136$

Homework

Words to Review

Give an example of the vocabulary word.

Scientific notation	Polynomial
Polynomial function	Synthetic substitution
End behavior	Prime polynomial
Factored completely	Factor by grouping

Quadratic form	Polynomial long division

Synthetic division	Repeated solution

Local maximum	Local minimum

Finite differences

Review your notes and Chapter 5 by using the Chapter Review on pages 402–406 of your textbook.

6.1 Evaluate nth Roots and Use Rational Exponents

Goal • Evaluate nth roots and study rational exponents.

Your Notes

VOCABULARY

nth root of a

Index of a radical

REAL nth ROOTS OF a

Let n be an integer ($n > 1$) and let a be a real number.

If n is an even integer:

- $a < 0$ No real nth roots.
- $a = 0$ One real nth root: $\sqrt[n]{0} = \underline{}$
- $a > 0$ Two real nth roots: $\pm\sqrt[n]{a} = \underline{}$

If n is an odd integer:

- $a < 0$ One real nth root: $\sqrt[n]{a} = \underline{}$
- $a = 0$ One real nth root: $\sqrt[n]{0} = \underline{}$
- $a > 0$ One real nth root: $\sqrt[n]{a} = \underline{}$

Example 1 Find nth roots

Find the indicated real nth root(s) of a.

a. $n = 3$, $a = -64$
b. $n = 6$, $a = 729$

Solution

a. Because $n = 3$ is odd and $a = -64$ ___ 0, -64 has _____. Because $(\underline{})^3 = -64$, you can write $\sqrt[3]{-64} = \underline{}$ or $(-64)^{1/3} = \underline{}$.

b. Because $n = 6$ is even and $a = 729$ ___ 0, 729 has _____. Because $\underline{}^6 = 729$ and $(\underline{})^6 = 729$, you can write $\pm\sqrt[6]{729} = \underline{}$ or $\pm 729^{1/6} = \underline{}$.

Your Notes

✓ **Checkpoint** Find the indicated real nth roots of a.

1. $n = 4$, $a = 256$	2. $n = 3$, $a = 512$

RATIONAL EXPONENTS

Let a be a real number, and let m and n be positive integers with $n > 1$.

$a^{m/n} = (a^{1/n})^m = (\underline{})^m$

$a^{-m/n} = \dfrac{1}{a^{m/n}} = \dfrac{1}{(a^{1/n})^m} = \dfrac{1}{(\underline{})^m}$, $a \neq 0$

Example 2 *Evaluate an expression with rational exponents*

Evaluate $8^{-4/3}$.

Solution

Rational Exponent Form

$8^{-4/3} =$ _____

$=$ _____

$=$ _____

$=$ _____

Radical Form

$8^{-4/3} =$ _____

$=$ _____

$=$ _____

$=$ _____

Example 3 *Solve equations using nth roots*

a. $2x^6 = 1458$
   $x^6 =$ _____
   $x =$ _____
   $x =$ _____

b. $(x + 4)^3 = 12$
   $x + 4 =$ _____
   $x =$ _____
   $x \approx$ _____

Your Notes

Example 4 — Use nth roots in problem solving

Animal Population The population P of a certain animal species after t months can be modeled by $P = C(1.21)^{t/3}$ where C is the initial population. Find the population after 19 months if the initial population was 75.

Solution

$P = C(1.21)^{t/3}$ Write model for population.

= _____   Substitute for C and t.

≈ _____   Use a calculator.

The population of the species is about _____ after 19 months.

✓ Checkpoint Complete the following exercises.

3. Evaluate $(-125)^{-2/3}$.	4. Solve $(y - 3)^4 = 200$.

5. The volume of a cone is given by $V = \dfrac{\pi r^2 h}{3}$, where h is the height of the cone and r is the radius. Find the radius of a cone whose volume is 25 cubic inches and whose height is 6 inches.

Homework

6.2 Apply Properties of Rational Exponents

Goal • Simplify expressions involving rational exponents.

Your Notes

VOCABULARY

Simplest form of a radical

Like radicals

PROPERTIES OF RATIONAL EXPONENTS

Let a and b be real numbers and let m and n be rational numbers. The following properties have the same names as those in Lesson 5.1, but now apply to rational exponents.

Property

1. $a^m \cdot a^n = a^{m+n}$ $\quad 4^{1/2} \cdot 4^{3/2} = 4^{(1/2 + 3/2)} = \underline{\quad}$

2. $(a^m)^n = a^{mn}$ $\quad (2^{5/2})^2 = 2^{(5/2 \cdot 2)} = \underline{\quad}$

3. $(ab)^m = a^m b^m$ $\quad (16 \cdot 4)^{1/2} = 16^{1/2} \cdot 4^{1/2} = \underline{\quad}$

4. $a^{-m} = \dfrac{1}{a^m}, a \neq 0$ $\quad 25^{-1/2} = \dfrac{1}{25^{1/2}} = \underline{\quad}$

5. $\dfrac{a^m}{a^n} = a^{m-n}, a \neq 0$ $\quad \dfrac{3^{5/2}}{3^{1/2}} = 3^{(5/2 - 1/2)} = \underline{\quad}$

6. $\left(\dfrac{a}{b}\right)^m = \dfrac{a^m}{b^m}, b \neq 0$ $\quad \left(\dfrac{27}{8}\right)^{1/3} = \dfrac{27^{1/3}}{8^{1/3}} = \underline{\quad}$

Your Notes

> **Example 1** — *Use properties of exponents*
>
> Use the properties of rational exponents to simplify the expression.
>
> a. $9^{1/2} \cdot 9^{3/4} =$ _____
>
> b. $(7^{2/3} \cdot 5^{1/6})^3 =$ _____
> $=$ _____
> $=$ _____
>
> c. $\dfrac{3^{5/6}}{3^{1/3}} =$ _____
>
> d. $\left(\dfrac{16^{2/3}}{4^{2/3}}\right)^4 =$ _____

PROPERTIES OF RADICALS

Product Property of Radicals

$\sqrt[n]{a \cdot b} =$ _____

Quotient Property of Radicals

$\sqrt[n]{\dfrac{a}{b}} =$ _____ , $b \neq 0$

> **Example 2** — *Use properties of radicals*
>
> Use the properties of radicals to simplify the expression.
>
> a. $\sqrt[5]{27} \cdot \sqrt[5]{9} =$ _____ $=$ _____ $=$ _____   Product property
>
> b. $\dfrac{\sqrt[3]{192}}{\sqrt[3]{3}} =$ _____ $=$ _____ $=$ _____   Quotient property

---

✓ **Checkpoint** Simplify the expression.

1. $(6^6 \cdot 5^6)^{-1/6}$	2. $\dfrac{\sqrt{245}}{\sqrt{5}}$

166 Lesson 6.2 • Algebra 2 Notetaking Guide

Your Notes

Example 3 — Write radicals in simplest form

Write the expression in simplest form.

$\sqrt[5]{128}$ = _____   Factor out perfect fifth power.

= _____ · _____   Product property

= _____   Simplify.

Example 4 — Add and subtract like radicals and roots

Simplify the expression.

a. $2(12^{2/3}) + 7(12^{2/3})$ = _____

b. $\sqrt[4]{48} - \sqrt[4]{3}$ = _____ · _____ − _____

= _____

✓ **Checkpoint** Write the expression in simplest form.

3. $\sqrt[3]{\dfrac{5}{9}}$	4. $6\sqrt[4]{6} + 2\sqrt[4]{6}$

Example 5 — Simplify expressions involving variables

Simplify the expression. Assume all variables are positive.

a. $\sqrt[5]{32x^{15}}$ = _____

b. $(36m^4 n^{10})^{1/2}$ = _____

= _____

c. $\sqrt[3]{\dfrac{a^9}{b^6}}$ = _____

d. $\dfrac{42x^4 z^7}{6x^{3/2} y^{-3} z^5}$ = _____

Your Notes

Example 6 — Write variable expressions in simplest form

Write the expression in simplest form. Assume all variables are positive.

$\sqrt[4]{\dfrac{a^2}{b^6}} =$ _____   Make denominator a perfect fourth power.

$=$ _____   Simplify.

$=$ _____   Quotient property.

$=$ _____   Simplify.

Example 7 — Add and subtract expressions involving variables

Perform the indicated operation. Assume all variables are positive.

a. $10\sqrt[5]{y} - 6\sqrt[5]{y} =$ _____

b. $3a^2 b^{1/4} + 4a^2 b^{1/4} =$ _____

✓ **Checkpoint** Simplify the expression. Assume all variables are positive.

5. $\sqrt[3]{8x^7 y^3 z^{11}}$

6. $7\sqrt[3]{2a^5} - a\sqrt[3]{128a^2}$

Homework

Lesson 6.2 • Algebra 2 Notetaking Guide

6.3 Perform Function Operations and Composition

Goal • Perform operations with functions.

Your Notes

VOCABULARY

Power function

Composition

OPERATIONS ON FUNCTIONS

Let f and g be any two functions. A new function h can be defined by performing any of the four basic operations on f and g.

Operation and Definition   **Example:** $f(x) = 3x$, $g(x) = x + 3$

Addition
$h(x) = f(x) + g(x)$ $h(x) = 3x + (x + 3)$
$= $ _____

Subtraction
$h(x) = f(x) - g(x)$ $h(x) = 3x - (x + 3)$
$= $ _____

Multiplication
$h(x) = f(x) \cdot g(x)$ $h(x) = 3x(x + 3)$
$= $ _____

Division
$h(x) = \dfrac{f(x)}{g(x)}$ $h(x) = $ _____

The domain of h consists of the x-values that are in the domains of _____. Additionally, the domain of a quotient does not include x-values for which $g(x) = $ ___.

Lesson 6.3 • Algebra 2 Notetaking Guide

Your Notes

Example 1 *Add and subtract functions*

Let $f(x) = 3x^{1/2}$ and $g(x) = -5x^{1/2}$. Find the following.

a. $f(x) + g(x)$
b. $f(x) - g(x)$
c. the domains of $f + g$ and $f - g$

Solution

a. $f(x) + g(x) = 3x^{1/2} + (-5x^{1/2})$
   $= \underline{}$

b. $f(x) - g(x) = 3x^{1/2} - (-5x^{1/2})$
   $= \underline{}$

c. The functions f and g each have the same domain: $\underline{}$. So, the domains of $f + g$ and $f - g$ also consist of $\underline{}$.

Example 2 *Multiply and divide functions*

Let $f(x) = 7x$ and $g(x) = x^{1/6}$. Find the following.

a. $f(x) \cdot g(x)$
b. $\dfrac{f(x)}{g(x)}$
c. the domains of $f \cdot g$ and $\dfrac{f}{g}$

Solution

a. $f(x) \cdot g(x) = (7x)(x^{1/6}) = \underline{}$

b. $\dfrac{f(x)}{g(x)} = \underline{}$

c. The domain of f consists of $\underline{}$, and the domain of g consists of $\underline{}$. So, the domain of $f \cdot g$ consists of $\underline{}$. Because $g(0) = \underline{}$, the domain of $\dfrac{f}{g}$ is restricted to $\underline{}$.

Your Notes

✓ **Checkpoint** Complete the following exercise.

1. Let $f(x) = 5x^{3/2}$ and $g(x) = -2x^{3/2}$. Find (a) $f + g$, (b) $f - g$, (c) $f \cdot g$, (d) $\dfrac{f}{g}$, and (e) the domains.

COMPOSITION OF FUNCTIONS

The composition of a function g with a function f is $h(x) = $ _____. The domain of h is the set of all x-values such that x is in the domain of ___ and $f(x)$ is in the domain of ___.

Domain of f — Input of f: x
Range of f — Output of f: $f(x)$
Domain of g — Input of g: $f(x)$
Range of g — Output of g: $g(f(x))$

Lesson 6.3 • Algebra 2 Notetaking Guide

Your Notes

Example 3 — Find compositions of functions

Let $f(x) = 6x^{-1}$ and $g(x) = 3x + 5$. Find the following.

a. $f(g(x))$ b. $g(f(x))$ c. $f(f(x))$

d. the domain of each composition

Solution

a. $f(g(x)) = f(3x + 5) = $ _____

b. $g(f(x)) = g(6x^{-1})$

= _____

c. $f(f(x)) = f(6x^{-1}) = $ _____

d. The domain of $f(g(x))$ consists of _____ except $x = $ ___ because $g($ ___ $) = 0$ is not in the _____. (Note that $f(0) = $ ___, which is _____.) The domains of $g(f(x))$ and $f(f(x))$ consist of _____ except $x = $ ___, again because _____.

✓ **Checkpoint** Complete the following exercise.

2. Let $f(x) = 5x - 4$ and $g(x) = 3x^{-1}$. Find (a) $f(g(x))$, (b) $g(f(x))$, (c) $f(f(x))$, and (d) the domain of each composition.

Homework

6.4 Use Inverse Functions

Goal • Find inverse functions.

Your Notes

VOCABULARY

Inverse relation

Inverse function

Example 1 *Find an inverse relation*

Find an equation for the inverse of the relation
$y = 7x - 4$.

$y = 7x - 4$ Write original equation.

_____   Switch x and y.

_____   Add ___ to each side.

_____   Solve for y. This is the inverse relation.

INVERSE FUNCTIONS

Functions f and g are inverses of each other provided:

$f(g(x)) =$ ___   and $g(f(x)) =$

The function g is denoted by f^{-1}, read as "f inverse."

Example 2 *Verify that functions are inverses*

Verify that $f(x) = 7x - 4$ and $f^{-1}(x) = \frac{1}{7}x + \frac{4}{7}$ are inverses.

Show that $f(f^{-1}(x)) = x$.   Show that $f^{-1}(f(x)) = x$.

$f(f^{-1}(x)) = f\left(\frac{1}{7}x + \frac{4}{7}\right)$ $f^{-1}(f(x)) = f^{-1}(7x - 4)$

= _____   = _____

= _____   = _____

= ___   = ___

Your Notes

✓ **Checkpoint** Find the inverse of the function. Then verify that your result and the original function are inverses.

1. $f(x) = -3x + 5$

Example 3 *Find the inverse of a power function*

Find the inverse of $f(x) = 4x^2$, $x \leq 0$. Then graph f and f^{-1}.

$f(x) = 4x^2$ Write original function.

$y = 4x^2$ Replace $f(x)$ with y.

_____   Switch x and y.

_____   Divide each side by 4.

_____   Take square roots of each side.

The domain of f is restricted to negative values of x. So, the range of f^{-1} must also be restricted to negative values, and therefore the inverse is $f^{-1}(x) = $ _____. (If the domain were restricted to $x \geq 0$, you would choose $f^{-1}(x) = $ _____.)

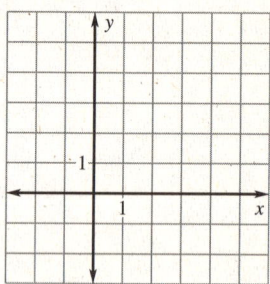

> You can check the solution by noting that the graph of $f^{-1}(x) = -\frac{1}{2}\sqrt{x}$ is the reflection of the graph of $f(x) = 4x^2$, $x \leq 0$, in the line $y = x$.

HORIZONTAL LINE TEST

The inverse of a function f is also a function if and only if no horizontal line intersects the graph of f _____ _____.

Function   Not a function

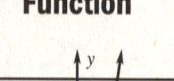

Lesson 6.4 • Algebra 2 Notetaking Guide

Your Notes

Example 4 — Find the inverse of a cubic function

Consider the function $f(x) = \frac{1}{4}x^3 + 3$. Determine whether the inverse of f is a function. Then find the inverse.

Solution

Graph the function f. Notice that no _____ intersects the graph more than once. So, the inverse of f is itself a _____. To find an equation for f^{-1}, complete the following steps.

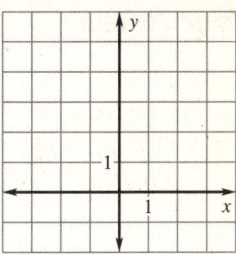

$f(x) = \frac{1}{4}x^3 + 3$ Write original function.

$y = \frac{1}{4}x^3 + 3$ Replace $f(x)$ with y.

_____   Switch x and y.

_____   Subtract ___ from each side.

_____   Multiply each side by ___.

_____   Take cube root of each side.

The inverse of f is $f^{-1}(x) =$ _____.

✓ **Checkpoint** Find the inverse of the function.

2. $f(x) = 2x^4 + 1$	3. $g(x) = \frac{1}{32}x^5$

Homework

6.5 Graph Square Root and Cube Root Functions

Goal • Graph square root and cube root functions.

Your Notes

VOCABULARY

Radical function

PARENT FUNCTIONS FOR SQUARE ROOT AND CUBE ROOT FUNCTIONS

- The parent function for the family of square root functions is $f(x) = \sqrt{x}$. The domain is x _____, and the range is y _____.

- The parent function for the family of cube root functions is $g(x) = \sqrt[3]{x}$. The domain and range are _____.

Example 1 Graph a square root function

Graph $y = 2\sqrt{x}$, and state the domain and range. Compare the graph with the graph of $y = \sqrt{x}$.

Solution

Make a table of values and sketch the graph.

x	0	1	2	3	4
y	___	___	___	___	___

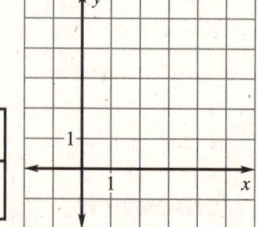

The radicand of a square root is always nonnegative. So, the domain is x ___ 0. The range is y ___ 0.

The graph of $y = 2\sqrt{x}$ is a vertical _____ of the parent graph of $y = \sqrt{x}$.

Your Notes

> **Example 2** *Graph a cube root function*
>
> Graph $y = -\frac{1}{2}\sqrt[3]{x}$, and state the domain and range. Compare the graph with the graph of $y = \sqrt[3]{x}$.
>
> **Solution**
>
> Make a table of values and sketch the graph.
>
> | x | −2 | −1 | 0 |
> |---|----|----|---|
> | y | ___ | ___ | ___ |
>
> | x | 1 | 2 |
> |---|---|---|
> | y | ___ | ___ |
>
>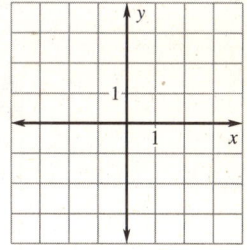
>
> The domain and range are _____.
>
> The graph of $y = -\frac{1}{2}\sqrt[3]{x}$ is a vertical _____ of the parent graph of $y = \sqrt[3]{x}$ by a factor of ___ followed by a reflection in the x-axis.

✓ **Checkpoint** Graph the function. Then state the domain and range.

1. $y = 2\sqrt[3]{x}$

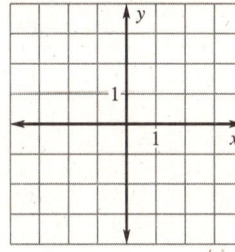

2. $y = -2\sqrt{x}$

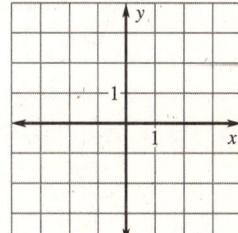

Lesson 6.5 • Algebra 2 Notetaking Guide

Your Notes

GRAPHS OF RADICAL FUNCTIONS

To graph $y = a\sqrt{x - h} + k$ or $y = a\sqrt[3]{x - h} + k$, follow these steps:

Step 1 _____ the graph of $y = a\sqrt{x}$ or $y = a\sqrt[3]{x}$.

Step 2 **Translate** the graph ___ units horizontally and ___ units vertically.

Example 3 *Graph a translated square root function*

Graph $y = 3\sqrt{x - 1} + 2$. Then state the domain and range.

Solution

1. **Sketch** the graph of $y = 3\sqrt{x}$. Notice that it begins at the origin and passes through the point (1, ___).

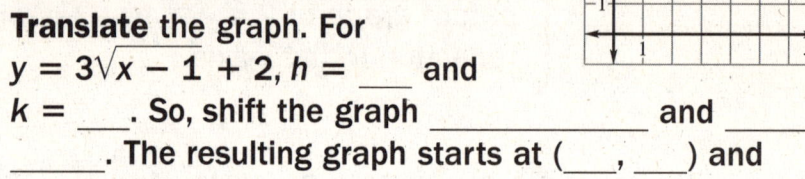

2. **Translate** the graph. For $y = 3\sqrt{x - 1} + 2$, $h =$ ___ and $k =$ ___. So, shift the graph _____ and _____. The resulting graph starts at (___, ___) and passes through (___, ___).

From the graph, you can see that the domain of the function is _____ and the range of the function is _____.

Your Notes

Example 4 Graph a translated cube root function

Graph $y = -2\sqrt[3]{x + 3} - 2$. Then state the domain and range.

Solution

1. Sketch the graph of $y = -2\sqrt[3]{x}$. Notice that it passes through the origin and the points (___, ___) and (___, ___).

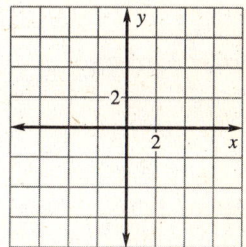

2. Note that for $y = -2\sqrt[3]{x + 3} - 2$, $h =$ ___ and $k =$ ___. So, shift the graph _____ and _____. The resulting graph passes through the points (___, ___), (___, ___), and (___, ___).

From the graph, you can see that the domain and range of the function are both _____.

✓ **Checkpoint** Graph the function. Then state the domain and range.

3. $y = -\frac{1}{2}\sqrt[3]{x + 3} + 2$

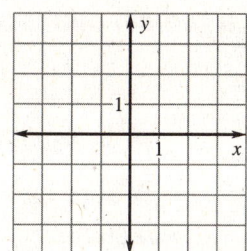

4. $y = 3\sqrt[3]{x} + 2$

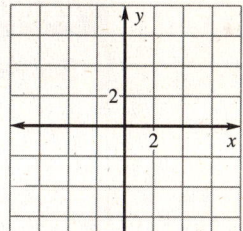

Homework

6.6 Solve Radical Equations

Goal • Solve radical equations.

Your Notes

VOCABULARY

Radical equation

SOLVING RADICAL EQUATIONS

To solve a radical equation, follow these steps:

Step 1 _____ the radical on one side of the equation, if necessary.

Step 2 Raise each side of the equation to the same _____ to eliminate the radical and obtain a linear, quadratic, or other polynomial equation.

Step 3 _____ the polynomial equation using techniques you learned in previous chapters. Check your solution.

Example 1 *Solve a radical equation*

Solve $\sqrt{x + 6} = 3$.

$\sqrt{x+6} = 3$		Write original equation.
_____ = _____		Square each side to eliminate the radical.
_____ = _____		Simplify.
_____ = _____		Subtract ___ from each side.

The solution is ___. Check this in the original equation.

✓ **Checkpoint** Solve the equation. Check your solution.

1. $\sqrt[3]{x - 5} + 1 = -1$

Your Notes

Example 2 *Solve an equation with a rational exponent*

$(3x + 4)^{2/3} = 16$ Original equation

_____ = _____ Raise each side to the power $\frac{3}{2}$.

_____ = _____ Apply properties of exponents.

_____ = _____ Simplify.

_____ = _____ Subtract ___ from each side.

_____ = _____ Divide each side by ___.

The solution is ___. Check this in the original equation.

Example 3 *Solve an equation with an extraneous solution*

$x - 2 = \sqrt{x + 10}$ Original equation

_____ = _____ Square each side.

_____ = _____ Expand left side and simplify right side.

_____ = 0 Write in standard form.

_____ = 0 Factor.

_____ = 0   or   _____ = 0 Zero product property

$x =$ ___ or $x =$ ___ Solve for x.

CHECK

Check $x =$ ___.   Check $x = -$ ___.

$x - 2 = \sqrt{x + 10}$ $x - 2 = \sqrt{x + 10}$

_____ $\stackrel{?}{=}$ _____   _____ $\stackrel{?}{=}$ _____

_____ $\stackrel{?}{=}$ _____   _____ $\stackrel{?}{=}$ _____

_____   _____

The only solution is ___. (The apparent solution ___ is extraneous.)

Your Notes

Example 4 *Solve an equation with two radicals*

Solve $\sqrt{x+6} + 2 = \sqrt{10-3x}$.

$\sqrt{x+6} + 2 = \sqrt{10-3x}$ Write original equation.

___ = ___   Square each side.

___ = ___   Expand left side and simplify right side.

___ = ___   Isolate radical expression.

___ = ___   Divide each side by 4.

___ = ___   Square each side again.

___ = ___   Simplify.

$0 =$ ___   Write in standard form.

$0 =$ ___   Factor.

___ $= 0$ or   ___ $= 0$ Zero product property

$x =$ ___   or $x =$ ___   Solve for x.

CHECK Check $x =$ ___.

___ $\stackrel{?}{=}$ ___

___ $\stackrel{?}{=}$ ___

___ $=$ ___

Check $x = -$ ___.

___ $\stackrel{?}{=}$ ___

___ $\stackrel{?}{=}$ ___

___ $=$ ___

The only solution is ___. (The apparent solution ___ is extraneous.)

Your Notes

✓ **Checkpoint** Solve the equation. Check for extraneous solutions.

2. $-2x^{4/3} - 21 = -53$

3. $x + 2 = \sqrt{2x + 7}$

4. $\sqrt{3x + 4} - 1 = \sqrt{x + 5}$

Homework

Words to Review

Give an example of the vocabulary word.

nth root of a	Index of a radical
Simplest form of a radical	Like radicals
Power function	Composition
Inverse relation	Inverse function
Radical function	Radical equation

Review your notes and Chapter 6 by using the Chapter Review on pages 466–468 of your textbook.

7.1 Graph Exponential Growth Functions

Goal • Graph and use exponential growth functions.

Your Notes

VOCABULARY

Exponential function

Exponential growth function

Growth factor

Asymptote

PARENT FUNCTION FOR EXPONENTIAL GROWTH FUNCTIONS

The function $y = b^x$, where b ____ 1, is the parent function for the family of exponential growth functions with base ____. The general shape of the graph of $y = b^x$ is shown below.

The *x*-axis is an asymptote of the graph. An asymptote is a line that a graph approaches more and more closely.

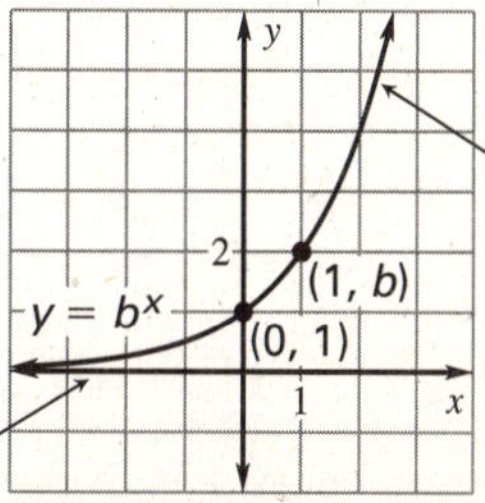

The graph rises from left to right, passing through the points (0,1) and (1,b).

The domain of $y = b^x$ is _____. The range is _____.

Your Notes

> **Example 1** Graph $y = ab^x$ for $b > 1$
>
> Graph the function $y = \frac{1}{4} \cdot 6^x$.
>
> **Solution**
>
> Plot $\left(0, \underline{}\right)$ and $\left(1, \underline{}\right)$. Then, from *left* to *right*, draw a curve that begins just _____ the *x*-axis, passes through the two points, and moves _____.

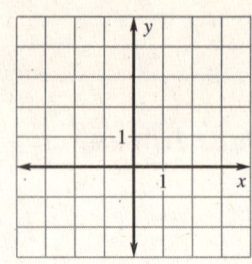

> **Example 2** Graph $y = ab^{x-h} + k$ for $b > 1$
>
> Graph $y = 2 \cdot 3^{x-2} - 2$. State the domain and range.
>
> **Solution**
>
> Begin by sketching the graph of $y = 2 \cdot 3^x$, which passes through $(0, \underline{})$ and $(1, \underline{})$. Then translate the graph _____ and _____.
>
> The graph's asymptote is the line _____. The domain is all real _____, and the range is _____.

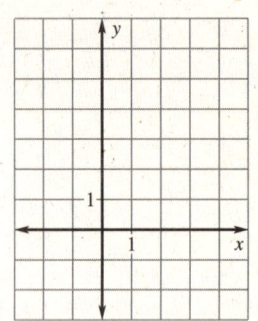

✓ **Checkpoint** Graph the function. State the domain and range.

1. $y = 2 \cdot 4^{x+1} - 3$

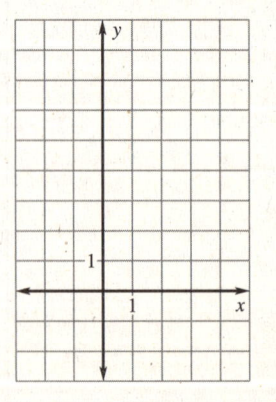

186   Lesson 7.1 • Algebra 2 Notetaking Guide

Your Notes

Example 3 — Solve a multi-step problem

Buffalo In the last 12 years, an initial population of 38 buffalo in a state park grew by about 7% per year.

a. Write an exponential growth model giving the number n of buffalo after t years. About how many buffalo were in the park after 7 years?

b. Graph the model. Use the graph to estimate the year when there were about 53 buffalo.

Solution

a. The initial amount is $a =$ ____ and the percent increase is $r =$ _____. So, the exponential growth model is:

$n = a(1 + r)^t$ Write exponential growth model.

$= $ _____   Substitute for a and r.

$= $ _____   Simplify.

Using this model, you can estimate the number of buffalo after 7 years ($t = 7$) to be

$n =$ _____ $\approx$ ____ buffalo.

b. The graph passes through the points (0, ____) and (1, _____). Plot a few other points. Then draw a smooth curve through the points. Using the graph, you can estimate that the number of buffalo was 53 after about ____ years.

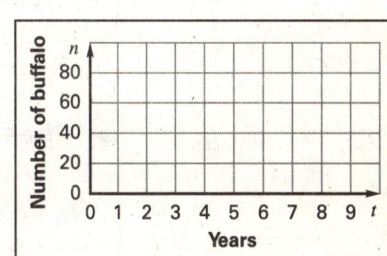

COMPOUND INTEREST

Consider an initial principal P deposited in an account that pays interest at an annual rate r (expressed as a decimal), compounded n times per year. The amount A in the account after t years is given by this equation:

$A =$ _____

Your Notes

Example 4 — Find the balance in an account

You deposit $2900 in an account that pays 3.5% annual interest. Find the balance after 1 year if the interest is compounded monthly and annually.

a. With interest compounded monthly, the balance after 1 year is:

$A = 2900$ _____ Substitute for *P*, *r*, *n*, and *t*.

$= 2900$ _____ Simplify.

$\approx$ _____ Use a calculator.

The balance at the end of 1 year is _____.

b. With interest compounded annually, the balance after 1 year is:

$A = 2900$ _____

$= 2900$ _____

$=$ _____

The balance at the end of 1 year is _____.

✓ Checkpoint Complete the following exercises.

2. From Example 3, how many buffalo were in the park after 11 years?

3. You deposit $5000 into an account that pays 3.72% annual interest. Find the balance after three years if the interest is compounded quarterly.

Homework

7.2 Graph Exponential Decay Functions

Goal • Graph and use exponential decay functions.

Your Notes

VOCABULARY

Exponential decay function

Decay factor

PARENT FUNCTION FOR EXPONENTIAL DECAY FUNCTIONS

The function $y = b^x$, where $0 < b < 1$, is the parent function for the family of exponential decay functions with base b. The general shape of the graph of $y = b^x$ is shown below.

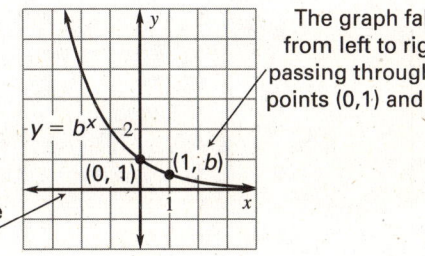

The graph falls from left to right, passing through the points (0,1) and (1,b)

The x-axis is an asymptote of the graph.

The domain of $y = b^x$ is _____. The range is _____.

Example 1 — Graph $y = ab^x$ for $0 < b < 1$

Graph the function $y = -2\left(\frac{3}{4}\right)^x$.

Plot (0, ___) and (1, ___). Then, from *right* to *left*, draw a curve that begins just _____ the x-axis, passes through the two points, and moves _____ to the left.

Your Notes

Example 2 Graph $y = ab^{x-h} + k$ for $0 < b < 1$

Graph $y = 2\left(\frac{3}{5}\right)^{x-1} + 1$. State the domain and range.

Solution

Begin by sketching the graph of $y = 2\left(\frac{3}{5}\right)^x$, which passes through (0, ___) and 1, (___). Then translate the graph _____ and _____. Notice that the graph passes through (1, ___) and (2, ___).

The graph's asymptote is the line _____. The domain is _____, and the range is _____.

✓ **Checkpoint** Graph the function. State the domain and range.

1. $y = -2\left(\frac{4}{5}\right)^x$

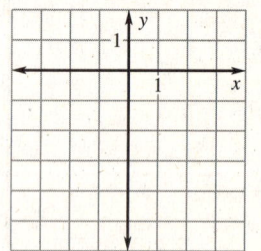

2. $y = 3\left(\frac{2}{3}\right)^{x+1} - 3$

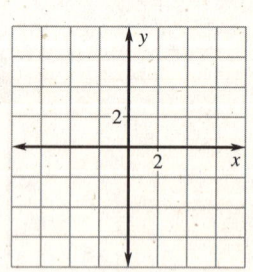

190 Lesson 7.2 • Algebra 2 Notetaking Guide

Your Notes

Example 3 Solve a multi-step problem

Televisions A new television costs $1200. The value of the television decreases by 21% each year. Write an exponential decay model giving the television's value y (in dollars) after t years. Estimate the value after 2 years. Graph the model. Use the graph to estimate when the value of the television will be $300.

Solution

a. The initial amount is $a =$ _____ and the percent decrease is $r =$ _____. So, the model is:

$y = a(1 - r)^t$ Write exponential decay formula.

$= $ _____   Substitute for a and r.

$= $ _____   Simplify.

When $t = 2$, the television's value is
$y = 1200(0.79)^2 = $ _____.

b. The graph passes through the points (0, _____) and (1, _____). It has the _____ as its asymptote. Plot a few other points. Then draw a smooth curve through the points.

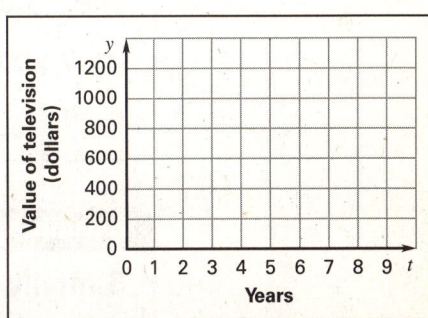

c. Using the graph, you can estimate that the value of the television will be $300 after about ___ years.

✓ **Checkpoint** Complete the following exercise.

3. Rework Example 3, with a 12% decrease each year.

Homework

7.3 Use Functions Involving e

Goal • Study functions involving the natural base e.

Your Notes

VOCABULARY

Natural base e

THE NATURAL BASE e

The natural base e is irrational. It is defined as follows:
As n approaches $+\infty$, $\left(1 + \frac{1}{n}\right)^n$ approaches

$e \approx$ _____ .

Example 1 Simplify natural base expressions

Simplify the expression.

a. $e^6 \cdot e^3 = e^{\_\_\_} = \_\_\_$

b. $\dfrac{18e^6}{2e^4} = _____ = \_\_\_$

c. $(4e^{3x})^2 = _____$
$= _____$

Example 2 Evaluate natural base expressions

Use a calculator to evaluate the expression.

Expression	Keystrokes	Display
a. e^{-2}	[2nd] [e^x] [−] ___ [)] [ENTER]	_____
b. $e^{0.3}$	[2nd] [e^x] ___ [)] [ENTER]	_____

Lesson 7.3 • Algebra 2 Notetaking Guide

Your Notes

✓ **Checkpoint** Complete the following exercises.

1. Simplify $e^{-3} \cdot e^6$.	2. Simplify $\dfrac{(4e^3)^2}{8e^5}$.
Use a calculator to evaluate the expression.	
3. e^{-4}	4. $e^{0.36}$

NATURAL BASE FUNCTIONS

A function of the form $y = ae^{rx}$ is called a natural base exponential function.

- If $a > 0$ and $r > 0$, the function is an exponential _____ function.
- If $a > 0$ and $r < 0$, the function is an exponential _____ function.

Example 3   Graph natural base functions

Graph the function. State the domain and range.

a. $y = 2e^{0.6x}$

b. $y = e^{-0.35(x + 1)} - 2$

Solution

a. Because $a =$ ___ is _____ and $r =$ _____ is _____, the function is an exponential _____ function. Plot the points (0, ___) and (1, _____) and draw the curve. The domain is _____, and the range is _____.

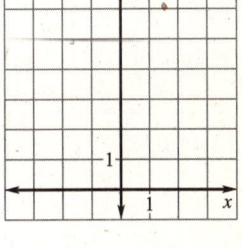

b. Because $a =$ ___ is _____ and $r =$ _____ is _____, the function is an exponential _____ function. Translate the graph of $y = e^{-0.35x}$ _____ and _____. The domain is _____, and the range is _____.

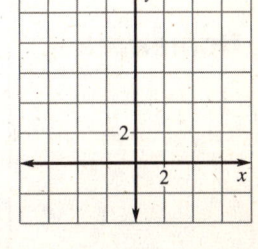

Your Notes

✓ **Checkpoint** Graph the function. State the domain and range.

5. $y = 2e^{0.7x} + 3$

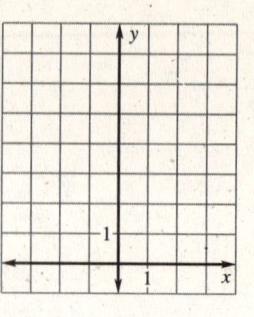

CONTINUOUSLY COMPOUNDED INTEREST

When interest is compounded continuously, the amount A in an account after t years is given by the formula

$A =$ _____ where P is the _____ and r is the _____ expressed as a decimal.

Example 4 *Model continuously compounded interest*

Compound Interest You deposit $3500 in an account that pays 4% annual interest compounded continuously. What is the balance after 1 year?

Solution

Use the formula for continuously compounded interest.

$A = Pe^{rt}$ Write formula.

$=$ _____   Substitute for P, r, and t.

$\approx$ _____

The balance at the end of 1 year is _____.

Homework

✓ **Checkpoint** Complete the following exercise.

6. You deposit $4800 in an account that pays 6.5% annual interest compounded continuously. What is the balance after 3 years?

7.4 Evaluate Logarithms and Graph Logarithmic Functions

Goal • Evaluate logarithms and graph logarithmic functions.

Your Notes

VOCABULARY

Logarithm of y with base b

Common logarithm

Natural logarithm

DEFINITION OF LOGARITHM WITH BASE b

Let b and y be positive numbers with $b \neq 1$. The logarithm of y with base b is denoted by $\log_b y$ is defined as follows:

$\log_b y =$ ____ if and only if $b^x =$ ____

The expression $\log_b y$ is read as "log base b of y."

Example 1 Rewrite logarithmic equations

Logarithmic Form	Exponential Form
a. $\log_2 32 = 5$	_____
b. $\log_7 1 = 0$	_____
c. $\log_{13} 13 = 1$	_____
d. $\log_{1/2} 2 = -1$	_____

✓ **Checkpoint** Rewrite the equation in exponential form.

1. $\log_{18} 1 = 0$	2. $\log_2 64 = 6$

Your Notes

Example 2 Evaluate logarithms

Evaluate the logarithm.

a. $\log_3 81$
b. $\log_4 0.25$
c. $\log_{1/4} 256$
d. $\log_{49} 7$

Solution

To help you find the value of $\log_b y$, ask yourself what power of b gives you y.

a. 3 to what power gives you 81?
   $3^{\underline{}} = 81$, so $\log_3 81 = \underline{}$.

b. 4 to what power gives you 0.25?
   $4^{\underline{}} = 0.25$, so $\log_4 0.25 = \underline{}$.

c. $\frac{1}{4}$ to what power gives you 256?
   $\left(\frac{1}{4}\right)^{\underline{}} = 256$, so $\log_{1/4} 256 = \underline{}$.

d. 49 to what power gives you 7?
   $49^{\underline{}} = 7$, so $\log_{49} 7 = \underline{}$.

✓ **Checkpoint** Evaluate the logarithm.

3. $\log_{1/3} 9$	4. $\log_{16} 4$

Example 3 Use inverse properties

Simplify the expression.

a. $10^{\log 6.7}$
b. $\log_2 16^x$

Solution

a. $10^{\log 6.7} = \underline{}$ $\log_b b^x = x$

b. $\log_2 16^x = \underline{}$ Express 16 as a power with base $\underline{}$.

   $= \underline{}$ Power of a power property

   $= \underline{}$ $\log_b b^x = x$

Your Notes

Example 4 *Find inverse functions*

Find the inverse of the function.

a. $y = \log_{3/2} x$ b. $y = \ln(x - 4)$

a. From the definition of logarithm, the inverse of $y = \log_{3/2} x$ is $y = \left(\dfrac{3}{2}\right)^x$.

b. $y = \ln(x - 4)$ Write original function.

 _____   Switch x and y.

 _____   Write in exponential form.

 _____ $= y$ Solve for y.

The inverse of $y = \ln(x - 4)$ is $y =$ _____.

✓ **Checkpoint** Complete the following exercises.

5. Simplify $10^{\log 7x}$.	6. Simplify $\log_3 27^x$.

Find the inverse of the function.

7. $y = 7^{2x}$	8. $y = \ln(x + 6)$

PARENT GRAPHS FOR LOGARITHMIC FUNCTIONS

The graph of $y = \log_b x$ is shown below for $b > 1$ and for $0 < b < 1$. Because $y = \log_b x$ and $y = b^x$ are _____ functions, the graph of $y = \log_b x$ is the reflection of the graph of $y = b^x$ in the line _____.

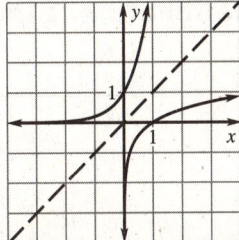 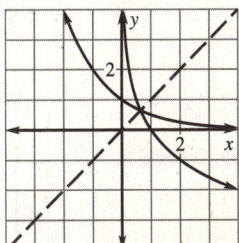

Note that the y-axis is a vertical asymptote of the graph of $y = \log_b x$. The domain of $y = \log_b x$ is _____, and the range is _____.

Your Notes

Example 5 — Graph logarithmic functions

Graph (a) $y = \log_2 x$ and (b) $y = \log_{1/3} x$.

a. Plot several convenient points, such as (1, ___), (2, ___), and (4, ___). The y-axis is a _____. From left to right, draw a curve that starts just to the _____ of the y-axis and moves _____ through the plotted points.

b. Plot several convenient points, such as (1, ___), (3, ___), and (9, ___). The y-axis is a _____. From left to right, draw a curve that starts just to the _____ of the y-axis and moves _____ through the plotted points.

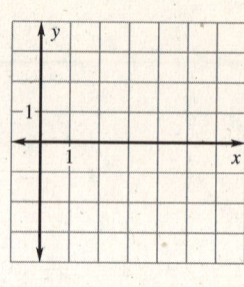

Example 6 — Translate a logarithmic graph

Graph $y = \log_3(x - 1) + 2$. State the domain and range.

Sketch the graph of the parent function $y = \log_3 x$, which passes through (1, ___), (3, ___), and (9, ___).

Translate the parent graph _____ and _____. The translated graph passes through (2, ___), (4, ___), and (10, ___). The graph's asymptote is _____. The domain is _____, and the range is _____.

✓ **Checkpoint** Graph the function. State the domain and range.

9. $y = \log_{1/2} x - 3$

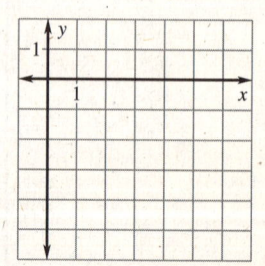

Homework

7.5 Apply Properties of Logarithms

Goal • Rewrite logarithmic expressions.

Your Notes

PROPERTIES OF LOGARITHMS

Let b, m, and n be positive numbers such that $b \neq 1$.

Product Property $\log_b mn = \log_b m \:\rule{1cm}{0.15mm}\: \log_b \rule{1cm}{0.15mm}$

Quotient Property $\log_b \frac{m}{n} = \log_b m \:\rule{1cm}{0.15mm}\: \log_b \rule{1cm}{0.15mm}$

Power Property $\log_b m^n = \rule{2cm}{0.15mm}$

Example 1 Use properties of logarithms

Use $\log_5 4 \approx 0.861$ and $\log_5 9 \approx 1.365$ to evaluate the logarithm.

a. $\log_5 \frac{4}{9} = \log_5 4 \:\rule{0.8cm}{0.15mm}\: \log_5 9$ Quotient property

$\approx \rule{3cm}{0.15mm}$ Use given values.

$= \rule{2cm}{0.15mm}$ Simplify.

b. $\log_5 36 = \log_5 (4 \cdot 9)$ Write 36 as $\rule{1.5cm}{0.15mm}$.

$= \log_5 4 \:\rule{0.8cm}{0.15mm}\: \log_5 9$ Product property

$\approx \rule{3cm}{0.15mm}$ Use given values.

$= \rule{2cm}{0.15mm}$ Simplify.

c. $\log_5 81 = \log_5 \rule{1cm}{0.15mm}$ Write 81 as $\rule{1cm}{0.15mm}$.

$= \rule{2cm}{0.15mm}$ Power property

$\approx \rule{2cm}{0.15mm}$ Use given value.

$= \rule{2cm}{0.15mm}$ Simplify.

✓ **Checkpoint** Use $\log_3 2 \approx 0.6309$ and $\log_3 8 \approx 1.8928$ to evaluate the logarithm.

1. $\log_3 4$	2. $\log_3 16$

Your Notes

> When you are expanding or condensing an expression involving logarithms, you may assume any variables are positive.

Example 2 — Expand a logarithmic expression

Expand $\log_3 \frac{7x^2}{y}$.

$\log_3 \frac{7x^2}{y} = $ _____ Quotient property

$= $ _____ Product property

$= $ _____ Power property

Example 3 — Condense a logarithmic expression

Condense $\log 2 + 3 \log 3 - \log 9$.

$\log 2 + 3 \log 3 - \log 9$

$= \log 2 + $ _____ $ - \log 9$ Power property

$= \log $ _____ $ - \log 9$ Product property

$= \log $ _____   Quotient property

$= $ _____   Simplify.

✓ **Checkpoint** Complete the following exercises.

3. Expand $\log \frac{7y^3}{4x^2}$.

4. Condense $\ln 3 + 2 \ln x - \ln y$.

200   Lesson 7.5 • Algebra 2 Notetaking Guide

Your Notes

CHANGE OF BASE FORMULA

If a, b, and c are positive numbers with $b \neq 1$ and $c \neq 1$, then

$$\log_c a = \frac{\log_b a}{\log_b c}$$

In particular $\log_c a = $ _____ and $\log_c a = $ _____ .

Example 4 *Use the change-of-base formula*

Evaluate $\log_6 11$ using common logarithms and natural logarithms.

Solution

Using common logarithms:

$\log_6 11 = $ _____ $\approx$ _____ $\approx$ _____

Using natural logarithms:

$\log_6 11 = $ _____ $\approx$ _____ $\approx$ _____

✓ **Checkpoint** Use the change-of-base formula to evaluate the logarithm.

5. $\log_{16} 26$	6. $\log_5 13$

Homework

7.6 Solve Exponential and Logarithmic Equations

Goal • Solve exponential and logarithmic equations.

Your Notes

VOCABULARY

Exponential equation

Logarithmic equation

PROPERTY OF EQUALITY FOR EXPONENTIAL EQUATIONS

Algebra If b is a positive number other than 1, then $b^x = b^y$ if and only if _____.

Example If $5^x = 5^4$, then $x =$ ___. If $x =$ ___, then $5^x = 5^4$.

Example 1 Solve by equating exponents

Solve $64^x = 16^{x+1}$.

$64^x = 16^{x+1}$	Write original equation.
$(\underline{\quad})^x = (\underline{\quad})^{x+1}$	Rewrite each power with base ___.
____ = ____	Power of a power property
____ = ____	Property of equality
$x =$ ___	Solve for x.

The solution is ___.

CHECK Substitute the solution into the original equation.

$64\underline{\quad} \stackrel{?}{=} 16\underline{\quad}{}^{+1}$ Substitute for x.

____ = ____   Solution checks.

Your Notes

Example 2 — Take a logarithm of each side

Solve $6^x = 27$.

$6^x = 27$		Write original equation.
____ = ____		Take ____ of each side.
$x =$ ____		$\log_b b^x = x$
$x =$ ____		Use change-of-base formula.
$\approx$ ____		Use a calculator.

The solution is about ____. Check this in the original equation.

Example 3 — Take a logarithm of each side

Solve $6e^{0.25x} + 8 = 20$.

$6e^{0.25x} + 8 = 20$		Write original equation.
$6e^{0.25x} =$ ____		Subtract ____ from each side.
____ = ____		Divide each side by ____.
____ = ____		Take natural log of each side.
____ = ____		$\ln e^x = \log_e e^x = x$
$x \approx$ ____		Divide each side by ____.

The solution is about ____. Check this in the original equation.

✓ Checkpoint — Solve the equation.

1. $3^{7x-3} = 9^{2x}$	2. $5^x = 72$
3. $8^{3x+2} - 6 = 5$	4. $3e^{0.5x} + 2 = 5$

Your Notes

PROPERTY OF EQUALITY FOR LOGARITHMIC EQUATIONS

Algebra If b, x, and y are positive numbers with $b \neq 1$, then $\log_b x = \log_b y$ if and only if _____.

Example If $\log_3 x = \log_3 8$, then $x = 8$. If $x =$ ___, then $\log_3 x = \log_3 8$.

Example 4 Solve a logarithmic equation

Solve $\log_7(6x - 16) = \log_7(x - 1)$.

$\log_7(6x - 16) = \log_7(x - 1)$ Write original equation.

_____ = _____   Property of equality

_____ = ____   Subtract ___ from each side.

____ = ____   Add ____ to each side.

___ = ___   Divide each side by ___.

The solution is ___.

CHECK Substitute the solution into the original equation.

$\log_7(6x - 16) = \log_7(x - 1)$ Write original equation.

$\log_7($_____$) \stackrel{?}{=} \log_7($_____$)$ Substitute for x.

____ = ____   Solution checks.

Example 5 Exponentiate each side of an equation

Solve $\log_5(3x - 8) = 2$.

$\log_5(3x - 8) = 2$ Write original equation.

_____ = ___   Exponentiate each side using base ___.

_____ = ___ $b^{\log_b x} = x$

___ = ___   Add ___ to each side.

___ = ___   Divide each side by ___.

The solution is ____.

CHECK $\log_5(3x - 8) = \log_5($_____$) = \log_5$ ____.

Because ____ = ____, $\log_5$ ____ = 2.

204 Lesson 7.6 • Algebra 2 Notetaking Guide

Your Notes

Example 6 — Check for extraneous solutions

Solve $\log 5x + \log(x - 1) = 2$.

$\log 5x + \log(x - 1) = 2$		Write original equation.
$\log[\underline{}] = 2$		Product property of logarithms
$\underline{} = \underline{}$		Exponentiate each side.
$\underline{} = \underline{}$		$b^{\log_b x} = x$
$\underline{} = \underline{}$		Distributive property
$\underline{} = \underline{}$		Write in standard form.
$\underline{} = \underline{}$		Divide each side by ___.
$\underline{} = \underline{}$		Factor.
$\underline{}$ or $\underline{}$		Zero product property

CHECK $x = 5$ $\log 5 \cdot \underline{} + \log(\underline{} - 1) \stackrel{?}{=} 2$

$\log \underline{} + \log \underline{} \stackrel{?}{=} 2$

$\log \underline{} \stackrel{?}{=} 2$

$\underline{} = 2$

So, ___ is a solution.

CHECK $x = -4$ $\log[5(\underline{})] + \log(\underline{} - 1) \stackrel{?}{=} 2$

$\log(\underline{}) + \log(\underline{}) \stackrel{?}{=} 2$

Because $\log(\underline{})$ and $\log(\underline{})$ are not defined, ___ is not a solution.

✓ **Checkpoint** Solve the equation. Check for extraneous solutions.

5. $\ln(7x - 13) = \ln(2x + 17)$	6. $\log_3(2x + 9) = 3$
7. $\log_4(10x + 624) = 5$	8. $\log_6(x - 9) + \log_6 x = 2$

Homework

7.7 Write and Apply Exponential and Power Functions

Goal • Write exponential and power functions.

Your Notes

Example 1 Write an exponential function

Write an exponential function $y = ab^x$ whose graph passes through (1, 10) and (4, 80).

Solution

1. Substitute the coordinates of the two given points into $y = ab^x$.

    ____ $= ab^1$ Substitute 10 for y and 1 for x.

    ____ $= ab^4$ Substitute 80 for y and 4 for x.

2. Solve for a in the first equation to obtain $a =$ ____ and substitute this expression for a into the second equation.

    $80 =$ ____ b^4 Substitute for a.

    $80 =$ ____   Simplify.

    ___ $=$ ___   Divide each side by ____.

    ___ $=$ ___   Take the positive cube root.

3. Because $b =$ ___, it follows that $a =$ _____.

    So, $y =$ _____.

✓ **Checkpoint** Complete the following exercise.

1. Write an exponential function $y = ab^x$ whose graph passes through the points (1, 8) and (2, 32).

Your Notes

Example 2 — Find an exponential model

Savings The table shows the amount A in a savings account t years after the account was opened.

t	0	1	2	3	4	5	6	7
A	210	255	310	377	459	557	677	822

- Draw a scatter plot of the data pairs $(t, \ln A)$. Is an exponential model a good fit for the original data pairs (t, A)?
- Find an exponential model for the original data.

Solution

1. Use a calculator to create a table of data pairs $(t, \ln A)$.

t	0	1	2	3	4
ln A	___	___	___	___	___

t	5	6	7
ln A	___	___	___

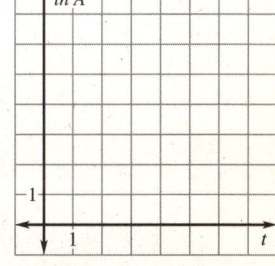

2. Plot the new points. The points lie close to a line, so an exponential model should be a good fit for the original data.

3. To find an exponential model $A = ab^t$, choose two points on the line, such as $(1, \underline{})$ and $(6, \underline{})$. Use these points to find an equation of the line. Then solve for A.

> Because the axes are t and $\ln A$, the point-slope form is rewritten as $\ln A - \ln A_1 = m(t - t_1)$.

$\ln A - \underline{} = \underline{}(t - 1)$ **Equation of line**

$\ln A = \underline{}$ **Simplify.**

$A = \underline{}$ **Exponentiate each side using base e.**

$A = \underline{}$ **Use properties of exponents.**

$A = \underline{}$ **Exponential model**

Your Notes

Example 3   *Write a power function*

Write a power function $y = ax^b$ whose graph passes through (2, 4) and (6, 10).

1. Substitute the coordinates of the two given points into $y = ax^b$.

   4 = _____   Substitute 4 for *y* and 2 for *x*.

   10 = _____   Substitute 10 for *y* and 6 for *x*.

2. Solve for *a* in the first equation to obtain $a =$ _____ and substitute for *a* into the second equation.

   10 = _____   Substitute for *a*.

   10 = _____   Simplify.

   ___ = ___   Divide each side by ___.

   _____ = ___   Take _____ of each side.

   _____ = ___   Change-of-base formula

   ___ = ___   Use a calculator.

3. Because $b =$ _____, it follows that $a =$ _____. So, $y =$ _____.

✓ **Checkpoint** Complete the following exercises.

2. Find an exponential model for the data:
   (0, 17.56), (1, 16.03), (2, 14.64), (3, 13.36), (4, 12.20), (5, 11.14), (6, 10.17)

3. Write a power function whose graph passes through the points (3, 8) and (6, 17).

Your Notes

Example 4: Find a power model

The table gives the approximate volume V of spheres with radius r. Draw a scatter plot of the data pairs ($\ln r$, $\ln V$). Is a power model a good fit for the original data pairs (r, V)? Find a power model for the original data.

r	1	2	3	4	5	6
V	4.189	33.510	113.097	268.083	523.599	904.779

1. Use a calculator to create a table of data pairs ($\ln r$, $\ln V$).

$\ln r$	0	0.693	1.099	1.386	1.609	1.792
$\ln V$	1.432	3.512	4.728	5.591	6.261	6.808

2. Plot the new points. The points appear linear, so a power model should be a good fit for the original data.

3. To find a power model $V = ar^b$, choose two points on the line, such as (1.099, _____) and (1.792, _____). Use these points to find an equation of the line. Then solve for V.

> Because the axes are $\ln r$ and $\ln V$, the point-slope form is rewritten as $\ln V - \ln V_1 = m(\ln r - \ln r_1)$.

$\ln V -$ _____ $=$ ___ $(\ln r -$ _____ $)$ Equation of line

$\ln V =$ _____   Power property of logarithms

$V =$ _____   Exponentiate each side.

$V =$ _____   Product of powers property

$V =$ _____   Simplify.

Homework

✓ **Checkpoint** Complete the following exercise.

4. Find a power model for the data: (1, 7.92), (2, 4.651), (3, 3.406), (4, 2.731), (5, 2.301), (6, 2.000)

Words to Review

Give an example of the vocabulary word.

Exponential function	Exponential growth function
Growth factor	Asymptote
Exponential decay function	Decay factor
Natural base e	Logarithm of y with base b
Common Logarithm	Natural logarithm
Exponential equation	Logarithmic equation

Review your notes and Chapter 7 by using the Chapter Review on pages 539–542 of your textbook.

8.1 Model Inverse and Joint Variation

Goal • Use inverse variation and joint variation models.

Your Notes

VOCABULARY

Inverse variation

Constant of variation

Joint variation

INVERSE VARIATION

Two variables x and y show inverse variation if they are related as follows: $y =$ _____ , $a \neq 0$

The constant a is the constant of variation, and y is said to _____ with x.

Example 1 *Classify direct and inverse variation*

Tell whether x and y show *direct variation*, *inverse variation*, or *neither*.

Given Equation	Rewritten Equation	Type of Variation
a. $\dfrac{y}{9} = x$	_____	_____
b. $xy = 3$	_____	_____

✓ **Checkpoint** Tell whether x and y show *direct variation*, *inverse variation*, or *neither*.

1. $y = x + 2$	2. $yx = 5$	3. $\dfrac{y}{2.6} = x$

Lesson 8.1 • Algebra 2 Notetaking Guide 211

Your Notes

Example 2 — Write an inverse variation equation

The variables x and y vary inversely, and $y = 3$ when $x = 6$. Write an equation that relates x and y. Find y when $x = -9$.

$y = \dfrac{a}{x}$ Write general equation for inverse variation.

$\underline{} = \dfrac{a}{\boxed{}}$ Substitute for y and for x.

$\underline{} = a$ Solve for a.

The inverse variation equation is $y = \underline{}$. When $x = -9$,

$y = \underline{} = \underline{}$.

✓ **Checkpoint** Complete the following exercise.

4. The variables x and y vary inversely, and $y = 4.4$ when $x = 5$. Write an equation that relates x and y. Find y when $x = 8$.

Example 3 — Check data for inverse variation

Determine whether m and n show inverse variation. If they do, write a model that gives n as a function of m. Find n when $m = 45$.

m	5	10	15	20	25
n	45	22.5	15	11.25	9

Calculate the product $m \cdot n$ for each data pair in the table.

$5(45) = \underline{}$ $10(22.5) = \underline{}$ $15(15) = \underline{}$

$20(11.25) = \underline{}$ $25(9) = \underline{}$

Each product is equal to $\underline{}$. So, the data $\underline{}$ inverse variation. A model relating m and n is

$m \cdot n = \underline{}$ or $n = \underline{}$.

The value of n when $m = 45$ is $n = \underline{} = \underline{}$.

Your Notes

✓ **Checkpoint** Do the data below show inverse variation? If so, write a model that gives y as a function of x.

5.
x	2	4	6	8	10
y	18	9	6	4.5	3.6

JOINT VARIATION

Joint variation occurs when a quantity varies directly with the product of _____ other quantities. In the equation below, a is a nonzero constant.

$z =$ _____

z varies jointly with x and y.

Example 4 *Write a joint variation equation*

The variable z varies jointly with x and y. Also, $z = -84$ when $x = -4$ and $y = 3$. Write an equation that relates x, y, and z. Find z when $x = 5$ and $y = 2$.

Write the general joint variation equation. Use the given values of z, x, and y to find the constant of variation a.

$z = axy$

____ $= a($____$)($____$)$ Substitute for z, x, and y.

____ $=$ ____ a Simplify.

____ $= a$ Solve for a.

The joint variation equation is $z =$ _____. Calculate z when $x = 5$ and $y = 2$ using substitution.

$z =$ _____ $=$ _____ $=$ _____

Your Notes

Example 5 — Compare different types of variation

Write an equation for the relationship.

Relationship	Equation
a. m varies jointly with n, p, and q.	$m = $ _____
b. r varies inversely with s.	$r = $ _____
c. x varies inversely with the cube of y.	$x = $ _____
d. k varies jointly with x and y and inversely with m.	$k = $ _____
e. t varies directly with u and inversely with w.	$t = $ _____

✓ **Checkpoint** Complete the following exercises.

6. The variable z varies jointly with x and y. Also, $z = -44$ when $x = 4$ and $y = -1$. Write an equation that relates x, y, and z. Find z when $x = 6$ and $y = 3$.

7. Write an equation for the relationship: x varies jointly with y and z and inversely with the square of t.

Homework

8.2 Graph Simple Rational Functions

Goal • Graph rational functions.

Your Notes

VOCABULARY

Rational function

PARENT FUNCTION FOR SIMPLE RATIONAL FUNCTIONS

- The graph of the parent function $f(x) = \frac{1}{x}$ is a _____, which consists of two symmetrical parts called _____.
- The domain and range are _____ _____.
- The asymptotes are $x =$ ___, and $y =$ ___.
- Any function of the form $g(x) = \frac{a}{x}$ ($a \neq 0$) has the same _____, _____, and _____ as the function $f(x) = \frac{1}{x}$.

Example 1 *Graph a rational function of the form $y = \frac{a}{x}$*

Graph the function $y = \frac{4}{x}$.

1. **Draw** the asymptotes $x =$ ___ and $y =$ ___.

2. **Plot** points to the left and to the right of the vertical asymptote, such as $(-2, \underline{})$, $(-1, \underline{})$, $(1, \underline{})$, and $(2, \underline{})$.

3. **Draw** the branches of the hyperbola so that they pass through the plotted points and approach the asymptotes.

The graph of $y = \frac{4}{x}$ is a vertical stretch of the graph of $y = \frac{1}{x}$ by a factor of 4.

Your Notes

✓ **Checkpoint** Graph the function.

1. $y = \dfrac{3}{x}$

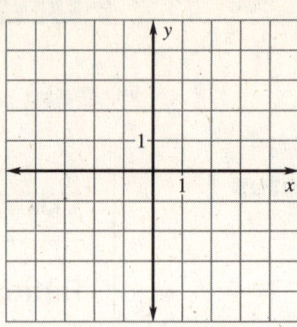

GRAPHING TRANSLATIONS OF SIMPLE RATIONAL FUNCTIONS

To graph a rational function of the form $y = \dfrac{a}{x-h} + k$, follow these steps:

Step 1 Draw the asymptotes $x = \underline{}$ and $y = \underline{}$.

Step 2 Plot points to the left and to the right of the \underline{}.

Step 3 Draw the two \underline{} of the hyperbola so that they pass through the plotted points and approach the asymptotes.

Example 2 Graph a rational function $y = \dfrac{a}{x-h} + k$

Graph $y = \dfrac{-6}{x+3} + 2$. State the domain and range.

1. Draw the asymptotes $x = \underline{}$ and $y = \underline{}$.

2. Plot points to the left and to the right of the vertical asymptote, such as $(-6, \underline{})$, $(-4, \underline{})$, $(-2, \underline{})$, and $(0, \underline{})$.

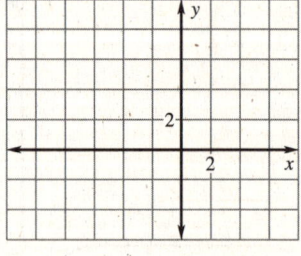

The graph of $y = \dfrac{-6}{x+3} + 2$ is the graph of $y = \dfrac{-6}{x}$ translated left 3 units and up 2 units.

3. Draw the two branches of the hyperbola so that they pass through the plotted points and approach the asymptotes.

The domain is \underline{}, and the range is \underline{}.

Your Notes

Example 3 Graph a rational function of the form $y = \dfrac{ax + b}{cx + d}$

Graph $y = \dfrac{4x - 2}{x - 1}$. State the domain and range.

Solution

1. **Draw** the asymptotes. Solve $x - 1 = 0$ for x to find the vertical asymptote $x =$ ___. The horizontal asymptote is the line

   $y = \dfrac{a}{c} = \dfrac{}{} =$ ___.

2. **Plot** points to the left of the vertical asymptote, such as $(-1,$ ___$)$ and $(0,$ ___$)$, and points to the right, such as $(2,$ ___$)$ and $(3,$ ___$)$.

3. **Draw** the two branches of the hyperbola so that they pass through the plotted points and approach the asymptotes.

The domain is _____. The range is _____.

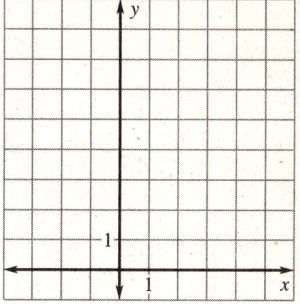

✓ **Checkpoint** Graph the function. State the domain and range.

2. $y = \dfrac{3}{x - 2} + 1$

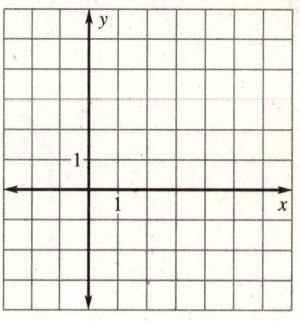

3. $y = \dfrac{-2x + 1}{-x - 2}$

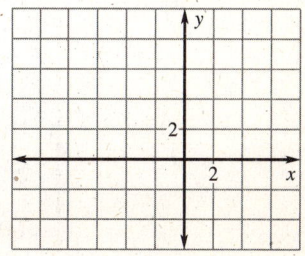

Homework

8.3 Graph General Rational Functions

Goal • Graph rational functions with higher-degree polynomials.

Your Notes

GRAPHS OF RATIONAL FUNCTIONS

Let $p(x)$ and $q(x)$ be polynomials with no common factors other than ± 1.

$$f(x) = \frac{p(x)}{q(x)} = \frac{a_m x^m + a_{m-1} x^{m-1} + \cdots + a_1 x + a_0}{b_n x^n + b_{n-1} x^{n-1} + \cdots + b_1 x + b_0}$$

1. The x-intercepts of the graph of f are the real zeros of _____.

2. The graph of f has a vertical asymptote at each real zero of _____.

3. The graph of f has at most one horizontal asymptote, determined by the degrees m and n of $p(x)$ and $q(x)$.

   • If $m < n$, the line _____ is a horizontal asymptote.

   • If $m = n$, the line _____ is a horizontal asymptote.

   • If $m > n$, the graph has _____.

   The end behavior is the same as $y = \frac{a_m}{b_n} x^{m-n}$.

Example 1 Graph a rational function ($m < n$)

Graph $y = \dfrac{3}{x^2 + 2}$. State the domain and range.

The numerator has no zeros, so there is no _____. The denominator has no real zeros, so there is no _____.

The degree of the numerator, ___, is less than the degree of the denominator, ___. So, the line _____ (the x-axis) is a horizontal asymptote.

The domain is _____, and the range is _____.

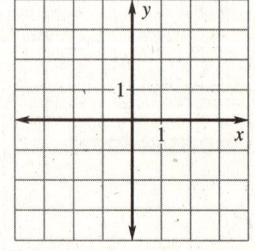

218 Lesson 8.3 • Algebra 2 Notetaking Guide   Copyright © McDougal Littell/Houghton Mifflin Company.

Your Notes

✓ **Checkpoint** Graph the function. State the domain and range.

1. $y = \dfrac{12}{x^2 + 4}$

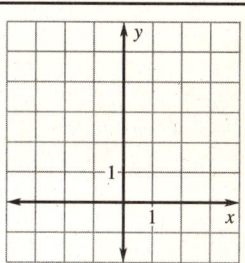

Example 2 Graph a rational function (m = n)

Graph $y = \dfrac{x^2 - 9}{x^2 - 4}$.

The zeros of the numerator $x^2 - 9$ are ____, so ____ and ____ are the x-intercepts. The zeros of the denominator $x^2 - 4$ are ____, so $x =$ ____ and $x =$ ____ are vertical asymptotes. The numerator and denominator have the same degree, so the horizontal asymptote is

$y = \dfrac{}{} =$ ____.

Plot points between and beyond the vertical asymptotes.

	x	y
To the left of x = −2	−5	____
	−3	____
Between x = −2 and x = 2	−1	____
	0	____
	1	____
To the right of x = −2	3	____
	5	____

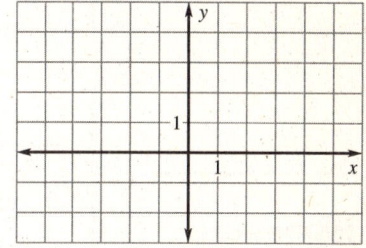

Lesson 8.3 • Algebra 2 Notetaking Guide

Your Notes

Example 3 *Graph a rational function (m > n)*

Graph $y = \dfrac{x^2 - 2x - 3}{x + 2}$.

The numerator factors as _____, so the x-intercepts are ___ and _____. The zero of the denominator $x + 2$ is _____, so the vertical asymptote is _____. The degree of the numerator, ___, is greater than the degree of the denominator, ___, so the graph has no horizontal asymptote. The graph has the same end behavior as the graph of $y = x$ ——— = ___.

Plot points on each side of the vertical asymptote.

To the left of $x = -2$

x	y
−7	___
−6	___
−4	___
−3	___

To the right of $x = -2$

x	y
−1	___
0	___
2	___

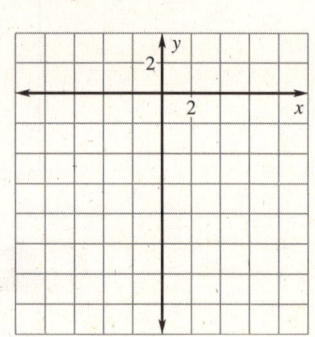

✓ **Checkpoint** Graph the function.

2. $y = \dfrac{3x^2}{x^2 - 16}$

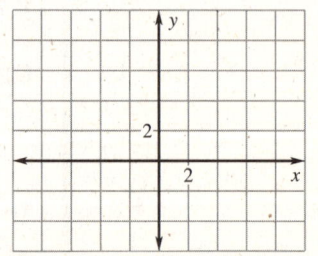

3. $y = \dfrac{x^2 + 2x - 8}{x - 1}$

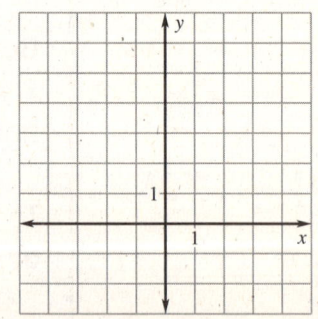

Homework

8.4 Multiply and Divide Rational Expressions

Goal • Multiply and divide rational expressions.

Your Notes

VOCABULARY

Simplified form of a rational expression

SIMPLIFYING RATIONAL EXPRESSIONS

Let a, b, and c be nonzero real numbers or variable expressions. Then the following property applies.

$\dfrac{a\cancel{c}}{b\cancel{c}} =$ _____   Divide out common factor c.

Example 1 *Simplify a rational expression*

$\dfrac{x^2 + 7x + 10}{x^2 - 4} = \dfrac{\boxed{}}{\boxed{}}$ Factor numerator and denominator.

$= \dfrac{\boxed{}}{\boxed{}}$ Divide out common factor.

$= \underline{}$ Simplified form.

MULTIPLYING RATIONAL EXPRESSIONS

Let a, b, c, and d be nonzero real numbers or variable expressions. The rule for multiplying rational expressions is the same as the rule for multiplying numerical fractions: multiply _____, multiply _____, and write the new fraction in simplified form.

$\dfrac{a}{b} \cdot \dfrac{c}{d} =$ _____   ← Simplify $\dfrac{ac}{bd}$ if possible.

Your Notes

Example 2 Multiply rational expressions

$$\frac{2x^2 + 4x}{x^2 - 4x - 12} \cdot \frac{x^2 - 9x + 18}{2x}$$

$= \dfrac{\boxed{}}{\boxed{}} \cdot \dfrac{\boxed{}}{\boxed{}}$ Factor numerator and denominator.

$= \dfrac{\boxed{}}{\boxed{}}$ Multiply numerator and denominator.

$= \underline{}$ Divide out common factors and write in simplified form.

✓ **Checkpoint** Complete the following exercises.

1. Simplify the expression.	2. Multiply the expression.
$\dfrac{x^2 - 2x - 15}{x^2 + 4x + 3}$	$\dfrac{6x^2 + 18x}{x^2 + x - 6} \cdot \dfrac{x^2 - x - 2}{x^2 - 7x - 8}$

Example 3 Multiply a rational expression by a polynomial

$$\frac{x - 4}{x^3 + 1} \cdot (x^2 - x + 1)$$

$= \dfrac{x - 4}{x^3 + 1} \cdot \dfrac{\boxed{}}{\boxed{}}$ Write polynomial as rational expression.

$= \dfrac{\boxed{}}{\boxed{}}$ Factor denominator.

$= \underline{}$ Divide out common factor and write in simplified form.

Your Notes

DIVIDING RATIONAL EXPRESSIONS

To divide one rational expression by another, multiply the first expression by the reciprocal of the second expression.

$$\frac{a}{b} \div \frac{c}{d} = \frac{a}{b} \cdot \frac{d}{c} = \underline{} \qquad \leftarrow \text{Simplify } \frac{ad}{bc} \text{ if possible.}$$

Example 4 *Divide rational expressions*

$$\frac{3}{x+7} \div \frac{8x^2 - 8x}{x^2 + 6x - 7}$$

$$= \frac{3}{x+7} \cdot \boxed{} \qquad \text{Multiply by reciprocal.}$$

$$= \frac{3}{x+7} \cdot \boxed{} \qquad \text{Factor.}$$

$$= \underline{} \qquad \text{Divide out common factors and write in simplified form.}$$

✓ **Checkpoint** *Multiply or divide the expression.*

3. $\dfrac{-2x^2}{x^3 - 27} \cdot (x^2 + 3x + 9)$

4. $\dfrac{x-5}{9x^2 - 18x} \div \dfrac{2x^2 - 11x + 5}{2x^2 - 5x + 2}$

Homework

8.5 Add and Subtract Rational Expressions

Goal • Add and subtract rational expressions.

Your Notes

VOCABULARY

Complex fraction

ADD (SUBTRACT) WITH LIKE DENOMINATORS

To add (or subtract) rational expressions with like denominators, simply add (or subtract) their _____. Then place the result over the common denominator. Let a, b, and c be polynomials with $c \neq 0$.

Addition $\dfrac{a}{c} + \dfrac{b}{c} =$ _____ Subtraction $\dfrac{a}{c} - \dfrac{b}{c} =$ _____

Example 1 *Add with like denominators*

$$\dfrac{9}{6x} + \dfrac{2}{6x} = \dfrac{\boxed{}}{6x} = \dfrac{\boxed{}}{6x}$$ Add numerators.

ADD (SUBTRACT) WITH UNLIKE DENOMINATORS

To add (or subtract) two rational expressions with unlike denominators, find the _____ (LCD), which is the _____ (LCM) of the denominators.

Rewrite each rational expression using the LCD, then add (or subtract) using the procedure for like denominators. Let a, b, c, and d be polynomials with $c \neq 0$ and $d \neq 0$.

Addition $\dfrac{a}{c} + \dfrac{b}{d} = \dfrac{ad}{cd} + \dfrac{bc}{cd} =$ _____

Subtraction $\dfrac{a}{c} - \dfrac{b}{d} = \dfrac{ad}{cd} - \dfrac{bc}{cd} =$ _____

Your Notes

Example 2 — Add with unlike denominators

Add: $\dfrac{5}{4x^2} + \dfrac{x+1}{2x^2+4x}$

To find the LCD, factor each denominator and write the highest power to which each factor occurs. Note that $4x^2 =$ _____ and $2x^2 + 4x =$ _____, so the LCD is _____ = _____.

$\dfrac{5}{4x^2} + \dfrac{x+1}{2x^2+4x}$

$= \dfrac{5}{4x^2} + \dfrac{x+1}{\boxed{}}$

$= \dfrac{5}{4x^2} \cdot \dfrac{\boxed{}}{\boxed{}} + \dfrac{x+1}{\boxed{}} \cdot \dfrac{\boxed{}}{\boxed{}}$

$= \dfrac{\boxed{}}{\boxed{}} + \dfrac{\boxed{}}{\boxed{}}$

$= \underline{}$

Example 3 — Subtract with unlike denominators

Subtract: $\dfrac{7}{3x-9} - \dfrac{x+4}{x^2-9}$

$\dfrac{7}{3x-9} - \dfrac{x+4}{x^2-9}$

$= \dfrac{7}{\boxed{}} - \dfrac{x+4}{\boxed{}}$

$= \dfrac{7}{\boxed{}} \cdot \dfrac{\boxed{}}{\boxed{}} - \dfrac{x+4}{\boxed{}} \cdot \dfrac{\boxed{}}{\boxed{}}$

$= \underline{} - \underline{}$

$= \underline{}$

Lesson 8.5 • Algebra 2 Notetaking Guide

Your Notes

✓ **Checkpoint** Perform the indicated operation and simplify.

1. $\dfrac{8x}{3+x} - \dfrac{7}{3+x}$	2. $\dfrac{13}{3x} + \dfrac{2}{3x}$
3. $\dfrac{x+1}{x^2 + 6x + 9} + \dfrac{6}{x^2 - 9}$	4. $\dfrac{8}{4x^2} - \dfrac{2+x}{8x^2 - 12x}$

SIMPLIFYING COMPLEX FRACTIONS

A complex fraction is a fraction that contains a fraction in its _____.

Method 1: If necessary, simplify the numerator and denominator by _____ _____. Then divide the numerator by the denominator.

Method 2: Multiply the numerator and the denominator by the _____ of every fraction in the numerator and denominator. Then simplify.

Example 4 *Simplify a complex fraction (Method 1)*

Simplify: $\dfrac{\dfrac{8}{5x}}{\dfrac{x+1}{15} + \dfrac{4}{15}}$

$\dfrac{\dfrac{8}{5x}}{\dfrac{x+1}{15} + \dfrac{4}{15}} = \dfrac{\dfrac{8}{5x}}{\underline{}}$ Write denominator as a single fraction.

$= \dfrac{8}{5x} \cdot \underline{}$ Divide numerator by denominator.

$= \underline{}$ Simplify.

Lesson 8.5 • Algebra 2 Notetaking Guide

Your Notes

Example 5 — Simplify a complex fraction (Method 2)

Simplify: $\dfrac{\frac{2x}{x+1}}{\frac{1}{3x}+\frac{2}{x+1}}$

The LCD of all the fractions in the numerator and denominator is _____.

$\dfrac{\frac{2x}{x+1}}{\frac{1}{3x}+\frac{2}{x+1}} = \dfrac{\frac{2x}{x+1}}{\frac{1}{3x}+\frac{2}{x+1}} \cdot \dfrac{\boxed{}}{\boxed{}}$ Multiply numerator and denominator by the LCD.

$= \dfrac{\boxed{}}{\boxed{}}$ Simplify.

$= \underline{}$ Simplify.

✓ **Checkpoint** Simplify the complex fraction.

5. $\dfrac{\frac{6x}{4}-\frac{x}{4}}{\frac{8}{2}+\frac{3x}{2}}$

6. $\dfrac{\frac{5}{2x}+\frac{7}{x^2}}{\frac{3}{x^2}-\frac{1}{2x}}$

Homework

8.6 Solve Rational Equations

Goal • Solve rational equations.

Your Notes

VOCABULARY

Cross multiplying

Example 1 Solve a rational equation by cross multiplying

$\dfrac{20}{3x-5} = \dfrac{5}{x-2}$ Original equation

$20\underline{(x-2)} = 5\underline{(3x-5)}$ Cross multiply.

$\underline{20x-40} = \underline{15x-25}$ Distributive property

$\underline{5x-40} = \underline{-25}$ Subtract __15x__ from each side.

$\underline{5x} = \underline{15}$ Add __40__ to each side

$\underline{x} = \underline{3}$ Divide each side by __5__.

CHECK $\dfrac{20}{3x-5} = \dfrac{20}{3(\boxed{3})-5} = \underline{5}$ and

$\dfrac{5}{x-2} = \dfrac{5}{\boxed{3}-2} = \underline{5}$

✓ **Checkpoint** Solve the equation by cross multiplying.

1. $\dfrac{3}{x+2} = \dfrac{6}{3x+8}$	2. $\dfrac{-6}{x+2} = \dfrac{-12}{x-1}$

Your Notes

Example 2 *Solve a rational equation with one solution*

$$\frac{8}{x} + \frac{11}{3} = \frac{-14}{x}$$ Original equation

$$\underline{\quad}\left(\frac{8}{x} + \frac{11}{3}\right) = \underline{\quad}\left(\frac{-14}{x}\right)$$ Multiply each side by the LCD, ____.

$$\underline{\quad\quad\quad} = \underline{\quad}$$ Simplify.

$$\underline{\quad} = \underline{\quad}$$ Solve for ____.

The solution is ____. Check this in the original equation.

Example 3 *Solve a rational equation with two solutions*

Solve: $\frac{3x+5}{x+3} = 2 + \frac{8}{(x+3)(x-4)}$

The LCD is _____.

$$\frac{3x+5}{x+3} = 2 + \frac{8}{(x+3)(x-4)}$$

$$\underline{\quad\quad}\left(\frac{3x+5}{x+3}\right) =$$

$$\underline{\quad\quad}\left(2 + \frac{8}{(x+3)(x-4)}\right)$$

$$\underline{\quad\quad} = \underline{\quad\quad}$$

$$\underline{\quad\quad} = \underline{\quad\quad}$$

$$\underline{\quad\quad} = 0$$

$$\underline{\quad\quad} = 0$$

$$x = \underline{\quad} \text{ or } x = \underline{\quad}$$

The solutions are ____ and ____. Check these in the original equation.

✓ **Checkpoint** Solve the equation by using the LCD.

3. $\frac{11}{4} - \frac{3}{x} = \frac{5}{2x}$	4. $1 + \frac{4}{x+2} = \frac{9}{x}$

Lesson 8.6 • Algebra 2 Notetaking Guide 229

Your Notes

Example 4 Check for extraneous solutions

Solve: $\dfrac{6x^2}{x^2-16} - \dfrac{3x}{x+4} = \dfrac{4}{x-4}$

The LCD is _____.

$$\dfrac{6x^2}{\boxed{}} - \dfrac{3x}{x+4} = \dfrac{4}{x-4}$$

$$\underline{} \left[\dfrac{6x^2}{\boxed{}} - \dfrac{3x}{x+4} \right] = \underline{} \cdot \dfrac{4}{x-4}$$

$$\underline{} = \underline{}$$

$$\underline{} = 0$$

$$\underline{} = 0$$

$$\underline{} = 0 \quad \text{or} \quad \underline{} = 0$$

$$x = \underline{} \quad \text{or} \quad x = \underline{}$$

You can use algebra to check whether either solution is extraneous.

CHECK The solution ____ checks, but the apparent solution ____ is extraneous, because substituting it in the equation results in _____, which is _____.

✓ **Checkpoint** Solve the equation by using the LCD. Check for extraneous solutions.

5. $\dfrac{8x^2}{x^2-9} - \dfrac{4x}{x+3} = \dfrac{2}{x-3}$

Homework

Words to Review

Give an example of the vocabulary word.

Inverse variation	Constant of variation
Joint variation	Rational function
Simplified form of a rational expression	Complex fraction
Cross multiplying	

Review your notes and Chapter 8 by using the Chapter Review on pages 603–606 of your textbook.

9.1 Apply the Distance and Midpoint Formulas

Goal • Find the length and midpoint of a line segment.

Your Notes

VOCABULARY

Distance formula

Midpoint formula

THE DISTANCE FORMULA

The distance d between (x_1, y_1) and (x_2, y_2) is
$d = \sqrt{(\underline{})^2 + (\underline{})^2}$.

Example 1 *Find the distance between two points*

Find the distance between $(-5, -3)$ and $(3, 6)$.

Let $(x_1, y_1) = (-5, -3)$ and $(x_2, y_2) = (3, 6)$.

$d = \sqrt{(x_2 - x_1)^2 + (y_2 - y_1)^2}$

$ = \sqrt{\underline{}} = \underline{}$

Example 2 *Classify a triangle using the distance formula*

Classify $\triangle ABC$ as scalene, isosceles, or equilateral.

$AB = \sqrt{\underline{}}$

$ = \underline{} = \underline{}$

$BC = \sqrt{\underline{}}$

$ = \underline{}$

$AC = \sqrt{\underline{}}$

$ = \underline{} = \underline{}$

$\triangle ABC$ is $\underline{}$.

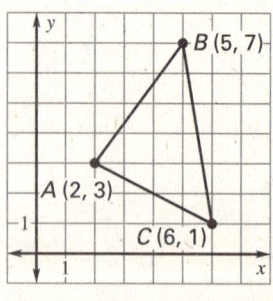

Your Notes

✓ **Checkpoint** Complete the following exercises.

1. Find the distance between $(-7, 3)$ and $(5, -2)$.

2. The vertices of a triangle are $T(2, 1)$, $U(4, 6)$, and $V(7, 3)$. Classify $\triangle TUV$ as *scalene*, *isosceles*, or *equilateral*.

THE MIDPOINT FORMULA

A line segment's midpoint is _____ from the segment's endpoints. The midpoint formula describes the _____ of a line segment joining $A(x_1, y_1)$ and $B(x_2, y_2)$ as follows:

$$M\left(\frac{x_1 + x_2}{2}, \frac{y_1 + y_2}{2}\right)$$

In words, each coordinate of M is the _____ of the corresponding coordinates of A and B.

Example 3 *Find the midpoint of a line segment*

Find the midpoint of the line segment joining $(-6, 5)$ and $(2, -3)$.

Let $(x_1, y_1) = (-6, 5)$ and $(x_2, y_2) = (2, -3)$.

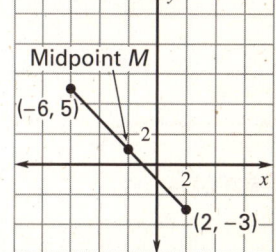

$$\left(\frac{x_1 + x_2}{2}, \frac{y_1 + y_2}{2}\right) = (\underline{}, \underline{})$$

$$= (\underline{}, \underline{})$$

Your Notes

Example 4 *Find a perpendicular bisector*

Write an equation for the perpendicular bisector of the line segment joining $A(-4, 1)$ and $B(2, 3)$.

Solution

1. **Find** the midpoint of the line segment.

   $\left(\dfrac{x_1 + x_2}{2}, \dfrac{y_1 + y_2}{2}\right) = \left(\underline{}, \underline{}\right) = (\underline{}, \underline{})$

2. **Calculate** the slope of $\overline{AB}$.

   $m = \dfrac{y_2 - y_1}{x_2 - x_1} = \underline{} = \underline{} = \underline{}$

3. **Find** the slope of the perpendicular bisector.

   $-\dfrac{1}{m} = \underline{} = \underline{}$

4. **Use** point-slope form: $y - \underline{} = \underline{}(x - (\underline{}))$ or
   $y = \underline{}$.

An equation for the perpendicular bisector of AB is
$y = \underline{}$.

✓ **Checkpoint** Complete the following exercises.

3. Find the midpoint of the line segment joining $(-6, 5)$ and $(1, 1)$.

4. Write an equation for the perpendicular bisector of the line segment joining $A(-5, 6)$ and $(3, -2)$.

Homework

9.2 Graph and Write Equations of Parabolas

Goal • Graph and write equations of parabolas that open left or right.

Your Notes

VOCABULARY

Focus

Directrix

STANDARD EQUATION OF A PARABOLA WITH VERTEX AT THE ORIGIN

The standard form of the equation of a parabola with vertex at (0, 0) is as follows:

Equation	Focus	Directrix	Axis of Symmetry
$x^2 = 4py$	$(0, p)$	$y =$ _____	Vertical (_____)
$y^2 = 4px$	$(p, 0)$	$x =$ _____	Horizontal (_____)

Your Notes

Example 1 — Graph an equation of a parabola

Graph $x = \frac{1}{2}y^2$. Identify the focus, directrix, and axis of symmetry.

1. **Rewrite** the equation in standard form.

   $x = \frac{1}{2}y^2$ Write original equation.

   ____ = ____   Multiply each side by ____.

2. **Identify** the focus, directrix, and axis of symmetry. The equation has the form $y^2 = 4px$ where $p =$ ____. The focus is $(p, 0)$, or $($ ____ $, 0)$. The directrix is $x = -p$, or $x =$ ____. Because y is squared, the axis of symmetry is the _____.

3. **Draw** the parabola by making a table of values and plotting points. Because p ____ 0, the parabola opens to the _____. So, use only _____ x-values.

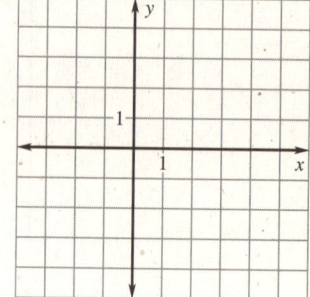

x	1	2	3	4	5
y	____	____	____	____	____

✓ **Checkpoint** Complete the following exercise.

1. Graph $y = -\frac{1}{4}x^2$. Identify the focus, directrix, and axis of symmetry.

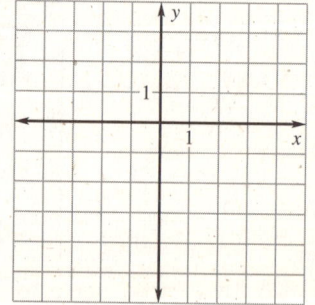

Your Notes

Example 2 Write an equation of a parabola

Write an equation of the parabola shown.

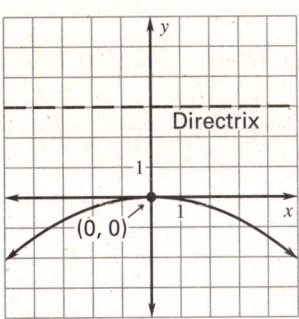

Solution

The graph shows that the vertex is _____ and the directrix is $y = -p =$ ___. Substitute _____ for p in the standard form of the equation of a parabola.

_____ Standard form, _____ axis of symmetry

_____ Substitute for p.

_____ Simplify.

✓ **Checkpoint** Complete the following exercise.

2. Write the standard form of the equation of the parabola with vertex at $(0, 0)$ and the directrix $x = -\frac{3}{4}$.

Homework

9.3 Graph and Write Equations of Circles

Goal • Graph and write equations of circles.

Your Notes

VOCABULARY

Circle

Center

Radius

STANDARD EQUATION OF A CIRCLE WITH CENTER AT THE ORIGIN

The standard form of the equation of a circle with center at (0, 0) and radius r is as follows:

$x^2 + y^2 = $ _____

Example 1 Graph an equation of a circle

Graph $y^2 = -x^2 + 16$. Identify the radius of the circle.

Solution

1. **Rewrite** the equation $y^2 = -x^2 + 16$ in standard form as _____.

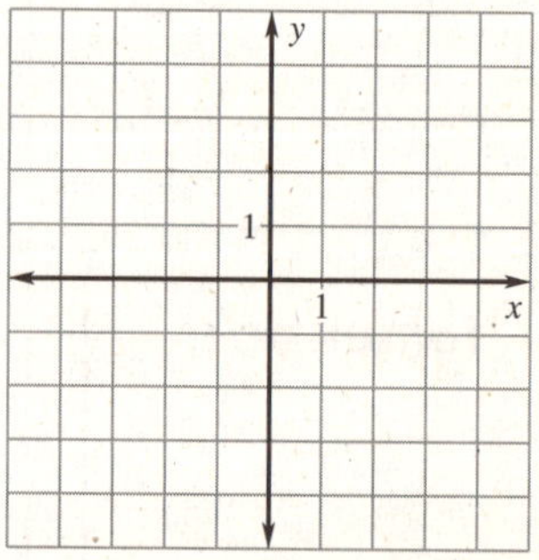

2. **Identify** the center and radius. From the equation, the graph is a circle centered at the origin with radius $r = $ _____ = ___.

3. **Draw** the circle. First plot several convenient points that are 4 units from the origin, such as (0, ___), (4, ___), (0, ___), and (−4, ___). Then draw the circle that passes through the points.

Your Notes

✓ **Checkpoint** Graph the equation. Identify the radius.

1. $x^2 = 4 - y^2$

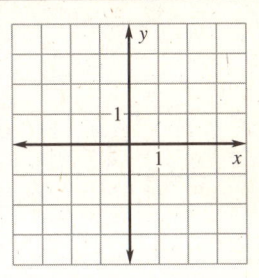

Example 2 *Write an equation of a circle*

The point $(-3, 4)$ lies on a circle whose center is the origin. Write the standard form of the equation of the circle.

The circle's radius r must be the distance between the center and $(-3, 4)$. Use the distance formula.

$r = \sqrt{(\underline{})^2 + (\underline{})^2}$

$= \sqrt{\underline{}} = \sqrt{\underline{}} = \underline{}$

Use the standard form with $r = \underline{}$ to write an equation of the circle.

$x^2 + y^2 = r^2$ Standard form

$x^2 + y^2 = \underline{}^2$ Substitute for r.

$x^2 + y^2 = \underline{}$ Simplify.

Example 3 *Find a tangent line*

Write an equation of the line tangent to the circle $x^2 + y^2 = 17$ at $(4, -1)$.

A line tangent to a circle and the radius to the point of tangency are perpendicular. The radius with endpoint $(4, -1)$ has slope $m = \underline{} = \underline{}$, so the slope of the tangent line at $(4, -1)$ is the negative reciprocal of $\underline{}$, or $\underline{}$. An equation of the tangent line is as follows:

$y + \underline{} = \underline{}(x - \underline{})$ Point-slope form

$y = \underline{}$ Solve for y.

Your Notes

> **Example 4** *Write a circular model*
>
> **Lighthouse** The beam from Oak Island Lighthouse in North Carolina can be seen for up to 24 miles. You are 18 miles east and 9 miles south of the lighthouse. Can you see the lighthouse beam?
>
> **Solution**
>
> 1. **Write** an inequality for the region lit by the beam. This region is all the points that satisfy the following inequality: $x^2 + y^2 <$ _____ ^{2}
>
> 2. **Substitute** the coordinates (18, 9) into the inequality.
>
> $x^2 + y^2 <$ _____ ^{2} Inequality
>
>   _____ $<$ _____ ^{2} Substitute for x and y.
>
>   _____   The inequality is _____.
>
>   You _____ see the lighthouse beam.

✓ **Checkpoint** Complete the following exercises.

> 2. Write the standard form of the equation of the circle with center at the origin that passes through the point (6, −3).
>
>
>
> 3. Write an equation of the line tangent to the circle $x^2 + y^2 = 34$ at (−3, −5).
>
>
>
> 4. From Example 4, suppose you are 16 miles east and 19 miles south of the lighthouse. Can you see the lighthouse beam?

Homework

9.4 Graph and Write Equations of Ellipses

Goal • Graph and write equations of ellipses.

Your Notes

VOCABULARY

Ellipse

Foci

Vertices

Major axis

Center

Co-vertices

Minor axis

STANDARD EQUATION OF AN ELLIPSE WITH CENTER AT THE ORIGIN

Equation	Major Axis	Vertices	Co-Vertices
$\dfrac{x^2}{a^2} + \dfrac{y^2}{b^2} = 1$	Horizontal	(±___, 0)	(0, ±___)
$\dfrac{x^2}{b^2} + \dfrac{y^2}{a^2} = 1$	Vertical	(0, ±___)	(±___, 0)

The major and minor axes are of lengths 2a and 2b, respectively, where a > b > 0. The foci of the ellipse lie on the major axis at a distance of c units from the center, where $c^2 =$ _____.

Your Notes

Example 1 Graph an equation of an ellipse

Graph the equation $9x^2 + 36y^2 = 324$. Identify the vertices, co-vertices, and foci of the ellipse.

1. **Rewrite** the equation in standard form.

   $9x^2 + 36y^2 = 324$ Write original equation.

   $\dfrac{}{} + \dfrac{}{} = \dfrac{}{}$ Divide each side by ____.

   $\dfrac{}{} + \dfrac{}{} = 1$ Simplify.

2. **Identify** the vertices, co-vertices, and foci. Note that $a^2 =$ ____ and $b^2 =$ ____, so $a =$ ____ and $b =$ ____. The denominator of the x^2-term is _____ that of the y^2-term, so the major axis is _____. The vertices of the ellipse are at $(\pm a, 0) = (\pm\underline{}, 0)$. The co-vertices are at $(0, \pm b) = (0, \pm\underline{})$. Find the foci.
   $c^2 = a^2 - b^2 =$ _____ = ____, so $c = \sqrt{\underline{}}$.
   The foci are at $(\pm\sqrt{\underline{}}, 0)$, or about $(\pm\underline{}, 0)$.

3. **Draw** the ellipse that passes through each vertex and co-vertex.

Example 2 Write an equation given a vertex and a co-vertex

Write an equation of the ellipse that has a vertex at $(0, 7)$, a co-vertex at $(-4, 0)$, and center at $(0, 0)$.

Sketch the ellipse as a check for your final equation. By symmetry, the ellipse must also have a vertex at $(0, \underline{})$ and a co-vertex at $(\underline{}, 0)$.

Because the vertex is on the _____ and the co-vertex is on the _____, the major axis is _____ with $a =$ ____, and the minor axis is _____ with $b =$ ____.

An equation is $\dfrac{}{} = 1$, or $\dfrac{}{} = 1$.

Your Notes

Example 3 *Write an equation given a vertex and a focus*

Write an equation of the ellipse that has a vertex at (−6, 0) and a focus at (5, 0).

Solution

Make a sketch of the ellipse. Because the vertex and focus lie on the _____, the major axis is _____, with $a =$ ___ and $c =$ ___. To find b, use the equation $c^2 = a^2 - b^2$.

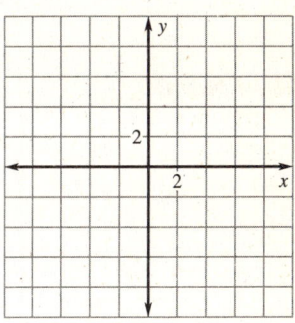

___ = ___ − b^2

$b^2 =$ ___ − ___ = ___

$b =$ ___

An equation is $\dfrac{}{} = 1$, or $\dfrac{}{} = 1$.

✓ **Checkpoint** Graph the equation. Identify the vertices, co-vertices, and foci of the ellipse.

1. $x^2 + \dfrac{y^2}{25} = 1$

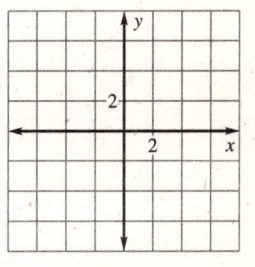

✓ **Checkpoint** Write an equation of the ellipse with the given characteristics and center at (0, 0).

2. Vertex: (−9, 0)
   Co-vertex: (0, 4)

3. Vertex: (0, 7)
   Focus: (0, −3)

Homework

9.5 Graph and Write Equations of Hyperbolas

Goal • Graph and write equations of hyperbolas.

Your Notes

VOCABULARY

Hyperbola

Foci

Vertices

Transverse Axis

Center

STANDARD EQUATION OF A HYPERBOLA WITH CENTER AT THE ORIGIN

Equation	Transverse Axis	Asymptotes	Vertices
$\dfrac{x^2}{a^2} - \dfrac{y^2}{b^2} = 1$	Horizontal	$y = \pm \underline{} x$	$(\pm \underline{}, 0)$
$\dfrac{y^2}{a^2} - \dfrac{x^2}{b^2} = 1$	Vertical	$y = \pm \underline{} x$	$(0, \pm \underline{})$

The foci lie on the transverse axis, c units from the center, where $c^2 =$ _____.

Your Notes

Example 1 *Graph an equation of a hyperbola*

Graph $36y^2 - 9x^2 = 324$. Identify the vertices, foci, and asymptotes of the hyperbola.

Solution

1. **Rewrite** the equation in standard form.

   $\underline{} = 1$

2. **Identify** the vertices, foci, and asymptotes. Note that $a^2 = \underline{}$ and $b^2 = \underline{}$, so $a = \underline{}$ and $b = \underline{}$. The y^2-term is \underline{}, so the transverse axis is \underline{} and the vertices are $(0, \pm\underline{})$. Find the foci.

   $c^2 = a^2 + b^2 = \underline{} = \underline{}$, so $c = \sqrt{\underline{}}$

   The foci are at $(0, \pm\sqrt{\underline{}}) \approx (0, \pm 6.7)$.

   The asymptotes are $y = \pm\frac{a}{b}x$, or $y = \underline{}$.

3. **Draw** the hyperbola. Draw a rectangle centered at the origin that is $2a = \underline{}$ units high and $2b = \underline{}$ units wide. The asymptotes pass through opposite corners of the rectangle. Then, draw the hyperbola passing through the vertices and approaching the asymptotes.

✓ **Checkpoint** Graph the equation. Identify the vertices, foci, and asymptotes of the hyperbola.

1. $\dfrac{x^2}{49} - \dfrac{y^2}{9} = 1$

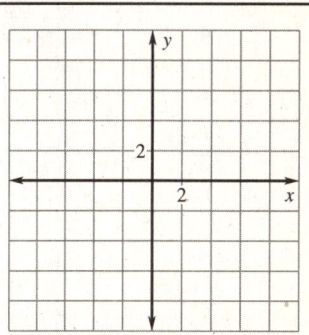

Your Notes

Example 2 *Write an equation of a hyperbola*

Write an equation of the hyperbola with foci at (−5, 0) and (5, 0) and vertices at (−4, 0) and (4, 0).

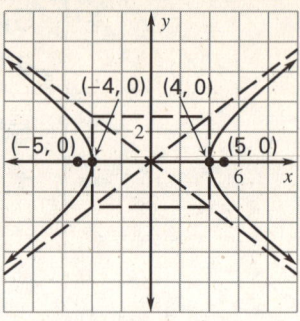

The foci and vertices lie on the ___-axis equidistant from the origin, so the transverse axis is _____ and the center is the origin. The foci are each ___ units from the center, so $c = $ ___. The vertices are each ___ units from the center, so $a = $ ___.

Because $c^2 = a^2 + b^2$, you have $b^2 = c^2 - a^2$. Find b^2.

$b^2 = c^2 - a^2 =$ _____ = ___

Because the transverse axis is horizontal, the standard form of the equation is as follows:

_____ = 1   Substitute 4 for *a* and 9 for b^2.

_____ = 1   Simplify.

✓ **Checkpoint** Write an equation of the hyperbola with the given foci and vertices.

2. Foci: (0, −8), (0, 8)
   Vertices: (0, −5), (0, 5)

Your Notes

Example 3 — Solve a multi-step problem

Lamp The diagram shows the hyperbolic cross section of a lamp. Write an equation for the cross section of the lamp. The lamp is 10 inches high. How wide is the base?

Solution

1. From the diagram, $a =$ ___ and $b =$ ___.

   Because the transverse axis is _____, an equation for the cross section of the lamp

   is $\dfrac{}{} = 1$,

   or $\dfrac{}{} = 1$.

   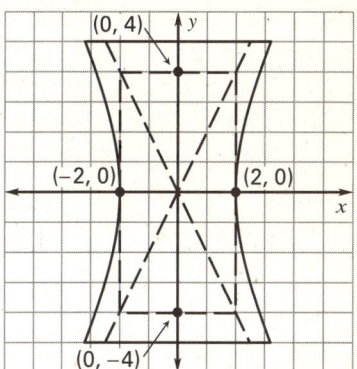

2. Find the x-coordinate at the lamp's bottom edge. Because the lamp is 10 inches tall, substitute $y =$ ___ into the equation and solve.

   $\dfrac{}{} = 1$

   $x^2 = $ _____

   $x \approx$ _____

   So, the lamp has a width of $2x$ or $2($ _____ $) = $ _____ inches.

✔ **Checkpoint** Complete the following exercise.

3. Write an equation for the hyperbolic cross section of the lamp in Example 3 if the vertices are at ($\pm 3, 0$) and the foci are at ($\pm 5, 0$). If the lamp is 15 inches high, how wide is the base?

Homework

9.6 Translate and Classify Conic Sections

Goal • Translate conic sections.

Your Notes

VOCABULARY

Conic sections

General second-degree equation

Discriminant

STANDARD FORM OF EQUATIONS OF TRANSLATED CONICS

In the following equations, the point (h, k) is the vertex of the parabola and the center of the other conics.

Circle $(x - h)^2 + (y - k)^2 = r^2$

Parabola $(y - k)^2 = 4p(x - h)$ Horizontal axis
$(x - h)^2 = 4p(y - k)$ Vertical axis

Ellipse $\dfrac{(x - h)^2}{a^2} + \dfrac{(y - k)^2}{b^2} = 1$ Horizontal axis

$\dfrac{(x - h)^2}{b^2} + \dfrac{(y - k)^2}{a^2} = 1$ Vertical axis

Hyperbola $\dfrac{(x - h)^2}{a^2} - \dfrac{(y - k)^2}{b^2} = 1$ Horizontal axis

$\dfrac{(y - k)^2}{a^2} - \dfrac{(x - h)^2}{b^2} = 1$ Vertical axis

Your Notes

Example 1 — Graph the equation of a translated circle

Graph $(x + 3)^2 + (y - 2)^2 = 4$.

1. **Compare** the given equation to the standard form of an equation of a circle. The graph is a circle with center at $(h, k) = (\underline{}, \underline{})$ and radius $r = \sqrt{\underline{}} = \underline{}$.

2. **Plot** the center. Then plot several points that are each ___ units from the center:

   $\underline{} = \underline{}$

   $\underline{} = \underline{}$

   $\underline{} = \underline{}$

   $\underline{} = \underline{}$

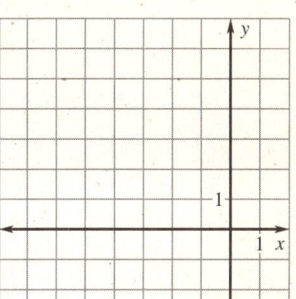

3. **Draw** a circle through the points.

Example 2 — Graph the equation of a translated hyperbola

Graph $\dfrac{(y + 2)^2}{16} - \dfrac{(x - 1)^2}{4} = 1$.

1. **Compare** the given equation to the standard forms of equations of hyperbolas. The graph is a hyperbola with a _____ transverse axis. The center is at $(h, k) = (\underline{}, \underline{})$. Because $a^2 = \underline{}$ and $b^2 = \underline{}$, you know that $a = \underline{}$ and $b = \underline{}$.

2. **Plot** the center, vertices, and foci. The vertices lie $a = \underline{}$ units above and below the center, at $(\underline{}, \underline{})$ and $(\underline{}, \underline{})$. Because $c^2 = a^2 + b^2 = \underline{}$, the foci lie $c = \sqrt{\underline{}} \approx \underline{}$ units above and below the center, at $(\underline{}, \underline{})$ and $(\underline{}, \underline{})$.

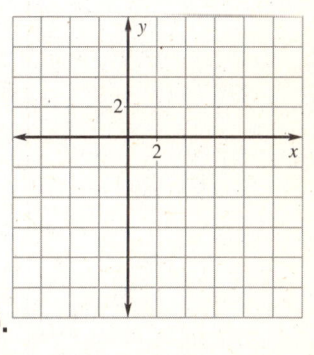

3. **Draw** the hyperbola. Draw a rectangle centered at $(\underline{}, \underline{})$ that is $2a = \underline{}$ units high and $2b = \underline{}$ units wide. Draw the asymptotes through the opposite corners of the rectangle. Then draw the hyperbola so that it passes through the vertices and approaches the asymptotes.

Your Notes

> **Example 3** *Write an equation of a translated parabola*
>
> Write an equation of the parabola whose vertex is at (2, 1) and whose focus is at (5, 1).
>
> 1. **Determine** the form of the equation. Sketch the parabola. The parabola opens to the _____ and has the form $(y - k)^2 = 4p(x - h)$ where p ___ 0.
>
>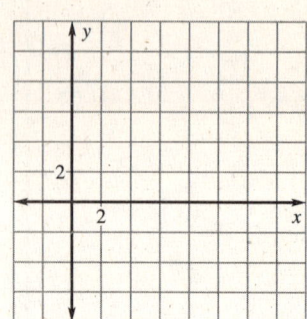
>
> 2. **Identify** h and k. The vertex is at (2, 1), so $h = $ ___ and $k = $ ___.
>
> 3. **Find** p. The vertex (2, 1) and focus (5, 1) both lie on the line _____, so the distance between them is $|p| = |\underline{}| = $ ___, and $p = $ ___ or $p = $ ___. Because p ___ 0, it follows that $p = $ ___, so $4p = $ ___.
>
> The equation is _____.

✓ **Checkpoint** Complete the following exercises.

---

1. Graph $(x - 2)^2 + (y + 3)^2 = 9$. Identify the center and radius.

   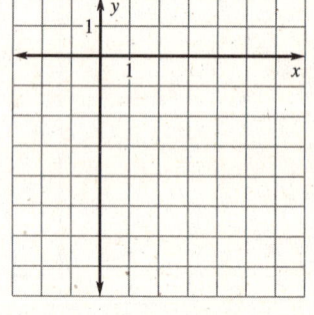

---

2. Graph $\dfrac{(x + 3)^2}{9} - \dfrac{(y - 1)^2}{25} = 1$.

   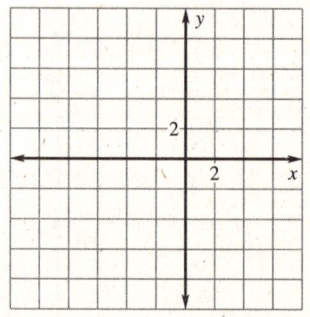

---

3. Write an equation of the parabola whose vertex is at (−3, −1) and whose focus is at (−3, 1).

Your Notes

Example 4 *Write an equation of a translated ellipse*

Write an equation of the ellipse with foci at (−2, 3) and (4, 3) and co-vertices at (1, 4) and (1, 2).

1. **Determine** the form of the equation. First sketch the ellipse. The foci lie on the major axis, so the axis is _____. The equation has the form:

$$\frac{(x-h)^2}{a^2} + \frac{(y-k)^2}{b^2} = 1$$

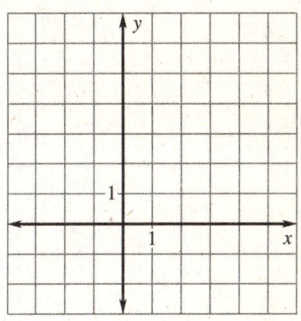

2. **Identify** h and k by finding the center, which is halfway between the foci (or the co-vertices).

$(h, k) = \left(\underline{\qquad}, \underline{\qquad} \right) = (\underline{\ }, \underline{\ })$

3. **Find** b, the distance between a co-vertex and the center, and c, the distance between a focus and the center:

$b = |\underline{\qquad}| = \underline{\ }$, $c = |\underline{\qquad}| = 3$.

4. **Find** a. For an ellipse,

$a^2 = b^2 + c^2 = \underline{\ } + \underline{\ } = \underline{\ }$, so $a = \sqrt{\underline{\ }}$.

The standard form of the equation is

_____.

✓ **Checkpoint** Complete the following exercise.

4. Write an equation of the ellipse with foci at (−3, 0) and (−3, −6) and co-vertices at (−1, −3) and (−5, −3).

Your Notes

CLASSIFYING CONICS USING THEIR EQUATIONS

Any conic can be described by a general second-degree equation in x and y:

$$Ax^2 + Bxy + Cy^2 + Dx + Ey + F = 0.$$

The expression $B^2 - 4AC$ is the discriminant of the conic equation and can be used to identify it.

Discriminant	Type of Conic
$B^2 - 4AC$ ___ 0, $B = 0$, and $A = C$	Circle
$B^2 - 4AC$ ___ 0 and either $B \neq 0$ or $A \neq C$	Ellipse
$B^2 - 4AC$ ___ 0	Parabola
$B^2 - 4AC$ ___ 0	Hyperbola

If B ___ 0, each axis of the conic is horizontal or vertical.

Example 5 *Classify a conic*

Classify the conic given by
$2x^2 + 2y^2 - 5x + 3y - 1 = 0.$

Solution

Note that $A =$ ___, $B =$ ___, and $C =$ ___, so the value of the discriminant is: $B^2 - 4AC =$ _____ = ___.

Because $B^2 - 4AC$ ___ 0 and A ___ C, the conic is a _____.

✓ **Checkpoint** Classify the conic.

5. $5x^2 - 3y^2 - 10x - 12y - 22 = 0$

Homework

9.7 Solve Quadratic Systems

Goal • Solve quadratic systems.

Your Notes

VOCABULARY

Quadratic system

Example 1 *Solve a linear-quadratic system by graphing*

Solve the system using a graphing calculator.

$y^2 - 3x - 1 = 0$ Equation 1
$2x - y = 6$ Equation 2

1. **Solve** each equation for y.

    Equation 1
    $y^2 - 3x - 1 = 0$
    $y^2 = $ _____
    $y = $ _____

    Equation 2
    $2x - y = 6$
    $-y = $ _____
    $y = $ _____

2. **Graph** the equations. Use the calculator's *intersect* feature to find the coordinates of the intersection points. The graphs of $y = $ _____ and $y = $ _____ intersect at (____, ____). The graphs of $y = $ _____ and $y = $ _____ intersect at (___, ___).

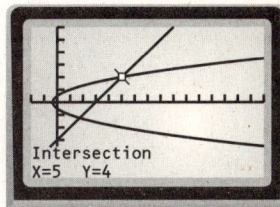

The solutions are (____, ____) and (___, ___). Check the solutions by substituting the coordinates of the points into each of the original equations.

✓ **Checkpoint** Use a graphing calculator to solve system.

1. $x^2 + y^2 = 18$ Equation 1
   $y = -x + 6$ Equation 2

Your Notes

Example 2 *Solve a linear-quadratic system by substitution*

Solve the system using substitution.

$x^2 + y^2 = 13$ Equation 1
$y = x + 5$ Equation 2

Solution

Substitute $x + 5$ for y in Equation 1 and solve for x.

$x^2 + y^2 = 13$	Equation 1
$x^2 + (\underline{})^2 = 13$	Substitute for y.
$x^2 + \underline{} = 13$	Expand the power.
$\underline{} = 0$	Combine like terms.
$\underline{} = 0$	Divide each side by ___.
$\underline{} = 0$	Factor.
$x = \underline{}$ or $x = \underline{}$	Zero product property

The corresponding y-values are $y = \underline{} = \underline{}$ and $y = \underline{} = \underline{}$. The solutions are (__ , __) and (__ , __).

✓ **Checkpoint** Solve the system using substitution.

2. $y^2 + 6x - 3 = 0$
   $y = 2x - 1$

Your Notes

Example 3 — Solve a quadratic system by elimination

Solve the system by elimination.

$5x^2 + y^2 + 48x + 99 = 0$ Equation 1
$x^2 - y^2 - 9 = 0$ Equation 2

Solution

Add the equations to eliminate the y^2-term and obtain a quadratic equation in x.

$5x^2 + y^2 + 48x + 99 = 0$
$\underline{x^2 - y^2 - 9 = 0}$

$6x^2 + 48x + 90 = 0$ Add.
$x^2 + 8x + 15 = 0$ Divide each side by __6__.
$(x+3)(x+5) = 0$ Factor.
$x = -3$ or $x = -5$ Zero product property

When $x = -3$, $y = 0$. When $x = -5$, $y = \pm 4$.

The solutions are $(-3, 0)$, $(-5, 4)$, and $(-5, -4)$.

✓ **Checkpoint** Solve the system by elimination.

3. $2x^2 + 2y^2 - 26 = 0$
   $-x^2 + y + 7 = 0$

Your Notes

> **Example 4** *Solve a real-life quadratic system*
>
> **Treasure Hunt** The class is having a treasure hunt that begins at the school.
>
> **Clue 1:** The treasure is 3 km from the school.
>
> **Clue 2:** The treasure is 5 km from the post office. (The post office is 4 km west and 6 km north of the school.)
>
> **Clue 3:** The treasure is 1 km from the town square. (The town square is 2 km north of the school.)
>
> **Solution**
>
> Let each unit represent 1 km. If the school is at (0, 0), then the post office is at _____ and the town square is at _____. Write equations of circles that represent the possible locations of the treasure. The intersection of the circles is the location of the treasure.
>
> **Clue 1:** _____
>
> **Clue 2:** _____
>
> **Clue 3:** _____
>
> Expand the equation from Clue 3, subtract Clue 1 from Clue 3, and solve for y.
>
> _____
> − (_____)
> _____ ⟹ y = ___
>
> Use y = ___ and the equation from Clue 1 to find x = ___. The treasure is _____ of the school.

✓ **Checkpoint** Find the location of the treasure.

---

4. **Clue 1:** The treasure is 4 blocks from the school.

   Clue 2: The treasure is 5 blocks from the library. (The library is 3 blocks north of the school.)

   Clue 3: The treasure is 2 blocks from the science center. (The science center is 2 blocks south and 4 blocks east of the school.)

Homework

Words to Review

Give an example of the vocabulary word.

Distance formula	Midpoint formula
Focus, foci	**Directrix**
Circle	**Center**
Radius	**Ellipse**
Vertices	**Major axis**

Co-vertices	Minor axis
Hyperbola	Transverse axis
Conic sections	General second-degree equation
Discriminant	Quadratic system

Review your notes and Chapter 9 by using the Chapter Review on pages 669–672 of your textbook.

10.1 Apply the Counting Principle and Permutations

Goal • Use the fundamental counting principle and find permutations.

Your Notes

VOCABULARY

Permutation

Factorial

FUNDAMENTAL COUNTING PRINCIPLE

Two Events If one event can occur in *m* ways and another event can occur in *n* ways, then the number of ways that both events can occur is _____.

Three or More Events The fundamental counting principle can be extended to three or more events. For example, if three events occur in *m*, *n*, and *p* ways, then the number of ways that all three events can occur is _____.

Example 1 Use the fundamental counting principle

Pizza You are buying a pizza. You have a choice of 3 crusts, 4 cheeses, 5 meat toppings, and 8 vegetable toppings. How many different pizzas with one crust, one cheese, one meat, and one vegetable can you choose?

Solution

Use the fundamental counting principle to find the total number of pizzas. Multiply the number of crusts (___), the number of cheeses (___), the number of meats (___), and the number of vegetables (___).

Number of pizzas = _____ = _____

Your Notes

✓ **Checkpoint** Complete the following exercise.

1. If the pizza crust was not a choice in Example 1, how many different pizzas could be made?

Example 2 *Use the counting principle with repetition*

Telephone Numbers A town has telephone numbers that all begin with 329 followed by four digits. How many different phone numbers are possible (a) if numbers can be repeated and (b) if numbers cannot be repeated?

a. There are ____ choices for each digit. Use the fundamental counting principle to find the total amount of phone numbers.

Phone numbers = _____ = _____

b. If you cannot repeat digits, there are still ____ choices for the first number, but then only ____ remaining choices for the second digit, ____ choices for the third digit, and ____ choices for the fourth digit. Use the fundamental counting principle.

Phone numbers = _____ = _____

Example 3 *Find the number of permutations*

Playoffs Eight teams are competing in a baseball playoff.

a. In how many different ways can the baseball teams finish the competition?

b. In how many different ways can 3 of the baseball teams finish first, second, and third?

Solution

a. There are 8! different ways that the teams can finish.
   8! = _____ = _____

b. Any of the ____ teams can finish first, then any of the ____ remaining teams can finish second, and then any of the remaining ____ teams can finish third.

   _____ = _____

Your Notes

PERMUTATIONS OF n OBJECTS TAKEN r AT A TIME

The number of permutations of r objects taken from a group of n distinct objects is denoted by $_nP_r$.

$$_nP_r = \frac{n!}{(n-r)!}$$

Example 4 *Find permutations of n objects taken r at a time*

Homework You have 6 homework assignments to complete over the weekend. However, you only have time to complete 4 of them on Saturday. In how many orders can you complete 4 of the assignments?

Solution

Find the number of permutations of 6 objects taken 4 at a time.

$$_6P_4 = \frac{\boxed{}!}{(\boxed{})!} = \frac{\boxed{}!}{\boxed{}!} = \frac{\boxed{}}{\boxed{}} = \underline{}$$

You can complete the 4 assignments in _____ different orders.

✓ **Checkpoint** Complete the following exercises.

2. How many different 7 digit telephone numbers are possible if all of the digits can be repeated?

3. In Example 3, how many different ways can the teams finish if there are 6 teams competing in the playoffs?

4. You were left a list of 9 chores to complete. In how many orders can you complete 5 of the chores?

Your Notes

PERMUTATIONS WITH REPETITION

The number of distinguishable permutations of n objects where one object is repeated s_1 times, another is repeated s_2 times, and so on, is:

$$\frac{n!}{s_1! \cdot s_2 \cdot \ldots \cdot s_k!}$$

Example 5 *Find permutations with repetition*

Find the number of distinguishable permutations of the letters in (a) EVEN and (b) CALIFORNIA.

Solution

a. EVEN has ___ letters of which ___ is repeated ___ times. So, the number of distinguishable permutations is $\dfrac{\boxed{}!}{\boxed{}!} = \dfrac{\boxed{}}{\boxed{}} = $ ___

b. CALIFORNIA has ___ letters of which ___ and ___ are each repeated ___ times. So, the number of distinguishable permutations is

  ___ = ___ = ___ .

✓ **Checkpoint** Find the number of distinguishable permutations of the letters in the word.

5. TOMORROW

6. YESTERDAY

Homework

10.2 Use Combinations and the Binomial Theorem

Goal • Use combinations and the binomial theorem.

Your Notes

VOCABULARY

Combination

Pascal's triangle

Binomial theorem

COMBINATIONS OF n OBJECTS TAKEN r AT A TIME

The number of combinations of r objects taken from a group of n distinct objects is denoted by $_nC_r$.

$$_nC_r = \frac{n!}{(n-r)! \cdot r!}$$

Example 1 Find combinations

Books You are picking 7 books from a stack of 32. If the order of the books you choose is not important, how many different 7 book groups are possible?

The number of ways to choose 7 books from 32 is:

$$_{32}C_7 = \frac{\boxed{}!}{\boxed{}! \cdot \boxed{}!}$$

= _____

= _____

Lesson 10.2 • Algebra 2 Notetaking Guide   263

Your Notes

Example 2 Decide to multiply or add combinations

Movie Rentals The local movie rental store is having a special on new releases. The new releases consist of 12 comedies, 8 action, 7 drama, 5 suspense, and 9 family movies.

a. You want exactly 2 comedies and 3 family movies. How many different movie combinations can you rent?

b. You can afford at most 2 movies. How many movie combinations can you rent?

Solution

a. You can choose 2 of the 12 comedies and 3 of the 9 family movies. So, the number of possible sets of movies is:

$$_{12}C_2 \cdot {_9}C_3 = \frac{\Box!}{\Box!\,\Box!} \cdot \frac{\Box!}{\Box!\,\Box!}$$

$$= \underline{\qquad} = \underline{\qquad}$$

b. You can rent 0, 1, or 2 movies. Because there are ____ movies to choose from, the number of possible sets of movies is:

____C_0 + ____C_1 + ____C_2 = _____ = ____

✓ Checkpoint Complete the following exercises.

1. Find $_7C_4$.	2. Find $_6C_3$.	3. Find $_{12}C_{11}$.

4. From Example 2, find the number of possible movie combinations if you can choose 2 action movies and 2 dramas.

Your Notes

Example 3 *Solve a multi-step problem*

Reading A popular magazine has 11 articles. You want to read at least 2 of the articles. How many different combinations of articles can you read?

Solution

For each of the 11 articles, you can choose to read or not read the article, so there are ____ total combinations. If you read at least ___ articles, you do not read only a total of ___ or ___ articles. So, the number of ways you can read at least 2 articles is:

____ − ($_{11}C$___ + $_{11}C$___) = _____ = ____

✓ **Checkpoint** Complete the following exercise.

5. Your school football team has 10 scheduled games for the season. You want to attend at least 4 games. How many different combinations of games can you attend?

PASCAL'S TRIANGLE

The first and last numbers in each row are ___. Every number other than ___ is the sum of the closest two numbers in the row directly above it.

Pascal's triangle: **As combinations**

$n = 0$ (0th row) $_0C$___

$n = 1$ (1st row) $_1C$___ $_1C$___

$n = 2$ (2nd row) $_2C$___ $_2C$___ $_2C$___

$n = 3$ (3rd row) $_3C$___ $_3C$___ $_3C$___ $_3C$___

As numbers

___

___ ___

___ ___ ___

___ ___ ___ ___

Lesson 10.2 • Algebra 2 Notetaking Guide

Your Notes

Example 4 — Use Pascal's triangle

Class Representatives Out of 5 finalists, your class must choose 3 class representatives. Use Pascal's triangle to find the number of combinations of 3 students that can be chosen as representatives.

Solution

Find $_5C\underline{}$ using the 5th row of Pascal's triangle.

$n = 5$
(5th row) $_5C\underline{}$ $_5C\underline{}$ $_5C\underline{}$ $_5C\underline{}$ $_5C\underline{}$ $_5C\underline{}$

The value of $_5C\underline{}$ is the _____ value in the 5th row of Pascal's triangle. Therefore, $_5C\underline{} = \underline{}$. There are _____ combinations of class representatives.

✓ **Checkpoint** Complete the following exercise.

6. In Example 4, use Pascal's triangle to find the number of combinations of 3 students that can be chosen from 8 finalists.

BINOMIAL THEOREM

- For any positive integer n, the binomial expansion of $(a + b)^n$ is:

$$(a + b)^n = {}_nC_0 a^n b^0 + {}_nC_1 a^{n-1} b^1 + \cdots + {}_nC_n a^0 b^n$$

Notice that each term in the expansion of $(a + b)^n$ has the form _____ where r is an integer from 0 to n.

Example 5 — Expand a power of a binomial sum

Use the binomial theorem to write the binomial expansion.

$(x + 4)^3$

= _____

= _____

= _____

Your Notes

Example 6 *Expand a power of a binomial difference*

Use the binomial theorem to write the binomial expansion.

$(2m - n)^4 = [2m + (\underline{})]^4$

= _____

= _____
_____

= _____

Example 7 *Find a coefficient in an expansion*

Find the coefficient of x^5 in the expansion of $(2x - 7)^9$.

Each term in the expansion has the form ${}_9C_r(2x)^{9-r}(-7)^r$. The term containing x^5 occurs when $r = 4$:

_____ = _____ = _____

The coefficient of x^5 is _____.

✓ **Checkpoint** Use the binomial theorem to write the binomial expansion.

7. $(a + 2b)^3$

8. $(6 - s)^4$

Homework

9. Find the coefficient of x^8 in the expansion of $(3x - 2)^{10}$.

10.3 Define and Use Probability

Goal • Find the likelihood that an event will occur.

Your Notes

VOCABULARY

Probability

Theoretical probability

Odds

Experimental probability

Geometric probability

THEORETICAL PROBABILITY OF AN EVENT

When all outcomes are equally likely, the theoretical probability that an event A will occur is:

$$P(A) = \frac{\text{Number of outcomes in event } A}{\boxed{}}$$

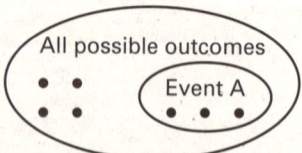

The theoretical probability of an event is often simply called the probability of the event.

Your Notes

✓ **Checkpoint** Complete the following exercises.

1. Using a standard deck of 52 playing cards, find the probability of drawing a red queen.

2. In Example 2, find the probability that 4 of the 7 male players on the baseball team bat first, in any order.

ODDS IN FAVOR OF OR ODDS AGAINST AN EVENT

When all outcomes are equally likely, the odds in favor of an event A and the odds against an event A are:

Odds in favor of event A = $\dfrac{\text{Number of outcomes in } A}{\boxed{}}$

Odds against event A = $\dfrac{\boxed{}}{\text{Number of outcomes in } A}$

You can write the odds in favor of or against an event in the form $\dfrac{a}{b}$ or in the form $a:b$.

Example 3 Find odds

Marbles A marble is drawn from a bag containing 6 red, 12 yellow, and 9 black marbles. Find (a) the odds in favor of drawing a red marble and (b) the odds against drawing a black marble.

Solution

a. Odds in favor of drawing red

= $\dfrac{\text{Number of red}}{\text{Number of non-red}}$ = ____ = ____ , or ____ : ____

b. Odds against drawing black

= $\dfrac{\text{Number of non-black}}{\text{Number of black}}$ = ____ = ____ , or ____ : ____

Your Notes

Example 2 Multiply rational expressions

$$\frac{2x^2 + 4x}{x^2 - 4x - 12} \cdot \frac{x^2 - 9x + 18}{2x}$$

$= \dfrac{\boxed{}}{\boxed{}} \cdot \dfrac{\boxed{}}{\boxed{}}$ Factor numerator and denominator.

$= \dfrac{\boxed{}}{\boxed{}}$ Multiply numerator and denominator.

$= \underline{}$ Divide out common factors and write in simplified form.

✓ **Checkpoint** Complete the following exercises.

1. Simplify the expression.

   $$\frac{x^2 - 2x - 15}{x^2 + 4x + 3}$$

2. Multiply the expression.

   $$\frac{6x^2 + 18x}{x^2 + x - 6} \cdot \frac{x^2 - x - 2}{x^2 - 7x - 8}$$

Example 3 Multiply a rational expression by a polynomial

$$\frac{x - 4}{x^3 + 1} \cdot (x^2 - x + 1)$$

$= \dfrac{x - 4}{x^3 + 1} \cdot \dfrac{\boxed{}}{\boxed{}}$ Write polynomial as rational expression.

$= \dfrac{\boxed{}}{\boxed{}}$ Factor denominator.

$= \underline{}$ Divide out common factor and write in simplified form.

Your Notes

EXPERIMENTAL PROBABILITY OF AN EVENT

When an experiment is performed that consists of a certain number of trials, the experimental probability of an event A is given by:

$$P(A) = \frac{\text{Number of trials where A occurs}}{\text{Total number of trials}}$$

Example 4 *Find an experimental probability*

Exam Grades Exam grades of students in a history class are shown in the bar graph. Find the probability that a randomly chosen student in this history class received a C or better.

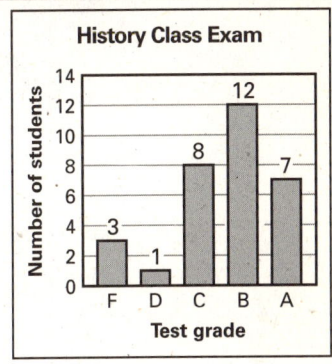

Solution

The total number of students who took the test is:

_____ = _____

Of those surveyed, _____ = _____ received at least a C.

P(at least a C) = _____ ≈ _____

✓ **Checkpoint** Complete the following exercises.

3. A marble is drawn from a bag containing 6 blue, 6 yellow, 9 white, and 11 green marbles. Find the odds in favor of drawing a yellow marble.

4. Using Example 4, find the experimental probability that a randomly selected student received a C or lower.

Homework

10.4 Find Probabilities of Disjoint and Overlapping Events

Goal • Find probabilities of compound events.

Your Notes

VOCABULARY

Compound Event

Disjoint or mutually exclusive events

PROBABILITY OF COMPOUND EVENTS

If A and B are two events, then the probability of A or B is: $P(A \text{ or } B) =$ _____

If A and B are disjoint events, then the probability of A or B is: $P(A \text{ or } B) =$ _____

Example 1 Find probability of disjoint events

You roll a six-sided number cube. What is the probability of rolling a 2 or a 5?

Let event A be rolling a 2 and event B be rolling a 5. A has ___ outcome and B has ___ outcome. Because A and B are mutually exclusive, the probability is:

$P(A \text{ or } B) =$ _____ = ___ + ___

= ___ = ___ ≈ ___

✓ **Checkpoint** Complete the following exercise.

1. You roll a six-sided number cube. What is the probability of rolling a 1 or an even number?

Your Notes

Example 2 Find probability of compound events

You roll a six-sided number cube. What is the probability of rolling an odd number or a number less than 3?

Solution

Let event A be rolling an odd number and event B be rolling a number less than 3. A has ___ outcomes and B has ___ outcomes. Of these, ___ outcome is common to A and B. So, the probability of rolling an odd number or a number less than 3 is:

P(A or B) = _____

     = _____ = ___ = ___ ≈ _____

Example 3 Use a formula to find P(A and B)

Music In a survey of 300 students, 150 like pop music *or* country music. There are 97 students who like pop music and there are 83 students who like country music. What is the probability that a randomly selected student likes both pop music *and* country music.

Solution

Let event A be selecting a student who likes pop music and event B be selecting a student who likes country music. From the given information you know that:

P(A) = ____ , P(B) = ____ , and P(A or B) = ____

The probability that a randomly selected student likes both pop music and country music is P(A and B).

P(A or B) = _____   Write general formula.

     = _____   Substitute.

P(A and B) = _____   Solve for P(A and B).

P(A and B) = _____ = _____ = _____   Simplify.

Your Notes

> Refer to the diagram in Example 4 of the textbook for the possible outcomes of rolling two six-sided dice.

Example 4 *Find the probability of complements*

When two six-sided dice are rolled, there are 36 possible outcomes. Find the probability that the sum is not 4 and the sum is greater than or equal to 3.

Solution

a. $P(\text{sum is not } 4) =$ _____

$= \underline{} = \underline{} = \underline{} \approx \underline{}$

b. $P(\text{sum} \geq 3) =$ _____

$= \underline{} \approx \underline{}$

PROBABILITY OF THE COMPLEMENT OF AN EVENT

The probability of the complement of A is
$P(\overline{A}) =$ _____ .

✓ **Checkpoint** Complete the following exercises.

2. You roll a six-sided number cube. What is the probability of rolling a number less than 4 or an even number?

3. In a survey of 125 people, 90 of them like orange juice or grape juice. There are 62 people who like orange juice and 43 people who like grape juice. What is the probability that a randomly selected person likes both orange juice and grape juice?

Homework

4. From Example 4, find the probability that the sum is not 8.

10.5 Find Probabilities of Independent and Dependent Events

Goals • Examine independent and dependent events.

Your Notes

VOCABULARY

Independent events

Dependent events

Conditional probability

PROBABILITY OF INDEPENDENT EVENTS

If A and B are independent events, then the probability that both A and B occur is: P(A and B) = _____

More generally, the probability that n independent events occur is the _____ of the n probabilities of the individual events.

Example 1 *Find probability of three independent events*

Attendance Every morning, one student in a class of 24 students is randomly chosen to take attendance. What is the probability that the same student will be chosen three days in a row?

Let events A, B, and C be the student being chosen on the first, second, and third day, respectively. The three events are independent. So, the probability is:

P(A and B and C) = _____

= _____ ≈ _____

Your Notes

Example 2 — Use a complement to find a probability

Manufacturing A manufacturer has found that 2 out of every 500 coffee pots produced are defective. What is the probability that at least one coffee pot is defective in the first 300 coffee pots made?

Solution

The probability of not making a defective coffee pot is:

$P(\text{coffee pot is not defective}) = \underline{} = \underline{}$

Each coffee pot made is an independent event. So, the probability of making at least one defective coffee pot is:

$P(\text{coffee pot is defective}) = 1 - [P(\text{coffee pot is not defective})]^{300}$

$= \underline{} \approx \underline{}$

✓ **Checkpoint** Complete the following exercises.

1. During a high school track meet, each race consists of 9 competitors who are randomly assigned lanes from 1 to 9. What is the probability that a runner will draw lanes 1, 2, or 3 in the three races in which he competes?

2. A manufacturer has found that 6 out of every 450 batteries produced is defective. What is the probability that at least one battery is defective in the first 100 produced?

PROBABILITY OF DEPENDENT EVENTS

If A and B are dependent events, then the probability that both A and B occur is:

$P(A \text{ and } B) = \underline{}$

Your Notes

Example 3 Find a conditional probability

Eye Color Find the probability that (a) a listed person has blue eyes and (b) a male has blue eyes.

	Green eyes	Blue eyes	Brown eyes	Hazel eyes
Male	27	35	15	23
Female	12	9	38	41

a. $P(\text{blue eyes}) = \dfrac{\text{Number of people with blue eyes}}{\text{Total number of people}}$

$= \dfrac{\underline{}}{\underline{}} = \underline{}$

b. $P(\text{blue eyes} \mid \text{male}) = \dfrac{\text{Number of blue-eyed males}}{\text{Total number of males}}$

$= \dfrac{\underline{}}{\underline{}} = \underline{}$

Example 4 Comparing independent and dependent events

You randomly select two marbles from a bag containing 15 yellow, 10 red, and 12 blue marbles. What is the probability that the first marble is yellow and the second marble is not yellow if (a) you replace the first marble before selecting the second, and (b) you do *not* replace the first marble?

Solution

Let A be "the first marble is yellow" and B be "the second marble is not yellow."

a. If you replace the first marble before selecting the second marble, then A and B are _____ events. So, the probability is:

$P(A \text{ and } B) = \underline{}$

$= \dfrac{\underline{}}{\underline{}} = \underline{} \approx \underline{}$

b. If you do not replace the first marble before selecting the second marble, then A and B are _____ events. So, the probability is:

$P(A \text{ and } B) = \underline{}$

$= \dfrac{\underline{}}{\underline{}} = \underline{} \approx \underline{}$

Your Notes

Example 5 *Find probability of three dependent events*

Pencils Your teacher passes around a box with 10 red pencils, 8 pink pencils, and 13 green pencils. If you and the two people in your group are the first to randomly select a pencil, what is the probability that all three of you select pink pencils?

Solution

Let A be that you choose a pink pencil, B be that the second group member chooses a pink pencil, and C be that the third group member chooses a pink pencil. These events are dependent. So, the probability is:

$P(A$ and B and $C) =$ _____

= _____ = _____ ≈ _____

✓ **Checkpoint** Complete the following exercises.

3. Use the table in Example 3 to find the probability that a female has hazel eyes.

4. From Example 4, find the probability that both marbles will be yellow if (a) you replace the first marble and (b) you do not replace the first marble.

Homework

5. From Example 5, what is the probability that you and your group members all choose a red pencil?

10.6 Construct and Interpret Binomial Distributions

Goal • Study probability distributions.

Your Notes

VOCABULARY

Random variable

Probability distribution

Binomial distribution

Binomial experiment

Symmetric

Skewed

PROBABILITY DISTRIBUTIONS

A probability distribution is a function that gives the probability of each possible outcome for a _____ _____. The sum of all the probabilities in a probability distribution must equal ___.

Your Notes

Example 1 Construct a probability distribution

Let X be a random variable that represent the sum when two four-sided dice are rolled. Make a table and histogram showing the probability distribution for X.

Solution

The possible values of X are the integers from 2 to 8. The table shows the number of outcomes for each value of X. Divide each value by _____ to get P(X).

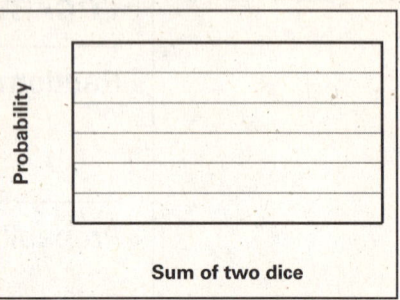
Sum of two dice

X (sum)	2	3	4	5	6	7	8
Outcomes	1	2	3	4	3	2	1
P(X)							

Example 2 Interpret a probability distribution

Use the probability distribution in Example 1 to answer each question. (a) What is the most likely outcome of rolling the two dice? (b) What is the probability that the sum of the two dice is at most 4?

Solution

a. The most likely outcome of rolling the two dice is the value of X for which P(X) is greatest. This probability is greatest for X = ____. So, the most likely outcome when rolling the two dice is a sum of ____.

b. The probability that the sum of the two dice is at most 4 is:

$P(X \leq 4) = $ _____

= _____ = _____ = _____

Your Notes

✓ **Checkpoint** Complete the following exercise.

1. Let X be the letter on a letter block randomly chosen from a bag containing 7 blocks labeled "A," 3 blocks labeled "B," 6 blocks labeled "C," and 5 blocks labeled "D." Make a table and histogram showing the probability distribution.

X				
Outcomes				
P(X)				

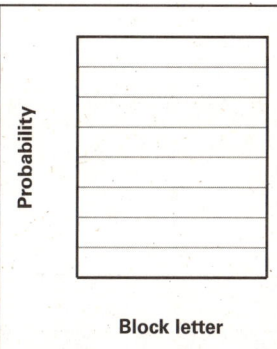

Block letter

BINOMIAL EXPERIMENTS

A binomial experiment meets the following conditions:

- There are n _____ trials.

- Each trial has only two possible outcomes: _____ and _____.

- The probability of success is the _____ for each trial. This probability is denoted by p. The probability for failure is given by $1 - p$.

For a binomial experiment, the probability of exactly k successes in n trials is:

$P(k \text{ successes}) = $ _____

Your Notes

Example 3 — Construct a binomial distribution

A survey taken in your school found that 68% of the students are not afraid to fly. Suppose you randomly survey 5 students. Draw a histogram of the binomial distribution for your survey.

The probability that a randomly selected student is not afraid to fly is $p =$ _____. Because you survey 5 students, $n =$ ___.

$P(k = 0) =$ _____ $\approx$ _____

$P(k = 1) =$ _____ $\approx$ _____

$P(k = 2) =$ _____ $\approx$ _____

$P(k = 3) =$ _____ $\approx$ _____

$P(k = 4) =$ _____ $\approx$ _____

$P(k = 5) =$ _____ $\approx$ _____

(Histogram: Probability vs. Number of students not afraid to fly)

Example 4 — Interpret a binomial distribution

Use the binomial distribution in Example 3.

a. What is the most likely outcome of the survey?

b. What is the probability that at least 3 students are not afraid to fly?

Solution

a. The most likely outcome of the survey is the value of k for which $P(k)$ is greatest. This probability is greatest for $k =$ ___. So, the most likely outcome is that ___ of the 5 students are not afraid to fly.

b. The probability that at least 3 students are not afraid to fly is:

$P(k \geq 3) =$ _____

$ =$ _____ $=$ _____

So, the probability is about ____ %.

Your Notes

✓ **Checkpoint** Complete the following exercises.

In a survey of your neighborhood, 57% of the families owned a pet. Suppose you randomly survey 6 families.

2. Draw a histogram showing the binomial distribution for your survey.

Probability

Number of families that own a pet

3. What is the most likely outcome of your survey? What is the probability that at most 2 families own a pet?

Homework

Words to Review

Give an example of the vocabulary word.

Permutation	Factorial
Combination	Pascal's triangle
Binomial theorem	Probability
Theoretical probability	Odds
Experimental probability	Geometric probability

Compound event	Disjoint or mutually exclusive events
Independent events	Dependent events
Conditional probability	Random variable
Probability distribution	Binomial distribution
Symmetric	Skewed
Binomial experiment	

Review your notes and Chapter 10 by using the Chapter Review on pages 734–736 of your textbook.

11.1 Find Measures of Central Tendency and Dispersion

Goal • Describe data using statistical measures.

Your Notes

VOCABULARY

Statistics

Measure of central tendency

Measure of dispersion

Standard deviation

Outlier

MEASURES OF CENTRAL TENDENCY

- The mean, or _____, of n numbers is the _____ of the numbers _____ by n. The mean is denoted by $\bar{x}$, which is read as "x-bar." For the data set $x_1, x_2, \ldots, x_n$, the mean is

    $\bar{x} = $ _____.

- The median of n numbers is the _____ number when the numbers are written in order. (If n is even, the median is the _____ of the two middle numbers.)

- The mode of n numbers is the number or numbers that occur _____. There may be _____ mode, _____ mode, or _____ mode.

286 Lesson 11.1 • Algebra 2 Notetaking Guide

Your Notes

Example 1 — Find measures of central tendency

Quiz Scores The data sets at the right give quiz scores for two different biology classes. Find the mean, median, and mode of each data set.

Class A	Class B
15, 17, 17, 17, 18, 19, 21, 22, 25	16, 18, 19, 21, 22, 22, 22, 24, 25

Class A: Mean: $\bar{x}$ = _____ = ____ = ____

   Median: ____   Mode: ____

Class B: Mean: $\bar{x}$ = _____ = ____ = ____

   Median: ____   Mode: ____

STANDARD DEVIATION OF A DATA SET

The standard deviation σ (read as "sigma") of $x_1, x_2, \ldots, x_n$ is:

$$\sigma = \sqrt{\frac{\rule{3cm}{0.4pt}}{n}}$$

Example 2 — Find the range and standard deviation

Find the range and standard deviation for the quiz scores in each data set from Example 1.

Class A: Range = ____ − ____ = ____

$\sigma = \sqrt{\dfrac{\rule{2cm}{0.4pt}}{\rule{1cm}{0.4pt}}}$

$\approx$ ____

Class B: Range = ____ − ____ = ____

$\sigma = \sqrt{\dfrac{\rule{2cm}{0.4pt}}{\rule{1cm}{0.4pt}}}$

$\approx$ ____

Because the range and standard deviation for Class ____ are greater, its quiz scores are _____ spread out.

Your Notes

Example 3 *Examine the effect of an outlier*

Soccer The winning scores for the first 9 games of the soccer season are: 3, 4, 2, 5, 3, 1, 4, 3, 2.

a. Find the mean, median, mode, range, and standard deviation of the data set.

b. The winning score in the next game is an outlier, 9. Find the new mean, median, mode, range, and standard deviation.

c. Which measure of central tendency does the outlier affect the most? the least?

d. What effect does the outlier have on the range and standard deviation?

Solution

a. Mean: $\bar{x} =$ _____ = ___

   Median: ___   Mode: ___   Range: _____ = ___

   Std. Dev.: $\sigma =$ _____

   $\approx$ _____

b. Mean: $\bar{x} =$ _____ = ____

   Median: ___   Mode: ___   Range: _____ = ___

   Std. Dev.:

   $\sigma =$ _____

   $\approx$ _____

c. The _____ is most affected by the outlier. The _____ and _____ are not affected by the outlier.

d. The outlier caused both the range and standard deviation to _____.

Your Notes

✓ **Checkpoint** Complete the following exercises.

The data set below gives the recorded speeds (in mi/h) for 10 different cars on a local highway.

69, 62, 64, 67, 62, 64, 63, 65, 60, 64

1. Find the mean, median, and mode of the data set.

2. Find the range and standard deviation of the data set.

3. The next car that drives by is having car trouble, so the recorded speed is 36 mi/h. Find the new mean, median, mode, range, and standard deviation.

Homework

Lesson 11.1 • Algebra 2 Notetaking Guide

11.2 Apply Transformations to Data

Goal • Learn how transformations of data affect statistics.

Your Notes

ADDING A CONSTANT TO DATA VALUES

When a constant is added to every value in a data set, the following are true:

• The mean, median, and mode of the new data set can be obtained by _____ the same constant to the mean, median, and mode of the original data set.

• The range and standard deviation are _____.

Example 1 Add a constant to data values

Midterm Scores The data set gives the midterm scores for a chemistry class:

84, 89, 98, 86, 96, 83, 87, 93, 91, 93

Every student in the class has also completed a bonus assignment, so the teacher adds 5 points to each score. Find the mean, median, mode, range and standard deviation of the test scores with and without the bonus points.

Solution

	Scores without bonus	Scores with bonus
Mean	90	95
Median	90	95
Mode	93	98
Range	15	15
Standard Deviation	4.80	4.80

MULTIPLYING DATA VALUES BY A CONSTANT

When each value of a data set is multiplied by a constant, the new mean, median, mode, range, and standard deviation can be found by _____ each original statistic by the same constant.

Your Notes

Example 2 — Multiply data values by a constant

Olympics The data set lists the winning distances (in meters) in the women's Olympic javelin throw from 1968 to 2004. Find the mean, median, mode, range, and standard deviation of the distances in meters and in yards. (*Note:* 1 m ≈ 1.094 yd)

19.61, 21.03, 21.16, 22.41, 20.48, 22.24, 21.06, 20.56, 20.56, 19.59

Solution

	Distance in meters	Distance in yards
Mean	_____	1.094(_____) = _____
Median	_____	1.094(_____) = _____
Mode	_____	1.094(_____) = _____
Range	_____	1.094(_____) = _____
Standard Deviation	_____	1.094(_____) = _____

✓ **Checkpoint** Complete the following exercises.

1. The data set gives the heights (in inches) of patients visiting a doctor's office: 64, 68, 72, 58, 61, 70, 74, 68.

   After the patients leave, the doctor realizes that all of the patients were wearing tennis shoes and must subtract 1 inch for each patient. Find the mean, median, mode, range, and standard deviation of the heights with and without tennis shoes.

Homework

2. From Example 2, find the mean, median, mode, range, and standard deviation of the distances in feet. (*Note:* 1 m ≈ 3.28 ft)

11.3 Use Normal Distributions

Goal • Study normal distributions.

Your Notes

VOCABULARY

Normal distribution

Normal curve

Standard normal distribution

z-score

AREAS UNDER A NORMAL CURVE

A normal distribution with mean $\bar{x}$ and standard deviation σ has these properties:

- The total area under the related normal curve is ____.
- About ____% of the area lies within 1 standard deviation of the mean.
- About ____% of the area lies within 2 standard deviations of the mean.
- About ____% of the area lies within 3 standard deviations of the mean.

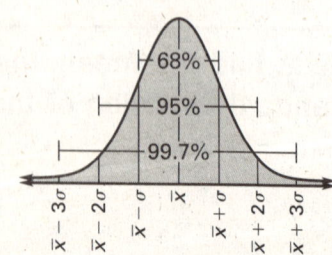 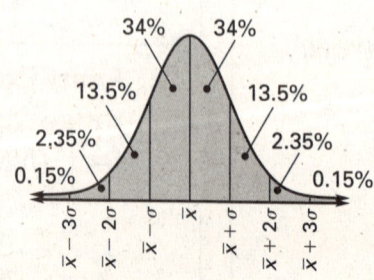

Your Notes

Example 1 — Find a normal probability

A normal distribution has mean $\bar{x}$ and standard deviation σ. For a randomly selected x-value from the distribution, find $P(\bar{x} \le x \le \bar{x} + 3\sigma)$

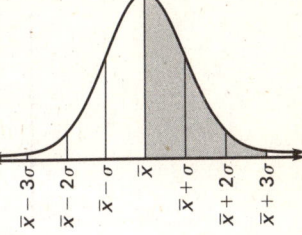

Solution

The probability that a randomly selected x-value lies between ___ and _____ is the shaded area under the normal curve. Therefore:

$P(\bar{x} \le x \le \bar{x} + 3\sigma) = $ _____ + _____ + _____

= _____

✓ **Checkpoint** Complete the following exercise.

1. A normal distribution has mean $\bar{x}$ and standard deviation σ. For a randomly selected x-value from the distribution, find $P(x \le \bar{x} - \sigma)$.

Example 2 — Interpret normally distributed data

Math Scores The math scores of the 2004 SAT exam are normally distributed with a mean of 518 and a standard deviation of 114.

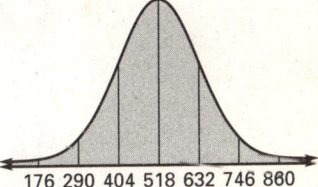

176 290 404 518 632 746 860
SAT Math scores

a. About what percent of the test-takers have scores between 518 and 746?

b. About what percent of the test-takers have scores less than 404?

Solution

a. The scores of 518 and 736 represent _____ standard deviations to the _____ of the mean. So, the percent of test-takers with scores between 518 and 736 is ____% + ____% = ____%.

b. A score of 404 is _____ standard deviation to the _____ of the mean. So, the percent of scores less than 404 is ____% + ____% + ____% = ____%.

Your Notes

Example 3 *Use a z-score and the standard normal table*

Height A survey of a group of women found that the height of the women is normally distributed with a mean height of 64.5 inches and a standard deviation of 2.5 inches. Find the probability that a woman is at most 58 inches tall.

Solution

1. Find the z-score corresponding to an x-value of 58.

$$z = \frac{x - \bar{x}}{\sigma} = \underline{\hspace{2cm}} = \underline{\hspace{1cm}}$$

2. Use the standard normal table to find $P(x \leq 58) = P(z \leq \underline{\hspace{1cm}})$. The table shows that $P(z \leq \underline{\hspace{1cm}}) = \underline{\hspace{1cm}}$. So, the probability that a woman is at most 58 inches tall is about $\underline{\hspace{1cm}}$.

z	.0	.1	.2	.3	.4
−2	.0228	.0179	.0139	.0107	.0082
2	.9772	.9821	.9861	.9893	.9918

z	.5	.6	.7	.8	.9
−2	.0062	.0047	.0035	.0026	.0019
2	.9938	.9953	.9965	.9974	.9981

✔ **Checkpoint** Complete the following exercises.

2. In Example 2, what percent of test-takers receive a score between 404 and 632?

3. In Example 3, find the probability that a woman is at most 70 inches tall.

Homework

11.4 Select and Draw Conclusions from Samples

Goal • Study different sampling methods for collecting data.

Your Notes

VOCABULARY

Population

Sample

Unbiased sample

Biased sample

Margin of error

Example 1 *Classify samples*

School Lunch A teacher wants to survey everyone at her school about the quality of the school lunches. Identify the type of sample described and tell if the sample is biased.

a. The teacher surveys every 7th student that goes through the lunch line.

b. From a random name lottery, the teacher chooses 150 students and teachers to survey.

Solution

a. The teacher is using a _____ to select students, so the sample is a _____ sample. This sample is _____ because the teacher surveys the students, but not the teachers.

b. The teacher chose from a random lottery, so the sample is a _____ sample. The sample is _____ because both students and teachers are being surveyed.

Your Notes

✓ **Checkpoint** Identify the type of sample described, and tell whether the sample is biased.

> 1. A local politician wants to survey his constituents. He mails surveys to the constituents that are members of his political party and uses only the surveys that are returned.

MARGIN OF ERROR FORMULA

When a random sample of size n is taken from a large population, the margin of error is approximated by:

Margin of error = $\pm$ _____

This means that if the percent of the sample responding a certain way is p (expressed as a decimal), then the percent of the population that would respond the same way is likely to be between $p -$ _____ and $p +$ _____ .

Example 2 Find a margin of error

Newspaper Survey In a survey of 1432 people, 26% said that they read the newspaper every day. (a) What is the margin of error for the survey? (b) Give an interval that is likely to contain the exact percent of all people who read the newspaper every day.

a. Margin of error = $\pm \dfrac{1}{\sqrt{n}} = \pm \dfrac{1}{\boxed{}} \approx$ _____

The margin of error for the survey is about _____ %.

b. To find the interval, add and subtract _____ %.

26% − _____ % = _____ %

26% + _____ % = _____ %

It is likely that the exact percent of all people who read the newspaper everyday is between _____ % and _____ %.

296 Lesson 11.4 • Algebra 2 Notetaking Guide

Your Notes

✓ **Checkpoint** Complete the following exercise.

2. In Example 2, suppose the sample size is 3236. What is the margin of error for the survey?

Example 3 Find a sample size

Community Survey A group of students survey the local community about their favorite beverage. How many people did they survey if the margin of error is ±7%?

Solution

Use the margin of error formula.

Margin of error $= \pm\dfrac{1}{\sqrt{n}}$

_____ $= \pm\dfrac{1}{\sqrt{n}}$

_____ $= \dfrac{1}{n}$

$n \approx$ _____

About _____ people were surveyed.

✓ **Checkpoint** Complete the following exercise.

3. In a poll about which movie channel its customers prefer to watch, a cable company wants a margin of error to be ±3%. How many people would they need to survey?

Homework

11.5 Choose the Best Model for Two-Variable Data

Goal • Choose the best model to represent a set of data.

Your Notes

Example 1 Use a linear model

Teacher's Salaries The table shows the teacher's salary y (in dollars) for a certain school district, where x is the number of years of teaching experience. Use a graphing calculator to find a model for the data.

x	1	2	3	4
y	30,624	32,436	34,167	35,989

x	5	6	7
y	37,684	39,311	41,098

1. **Make** a scatter plot. The points lie approximately on a _____. This suggests a _____ model.

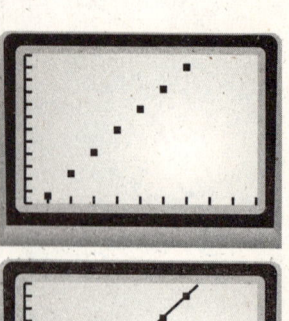

2. **Use** the _____ regression feature to find an equation of the model.

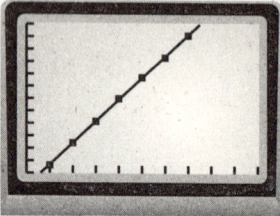

3. **Graph** the model along with the data to verify that the model fits the data well.

A model for the data is $y = $ _____.

✓ Checkpoint Complete the following exercise.

1. Use a graphing calculator to find a model for the data. Graph the model and data.

x	0	1	2	3
y	2	9	19	29

x	4	5	6	7
y	40	51	61	73

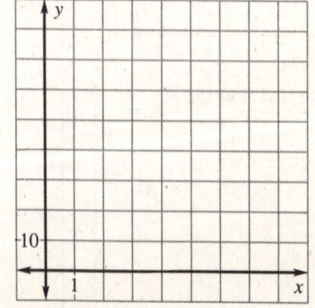

Your Notes

Example 2 Use an exponential model

Deer Population An environmental group observes a deer population in a park where hunting has been banned. The table shows the population y counted x years after the ban began. Use a graphing calculator to find a model for the data.

x	0	5	10	15	20
y	500	729	1271	2206	3765

Solution

1. **Make** a scatter plot. The points are level at first and then begin to _____ rapidly. This suggests an _____ growth model.

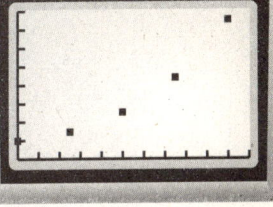

2. **Use** the _____ regression feature to find an equation of the model.

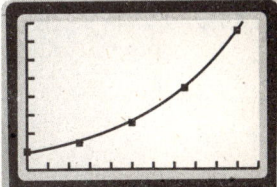

3. **Graph** the model along with the data to verify that the model fits the data well.

A model for the data is y = _____.

✓ **Checkpoint** Complete the following exercise.

2. Use a graphing calculator to find a model for the data. Then graph the model and the data in the same coordinate plane.

x	1	2	3	4	5	6	7
y	462	318	181	107	75	62	55

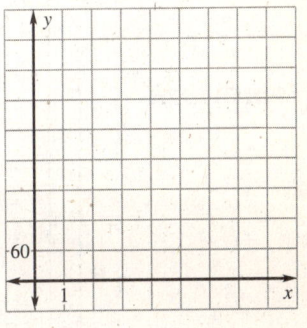

Your Notes

Example 3 Use a quadratic model

Roller Coaster Riders A manager at a local amusement park kept a record of the number of people to ride the most popular roller coaster at the park. The table shows the number of people y that rode the roller coaster x hours after the park had opened. Use a graphing calculator to find a model for the data.

x	0	2	4	6	8	10	12
y	85	163	282	341	398	381	304

Solution

1. **Make** a scatter plot. The points form an _____. This suggests a _____ model.

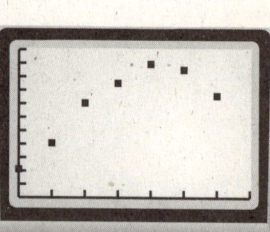

2. **Use** the _____ regression feature to find an equation of the model.

3. **Graph** the model along with the data to verify that the model fits the data well.

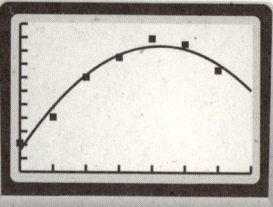

A model for the data is y = _____.

✓ Checkpoint Complete the following exercise.

3. Use a graphing calculator to find a model for the data. Then graph the model and the data in the same coordinate plane.

x	0	2	4	6	8	10	12
y	100	178	273	314	349	324	289

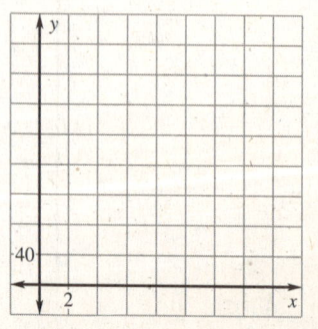

Homework

Words to Review

Give an example of the vocabulary word.

Statistics	Outlier
Measure of central tendency Mean: Median: Mode:	Measure of dispersion Range: Standard Deviation:
Normal distribution	Normal curve
Standard normal distribution	z-score
Population	Sample

Unbiased sample	Biased sample

Margin of error

Review your notes and Chapter 11 by using the Chapter Review on pages 784–786 of your textbook.

12.1 Define and Use Sequences and Series

Goal • Recognize and write rules for number patterns.

Your Notes

VOCABULARY

Sequence

Terms

Series

Summation notation

Sigma notation

SEQUENCES

A sequence is a function whose domain is a set of _____ integers. If a domain is not specified, it is understood that the domain starts with 1. The values in the range are called the _____ of the sequence.

Domain: 1   2   3   4 ... n   The relative position of each term

Range: a_1 a_2 a_3 a_4 ... a_n Terms of the sequence

A _____ sequence has a limited number of terms.
An _____ sequence continues without stopping.

Finite sequence: 2, 4, 6, 8
Infinite Sequence: 2, 4, 6, 8, ···

A sequence can be specified by an equation, or _____. For example, both sequences above can be described by the rule $a_n = 2n$ or $f(n) = 2n$.

Your Notes

> **Example 1** *Write terms of sequences*
>
> Write the first six terms of $a_n = 2^n + 1$.
>
> $a_1 = $ _____ = ____ 1st term
> $a_2 = $ _____ = ____ 2nd term
> $a_3 = $ _____ = ____ 3rd term
> $a_4 = $ _____ = ____ 4th term
> $a_5 = $ _____ = ____ 5th term
> $a_6 = $ _____ = ____ 6th term

> **Example 2** *Write rules for sequences*
>
> Describe the pattern, write the next term, and write a rule for the *n*th term of the sequence
> (a) 1, 4, 9, 16, . . . and (b) 0, 7, 26, 63, ...
>
> **Solution**
>
> a. You can write the terms as ___^{2}, ___^{2}, ___^{2}, ___^{2}, ...
>   The next term is $a_5 = $ ___ = ___. A rule for the *n*th term is $a_n = $ ___.
>
> b. You can write the terms as ____ – 1, ____ – 1, ____ – 1, ____ – 1, ... The next term is
> $a_5 = $ ___ – 1 = ____. A rule for the *n*th term is
> $a_n = $ _____.

✔ **Checkpoint** Complete the following exercises.

1. Write the first six terms of the sequence $f(n) = 3n - 7$.

2. For the sequence –3, 9, –27, 81, . . ., describe the pattern, write the next term, and write a rule for the *n*th term.

Your Notes

SERIES AND SUMMATION NOTATION

When the terms of a sequence are added together, the resulting expression is a series. A series can be finite or infinite.

Finite series: $2 + 4 + 6 + 8$

Infinite series: $2 + 4 + 6 + 8 \cdots$

You can use _____ notation to write a series.

$$2 + 4 + 6 + 8 = \sum_{i=1}^{4} 2i$$

$$2 + 4 + 6 + 8 + \cdots = \sum_{i=1}^{\infty} 2i$$

For both series, the index of summation is ___ and the lower limit of summation is ___. The upper limit of summation is ___ for the finite series and ___ (_____) for the infinite series. Summation notation is also called _____ notation because it uses the uppercase Greek letter sigma, written Σ.

Example 3 Write series using summation notation

Write the series using summation notation.

a. $4 + 7 + 10 + \cdots + 46$ b. $1 + \frac{1}{8} + \frac{1}{27} + \frac{1}{64} + \cdots$

Solution

a. Notice that the first term is $3(1) + 1$, the second is _____, the third is _____, and the last is _____. So, $a_i =$ _____ where $i = 1, 2, 3, \ldots,$ ____. The lower limit of summation is ___ and the upper limit of summation is ____.

  The summation notation for the series is _____.

b. Notice that for each term, the denominator is a perfect cube. So, $a_i =$ _____ where $i = 1, 2, 3, 4, \ldots$. The lower limit of summation is ___ and the upper limit of summation is _____.

  The summation notation for the series is _____.

Your Notes

✓ **Checkpoint** Write the series using summation notation.

3. $7 + 14 + 21 + \cdots + 77$

4. $-4 - 8 - 12 - 16 - \cdots$

Example 4 *Find the sum of a series*

Find the sum of the series.

$\sum_{k=3}^{5} 2 - 3k = [2 - 3(\underline{})] + [2 - 3(\underline{})] + [2 - 3(\underline{})]$

$\phantom{\sum_{k=3}^{5} 2 - 3k} = \underline{} = \underline{}$

FORMULAS FOR SPECIAL SERIES

Sum of n terms of 1	Sum of first n positive integers	Sum of squares of first n positive integers
$\sum_{i=1}^{n} 1 = n$	$\sum_{i=1}^{n} i = \dfrac{n(n+1)}{2}$	$\sum_{i=1}^{n} i^2 = \dfrac{n(n+1)(2n+1)}{6}$

Example 5 *Use a formula for a sum*

Use a formula for special series to find the sum of $\sum_{i=1}^{32} i$.

$\sum_{i=1}^{32} i = \underline{} = \underline{} = \underline{}$

Homework

✓ **Checkpoint** Find the sum of the series.

5. $\sum_{k=4}^{8} (k^2 - 6)$

6. $\sum_{i=1}^{28} i^2$

12.2 Analyze Arithmetic Sequences and Series

Goal • Study arithmetic sequences and series.

Your Notes

VOCABULARY

Arithmetic sequence

Common difference

Arithmetic series

Example 1   Identify arithmetic sequences

Tell whether the sequence $-5, -3, -1, 1, 3, \ldots$ is arithmetic.

Find the differences of consecutive terms.

$a_2 - a_1 =$ _____ = ___
$a_3 - a_2 =$ _____ = ___
$a_4 - a_3 =$ _____ = ___
$a_5 - a_4 =$ _____ = ___

Each difference is ___, so the sequence ___ arithmetic.

✓ **Checkpoint** Decide whether the sequence is arithmetic.

1. $32, 27, 21, 17, 10, \ldots$

RULE FOR AN ARITHMETIC SEQUENCE

The nth term of an arithmetic sequence with first term a_1 and common difference d is given by:

$a_n = a_1 + (n-1)d$

Your Notes

Example 2 — Write a rule for the nth term

Write a rule for the *n*th term of the sequence. Then find a_{19}.

a. 2, 9, 16, 23, ...   b. 57, 45, 33, 21, ...

Solution

a. The sequence is arithmetic with first term $a_1 = 2$ and common difference $d =$ _____ = ____. So, a rule for the *n*th term is:

$a_n = a_1 + (n - 1)d$ Write general rule.

$= \underline{} + (n - 1)\underline{}$ Substitute for a_1 and d.

$= \underline{}$ Simplify.

The 19th term is $a_{19} = \underline{} = \underline{}$.

b. The sequence is arithmetic with first term $a_1 = 57$ and common difference $d =$ _____ = _____. So, a rule for the *n*th term is:

$a_n = a_1 + (n - 1)d$ Write general rule.

$= \underline{} + (n - 1)(\underline{})$ Substitute for a_1 and d.

$= \underline{}$ Simplify.

The 19th term is $a_{19} = \underline{} = \underline{}$.

✓ **Checkpoint** Write a rule for the *n*th term of the arithmetic sequence. Then find a_{22}.

2. 9, 5, 1, −3, ...

3. −15, −9, −3, 3, ...

Your Notes

Example 3 — Write a rule given a term and common difference

One term of an arithmetic sequence is $a_{11} = 41$. The common difference is $d = 5$. (a) Write a rule for the nth term. (b) Graph the sequence.

a. Use the general rule to find the first term.

$a_n = a_1 + (n-1)d$ Write general rule.

_____ $= a_1 +$ (_____ $- 1$)_____   Substitute for a_n, n, and d.

_____ $= a_1$ Solve for a_1.

So, a rule for the nth term is:

$a_n =$ _____ $+ (n-1)$_____   Substitute for a_1 and for d.

$=$ _____   Simplify.

b. Create a table of values for the sequence. Notice that the points lie on a line.

n	1	2	3	4	5	6
a_n						

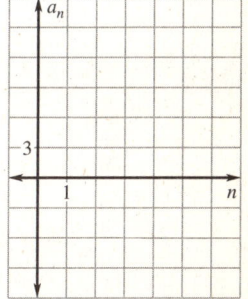

Example 4 — Write a rule given two terms

Two terms of the arithmetic sequence are $a_6 = 7$ and $a_{22} = 87$. Find a rule for the nth term.

1. Write a system of equations using $a_n = a_1 + (n-1)d$ and substituting 22 for n (Equation 1) and then 6 for n (Equation 2).

$a_{22} = a_1 + (22-1)d$ ⟹ ____ $= a_1 +$ ____ d

$a_6 = a_1 + (6-1)d$ ⟹ ____ $= a_1 +$ ____ d

2. Solve the system.

____ $=$ ____ d

____ $= d$

____ $= a_1 +$ ____ (____)

____ $= a_1$

3. Find a rule for a_n. $a_n = a_1 + (n-1)d$

$=$ ____ $+ (n-1)$ ____

$=$ ____

Your Notes

✓ **Checkpoint** Write a rule for the nth term of the arithmetic sequence. Then find a_{22}.

4. $a_{15} = 107$, $d = 12$

5. $a_5 = 91$, $a_{20} = 1$

THE SUM OF A FINITE ARITHMETIC SERIES

The sum of the first n terms of an arithmetic series is:

$$S_n = n\left(\frac{a_1 + a_n}{2}\right)$$

In words, S_n is the _____ of the _____ terms, _____ by _____.

Example 5 Find a sum

Find the sum of the arithmetic series $\sum_{i=1}^{15}(9 + 3i)$.

$a_1 = 9 + 3(\_\_) = \_\_$ Identify first term.

$a_{15} = 9 + 3(\_\_) = \_\_$ Identify last term.

$S_{15} = $ _____   Write rule for S_{15}.

$= $ _____   Simplify.

Homework

✓ **Checkpoint** Find the sum of the arithmetic series.

6. $\sum_{i=1}^{18}(77 - 4i)$

12.3 Analyze Geometric Sequences and Series

Goal • Study geometric sequences and series.

Your Notes

VOCABULARY

Geometric sequence

Common ratio

Geometric series

Example 1 *Identify geometric sequences.*

Tell whether the sequence 1, −4, 16, −64, 256, ... is geometric.

To decide whether a sequence is geometric, find the ratios of consecutive terms.

$\dfrac{a_2}{a_1} = \dfrac{-4}{1} = -4$ $\dfrac{a_3}{a_2} = \underline{\quad} = \underline{\quad}$

$\dfrac{a_4}{a_3} = \underline{\quad} = \underline{\quad}$ $\dfrac{a_5}{a_4} = \underline{\quad} = \underline{\quad}$

Each ratio is _____, so the sequence _____ geometric.

✓ **Checkpoint** Tell whether the sequence is geometric.

1. 512, 128, 64, 8, ...

RULE FOR A GEOMETRIC SEQUENCE

The nth term of a geometric sequence with first term a_1 and common ratio r is given by: $a_n = a_1 r^{n-1}$

Your Notes

Example 2 — Write a rule for the nth term

Write a rule for the nth term of the sequence 972, -324, 108, -36, ... Then find a_{10}.

Solution

The sequence is geometric with first term $a_1 = $ _____ and common ratio $r = $ ___ = ___ . So, a rule for the nth term is:

$a_n = a_1 r^{n-1}$ Write general rule.

$= $ ___$($ ___$)^{n-1}$ Substitute for a_1 and r.

The 10th term is $a_{10} = $ _____ = ___ .

Example 3 — Write a rule given a term and common ratio

One term of a geometric sequence is $a_3 = -18$. The common ratio is $r = 3$. (a) Write a rule for the nth term. (b) Graph the sequence.

a. Use the general rule to find the first term.

$a_n = a_1 r^{n-1}$ Write general rule.

___ $= a_1($___$)$___$^{-1}$ Substitute for a_n, r, and n.

___ $= a_1$ Solve for a_1.

So, a rule for the nth term is:

$a_n = a_1 r^{n-1}$ Write general rule.

$= $ _____   Substitute for a_1 and r.

b. Create a table of values for the sequence. Notice that the points lie on an exponential curve.

n	1	2	3
a_n			

n	4	5
a_n		

Your Notes

✓ **Checkpoint** Write a rule for the nth term of the geometric sequence. Then find a_9.

2. 14, 28, 56, 112, . . .

3. $a_5 = 324$, $r = -3$

Example 4 Write a rule given two terms

Two terms of a geometric sequence are $a_2 = 10$ and $a_7 = -320$. Find a rule for the nth term.

1. **Write** a system of equations using $a_n = a_1 r^{n-1}$ and substituting 2 for n (Equation 1) and then 7 for n (Equation 2).

   $a_2 = a_1 r^{2-1}$ ⟹ _____ Equation 1
   $a_7 = a_1 r^{7-1}$ ⟹ _____ Equation 2

2. **Solve** the system.   ___ = a_1 Solve Equation 1 for a_1.

   $-320 = $ ___ (r^6) Substitute for a_1 in Equation 2.

   $-320 = $ ___   Simplify.

   ___ = r Solve for r.

   $10 = a_1($ ___ $)$ Substitute in Equation 1

   ___ = a_1 Solve for a_1.

3. **Find** a rule for a_n. $a_n = a_1 r^{n-1}$ Write general rule.

   $a_n = $ _____   Substitute.

Your Notes

✓ **Checkpoint** Write a rule for the nth term of the geometric sequence. Then find a_9.

4. $a_3 = 224$, $a_6 = 28$

THE SUM OF A FINITE GEOMETRIC SERIES

The sum of the first n terms of a geometric series with common ratio $r \neq 1$ is:

$$S_n = a_1\left(\frac{1 - r^n}{1 - r}\right)$$

Example 5 *Find the sum of a geometric series*

Find the sum of the geometric series $\sum_{i=1}^{13} 3(4)^{i-1}$.

$a_1 = \underline{} = \underline{}$ Identify first term.

$r = \underline{}$ Identify common ratio.

$S_{13} = a_1\left(\dfrac{1 - r^{13}}{1 - r}\right)$ Write rule for S_{13}.

$= \underline{} = \underline{}$ Substitute and simplify.

✓ **Checkpoint** Find the sum of the geometric series.

5. $\sum_{i=1}^{11} 7(-5)^{n-1}$

Homework

314 Lesson 12.3 • Algebra 2 Notetaking Guide

12.4 Find Sums of Infinite Geometric Series

Goal • Find the sums of infinite geometric series.

Your Notes

VOCABULARY

Partial sum

THE SUM OF AN INFINITE GEOMETRIC SERIES

The sum of an infinite geometric series with first term a_1 and common ratio r is given by

$$S = \frac{a_1}{1-r}$$

provided $|r| < 1$. If $|r| \geq 1$, the series has _____.

Example 1 *Find sums of infinite geometric series*

Find the sum of the infinite geometric series.

a. $\sum_{i=1}^{\infty} 6(0.6)^{i-1}$ b. $1 - \frac{2}{3} + \frac{4}{9} - \frac{8}{27} + \ldots$

c. $1 - 2 + 4 - 8 + \ldots$

Solution

a. For this series, $a_1 =$ ___ and $r =$ ____.

$$S = \frac{a_1}{1-r} = \underline{\qquad} = \underline{\quad}$$

b. For this series, $a_1 =$ ___ and $r =$ ____.

$$S = \frac{a_1}{1-r} = \underline{\qquad} = \underline{\quad}$$

c. You know that $a_1 =$ ___ and $a_2 =$ ____. So,

$r = \underline{\quad} = \underline{\quad}$. Because $|\underline{\quad}| \underline{\quad} 1$, the sum _____.

Your Notes

✓ **Checkpoint** Find the sum of the infinite geometric series, if it exists.

1. $\sum_{k=1}^{\infty} 5\left(\frac{9}{7}\right)^{k-1}$

2. $\sum_{n=1}^{\infty} 9\left(\frac{5}{6}\right)^{n-1}$

3. $6 + \frac{10}{3} + \frac{50}{27} + \frac{250}{243} + \cdots$

Example 2 *Use an infinite series as a model*

Swings A person is given one push on a swing. On the first swing, the person travels a distance of 4 feet. On each successive swing, the person travels 75% of the distance of the previous swing. What is the total distance the person swings?

Solution

The total distance traveled by the person is:

$d = 4 + 4(\underline{}) + 4(\underline{})^2 + 4(\underline{})^3 + \cdots$

$= \dfrac{a_1}{1-r}$ Write formula for sum.

$= \underline{}$ Substitute for a_1 and r.

$= \underline{}$ Simplify.

The swing travels a total distance of _____ feet.

Your Notes

✓ **Checkpoint** Complete the following exercise.

> **4.** In Example 2, suppose the person travels 3 feet on the first swing. What is the total distance the person swings?

Example 3 *Write a repeating decimal as a fraction*

Write 0.474747 . . . as a fraction in lowest terms.

Solution

0.474747 . . .

= 47(____) + 47(____)^2 + 47(____)^3 + . . .

= $\dfrac{a_1}{1-r}$ Write formula for sum.

= _____ Substitute for a_1 and r.

= ____ Simplify.

= ____ Write as a quotient of integers.

The repeating decimal 0.474747 . . . is ____ as a fraction.

✓ **Checkpoint** Write the repeating decimal as a fraction.

5. 0.888 . . .	6. 0.636363 . . .

Homework

12.5 Use Recursive Rules with Sequences and Functions

Goal • Use recursive rules for sequences.

Your Notes

VOCABULARY

Explicit rule

Recursive rule

Iteration

Example 1 Evaluate recursive rules

Write the first six terms of the sequence.

$a_0 = 2, a_n = a_{n-1} - 3$

Solution

$a_0 = 2$

$a_1 = a_0 - 3 = \underline{\qquad} = \underline{\qquad}$

$a_2 = a_1 - 3 = \underline{\qquad} = \underline{\qquad}$

$a_3 = a_2 - 3 = \underline{\qquad} = \underline{\qquad}$

$a_4 = a_3 - 3 = \underline{\qquad} = \underline{\qquad}$

$a_5 = a_4 - 3 = \underline{\qquad} = \underline{\qquad}$

✓ **Checkpoint** Write the first five terms of the sequence.

1. $a_0 = 4, a_n = 1.5 a_{n-1}$

Your Notes

> **RECURSIVE EQUATIONS FOR ARITHMETIC AND GEOMETRIC SEQUENCES**
>
> **Arithmetic Sequence** $a_n = a_{n-1} + d$ where d is the common difference
>
> **Geometric Sequence** $a_n = r \cdot a_{n-1}$ where r is the common ratio

Example 2 *Write recursive rules*

Write a recursive rule for the sequence.

a. 1, 7, 13, 19, 25, . . .   b. 4, 12, 36, 108, 324, . . .

Solution

a. The sequence is _____ with first term
$a_1 =$ ___ and common difference $d =$ _____ = ___.

$a_n = a_{n-1} + d$ General recursive equation for a_n.

= _____   Substitute for d.

So, a recursive rule for the sequence is $a_1 =$ ___,
$a_n =$ _____.

b. The sequence is _____ with first term $a_1 =$ ___
and common ratio $r =$ ___ = ___.

$a_n = r \cdot a_{n-1}$ General recursive equation for a_n.

= _____   Substitute for r.

So, a recursive rule for the sequence is $a_1 =$ ___,
$a_n =$ _____.

Example 3 *Write recursive rules for special sequences*

Write a recursive rule for the sequence 3, 5, 2, −3, −5, ...

Solution

Beginning with the _____ term in the sequence, each term is the _____ between the two previous terms.

So, a recursive rule is: $a_1 =$ ___, $a_2 =$ ___,
$a_n =$ _____ − _____

Your Notes

✓ **Checkpoint** Write a recursive rule for the sequence.

2. 3, 27, 243, 2187, 19,683, . . .

---

3. 89, 78, 67, 56, 45, . . .

---

4. 9, 4, 13, 17, 30, . . .

Example 4 Iterate a function

Find the first three iterates x_1, x_2, and x_3 of the function $f(x) = 2x - 5$ for an initial value of $x_0 = 3$.

Solution

$x_1 = f(x_0)$ $x_2 = f(x_1)$ $x_3 = f(x_2)$

$= f(\_\_)$ $= f(\_\_)$ $= f(\_\_)$

$= 2(\_\_) - 5$ $= 2(\_\_) - 5$ $= 2(\_\_) - 5$

$= \_\_$ $= \_\_$ $= \_\_$

The first three iterates are _____.

✓ **Checkpoint** Find the first three iterates of the function for the given initial value.

Homework

5. $f(x) = x^2 + 3$, $x_0 = -2$

Words to Review

Give an example of the vocabulary word.

Sequence	Terms
Series	Summation (Sigma) notation
Arithmetic sequences	Common difference
Arithmetic series	Geometric sequences
Common ratio	Geometric series

Partial sum	Explicit rule
Recursive rule	Iteration

Review your notes and Chapter 12 by using the Chapter Review on pages 840–842 of your textbook.

13.1 Use Trigonometry with Right Triangles

Goal • Use trigonometric functions to find lengths.

Your Notes

VOCABULARY

Sine, cosine, tangent, cosecant, secant, cotangent

RIGHT TRIANGLE DEFINITIONS OF TRIGONOMETRIC FUNCTIONS

Let θ be an acute angle of a right triangle. The six trigonometric functions of θ are defined as follows:

$\sin \theta = \dfrac{\boxed{}}{\text{hypotenuse}}$ $\qquad$ $\csc \theta = \dfrac{\text{hypotenuse}}{\boxed{}}$

$\cos \theta = \dfrac{\text{adjacent}}{\boxed{}}$ $\qquad$ $\sec \theta = \dfrac{\boxed{}}{\text{adjacent}}$

$\tan \theta = \dfrac{\boxed{}}{\text{adjacent}}$ $\qquad$ $\cot \theta = \dfrac{\text{adjacent}}{\boxed{}}$

The abbreviations *opp*, *adj*, and *hyp* are often used to represent the side lengths of the right triangle. Note that the ratios in the second column are reciprocals of the ratios in the first column:

$\csc \theta = \dfrac{1}{\boxed{}}$ $\qquad$ $\sec \theta = \dfrac{1}{\boxed{}}$ $\qquad$ $\cot \theta = \dfrac{1}{\boxed{}}$

Your Notes

Example 1 *Evaluate trigonometric functions*

Evaluate the six trigonometric functions of the angle θ.

From the Pythagorean theorem, the length of the hypotenuse is
$\sqrt{8^2 + 15^2} = \sqrt{\underline{}} = \underline{}$.

$\sin \theta = \dfrac{\boxed{}}{\text{hyp}} = \dfrac{\boxed{}}{\boxed{}}$ $\csc \theta = \dfrac{\text{hyp}}{\boxed{}} = \dfrac{\boxed{}}{\boxed{}}$

$\cos \theta = \dfrac{\text{adj}}{\boxed{}} = \dfrac{\boxed{}}{\boxed{}}$ $\sec \theta = \dfrac{\boxed{}}{\text{adj}} = \dfrac{\boxed{}}{\boxed{}}$

$\tan \theta = \dfrac{\boxed{}}{\text{adj}} = \dfrac{\boxed{}}{\boxed{}}$ $\cot \theta = \dfrac{\text{adj}}{\boxed{}} = \dfrac{\boxed{}}{\boxed{}}$

TRIGONOMETRIC VALUES FOR SPECIAL ANGLES

The table below gives the values of the six trigonometric functions for the angles 30°, 45°, and 60°. You can obtain these values from the triangles shown.

θ	$\sin \theta$	$\cos \theta$	$\tan \theta$
30°	$\dfrac{1}{2}$	$\dfrac{\sqrt{3}}{2}$	___
45°	$\dfrac{\sqrt{2}}{2}$	___	1
60°	___	$\dfrac{1}{2}$	$\sqrt{3}$

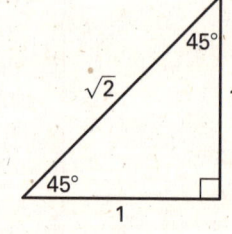

θ	$\csc \theta$	$\sec \theta$	$\cot \theta$
30°	2	$\dfrac{2\sqrt{3}}{3}$	___
45°	$\sqrt{2}$	___	1
60°	___	2	$\dfrac{\sqrt{3}}{3}$

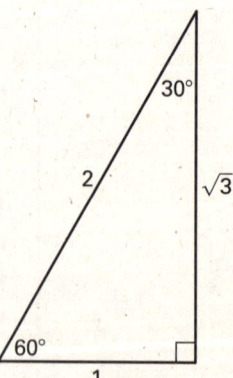

324 Lesson 13.1 • Algebra 2 Notetaking Guide

Your Notes

Example 2 — Use a calculator to solve a right triangle

Solve △ABC.

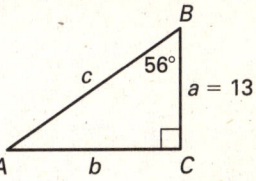

Solution

A and B are complementary angles, so A = 90° − ____ = ____.

$\tan 56° = \dfrac{\Box}{\text{adj}}$ $\qquad$ $\sec 56° = \dfrac{\Box}{\text{adj}}$

$\tan 56° = \dfrac{b}{\Box}$ $\qquad$ $\sec 56° = \dfrac{c}{\Box}$

_____ = b $\qquad$ _____ $\left(\dfrac{1}{\boxed{}}\right)$ = c

_____ ≈ b $\qquad$ _____ ≈ c

So, A = ____, b ≈ _____, and c ≈ _____.

✓ **Checkpoint** Complete the following exercises.

1. Evaluate the six trigonometric functions of the angle θ.

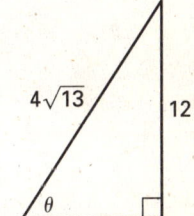

---

2. Solve △ABC.

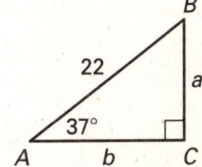

Lesson 13.1 • Algebra 2 Notetaking Guide 325

Your Notes

Example 3 — Use an angle of elevation

Building Height You are measuring the height of your school building. You stand 25 feet from the base of the school. The angle of elevation from a point on the ground to the top of the school is 62°. Estimate the height of the school to the nearest foot.

Solution

1. **Draw** a diagram that represents the situation.
2. **Write** and solve an equation to find the height h.

$$\tan \underline{} = \frac{\boxed{}}{\boxed{}}$$

$$\underline{}(\tan 62°) = h$$

$$\underline{} \approx h$$

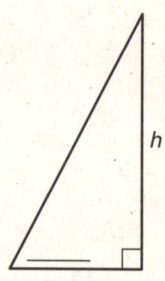

The height of the school is about _____ feet.

✓ Checkpoint Complete the following exercise.

3. A kite makes an angle of 59° with the ground. If the string on the kite is 40 feet, how far above the ground is the kite itself? Round to the nearest foot.

Homework

13.2 Define General Angles and Use Radian Measure

Goal • Use general angles that may be measured in radians.

Your Notes

VOCABULARY

Initial side and terminal side

Standard position

Coterminal

Radian

Sector

Central angle

ANGLES IN STANDARD POSITION

In a coordinate plane, an angle can be formed by fixing one ray, called the _____ side, and rotating the other ray, called the _____ side, about the _____.

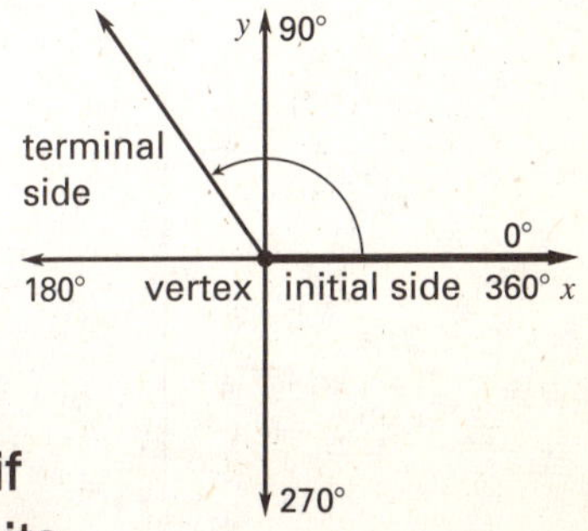

An angle is in standard position if its vertex is at _____ and its initial side lies on the positive _____.

Lesson 13.2 • Algebra 2 Notetaking Guide 327

Your Notes

Example 1 — Draw angles in standard position

Draw an angle with the given measure in standard position.

a. 405° b. −65°

a. Because 405° is _____ more than 360°, the terminal side makes one whole revolution _____ plus _____ more.

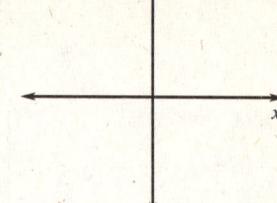

b. Because −65° is negative, the terminal side is _____ _____ from the positive x-axis.

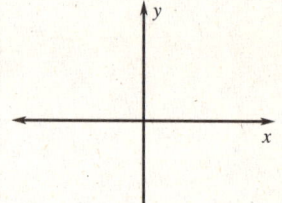

Example 2 — Find coterminal angles

Find one positive angle and one negative angle that are coterminal with 210°.

There are many such angles, depending on what multiple of 360° is added or subtracted.

210° + 360° = _____   210° − 360° = _____

✓ **Checkpoint** Draw an angle with the given measure in standard position. Then find one positive coterminal angle and one negative coterminal angle.

1. 485°

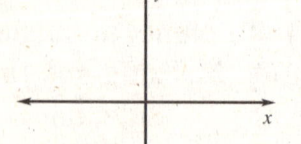

2. −75°

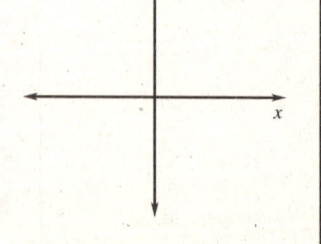

Your Notes

CONVERTING BETWEEN DEGREES AND RADIANS

Degrees to radians

Multiply degree measure by $\dfrac{\pi \text{ radians}}{180°}$.

Radians to Degrees

Multiply radian measure by $\dfrac{180°}{\pi \text{ radians}}$.

Example 3   *Convert between degrees and radians*

Convert (a) 315° to radians and (b) $\dfrac{\pi}{6}$ radians to degrees.

a. $315° = 315°\left(\underline{}\right) = \underline{}$

b. $\dfrac{\pi}{6} = \left(\dfrac{\pi}{6} \text{ radians}\right)\left(\underline{}\right) = \underline{}$

✓ **Checkpoint** Convert the degree measure to radians or the radian measure to degrees.

3. 200°	4. $\dfrac{\pi}{5}$

ARC LENGTH AND AREA OF A SECTOR

The arc length *s* and area *A* of a sector with radius *r* and central angle θ (measured in radians) are as follows.

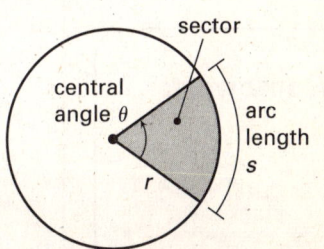

Arc length: $s = r\theta$

Area: $A = \dfrac{1}{2}r^2\theta$

Lesson 13.2 • Algebra 2 Notetaking Guide

Your Notes

Example 4 *Solve a multi-step problem*

Find the arc length and area of a sector with a radius of 15 inches and a central angle of 60°.

Solution

1. **Convert** the measure of the central angle to radians.

   $60° = 60°\left(\underline{}\right) = \underline{}$ radians

2. **Find** the arc length and the area of the sector.

   Arc length: $s = r\theta$

   $= \underline{}(\underline{})$

   $= \underline{}$

   $\approx \underline{}$ inches

   Area: $A = \frac{1}{2}r^2\theta$

   $= \frac{1}{2}(\underline{})^2(\underline{})$

   $= \underline{}$

   $\approx \underline{}$ square inches.

✓ **Checkpoint** Find the arc length and area of the sector with given radius and angle.

5. $r = 5$ ft, $\theta = 75°$

Homework

13.3 Evaluate Trigonometric Functions of Any Angle

Goal • Evaluate trigonometric functions of any angle.

Your Notes

VOCABULARY

Unit circle

Quadrantal angle

Reference angle

GENERAL DEFINITIONS OF TRIGONOMETRIC FUNCTIONS

Let θ be an angle in standard position, and let (x, y) be the point where the terminal side of θ intersects the circle $x^2 + y^2 = r^2$. The six trigonometric functions of θ are defined as follows:

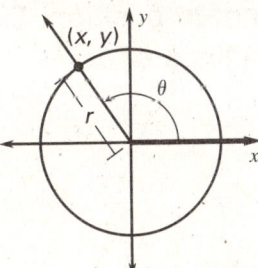

$\sin \theta = \dfrac{\boxed{}}{r}$ $\qquad$ $\csc \theta = \dfrac{\boxed{}}{y}, y \neq 0$

$\cos \theta = \dfrac{x}{\boxed{}}$ $\qquad$ $\sec \theta = \dfrac{\boxed{}}{x}, x \neq 0$

$\tan \theta = \dfrac{\boxed{}}{x}, x \neq 0$ $\qquad$ $\cot \theta = \dfrac{\boxed{}}{y}, y \neq 0$

Your Notes

Example 1 — Evaluate trigonometric functions given a point

Let $(-12, 5)$ be a point on the terminal side of an angle θ in standard position. Evaluate the six trigonometric functions of θ.

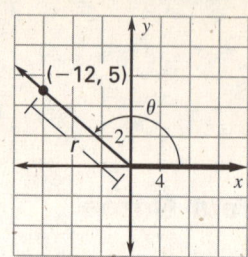

Use the Pythagorean theorem to find the value of r.

$r = \sqrt{x^2 + y^2} = \sqrt{(\underline{})^2 + \underline{}^2} = \sqrt{\underline{}} = \underline{}$

Using $x = -12$, $y = 5$, and $r = \underline{}$, you can write:

$\sin \theta = \dfrac{\Box}{r} = \underline{}$ $\qquad$ $\csc \theta = \dfrac{\Box}{y} = \underline{}$

$\cos \theta = \dfrac{x}{\Box} = \underline{}$ $\qquad$ $\sec \theta = \dfrac{\Box}{x} = \underline{}$

$\tan \theta = \dfrac{\Box}{x} = \underline{}$ $\qquad$ $\cot \theta = \dfrac{\Box}{y} = \underline{}$

✓ **Checkpoint** Complete the following exercise.

1. Let $(6, -8)$ be a point on the terminal side of an angle θ in standard position. Evaluate the six trigonometric functions of θ.

THE UNIT CIRCLE

The circle $x^2 + y^2 = 1$, which has center $(0, 0)$ and radius 1, is called the unit circle.

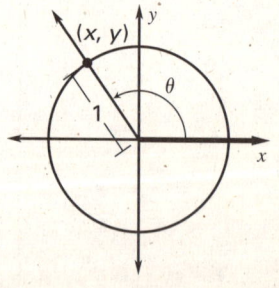

$\sin \theta = \dfrac{y}{r} = \dfrac{y}{1} = \underline{}$

$\cos \theta = \dfrac{x}{r} = \dfrac{x}{1} = \underline{}$

Your Notes

Example 2 — Use the unit circle

Use the unit circle to evaluate the six trigonometric functions of $\theta = 450°$.

Draw the unit circle, then draw the angle $\theta = 450°$ in standard position. The terminal side of θ intersects the unit circle at (___, ___), so use $x =$ ___ and $y =$ ___ to evaluate the trigonometric functions.

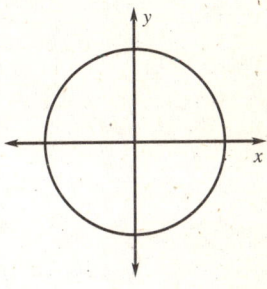

$\sin \theta = \dfrac{y}{r} = \dfrac{}{} = \underline{}$ $\csc \theta = \dfrac{r}{y} = \dfrac{}{} = \underline{}$

$\cos \theta = \dfrac{x}{r} = \dfrac{}{} = \underline{}$ $\sec \theta = \dfrac{r}{x}$

$ = \dfrac{}{}$

$\tan \theta = \dfrac{y}{x} = \underline{}$ $\cot \theta = \dfrac{x}{y} = \dfrac{}{} = \underline{}$

✓ **Checkpoint** Complete the following exercise.

2. Use the unit circle to evaluate the six trigonometric functions of $\theta = 360°$.

Your Notes

REFERENCE ANGLE RELATIONSHIPS

Let θ be an angle in standard position. The reference angle for θ is the acute angle θ' formed by the terminal side of θ and the x-axis. The relationship between θ and θ' is shown below for nonquadrantal angles θ such that $90° < \theta < 360° \left(\frac{\pi}{2} < \theta < 2\pi\right)$.

Quadrant II	Quadrant III	Quadrant IV
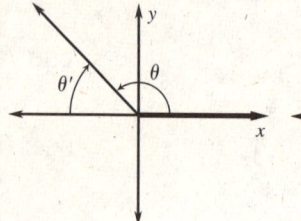	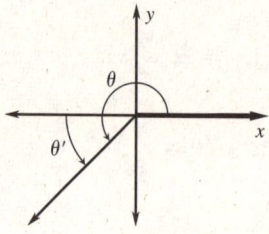	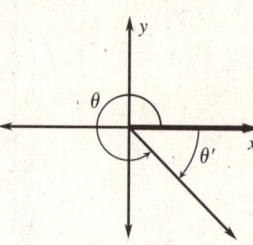

Degrees:
$\theta' = 180° - \theta$ $\theta' = \theta - 180°$ $\theta' = 360° - \theta$

Radians:
$\theta' = \pi - \theta$ $\theta' = \theta - \pi$ $\theta' = 2\pi - \theta$

Example 3 *Find reference angles*

Find the reference angle θ' for (a) $\theta = -165°$ and (b) $\theta = \frac{7\pi}{4}$.

Solution

a. Note that θ is coterminal with _____, whose terminal side lies in Quadrant ____. So,

$\theta' = $ _____ $-$ _____ $=$ _____.

b. The terminal side of θ lies in Quadrant ____. So,

$\theta' = $ ____ $-$ ____ $=$ ____.

Your Notes

EVALUATING TRIGONOMETRIC FUNCTIONS

Use these steps to evaluate a trigonometric function for any angle θ:

STEP 1 **Find** the reference angle ____.

STEP 2 **Evaluate** the trigonometric functions for ____.

STEP 3 **Determine** the sign of the trigonometric function value from the quadrant in which ____ lies.

Signs of Function Values

Quadrant II	Quadrant I
$\sin\theta, \csc\theta: +$	$\sin\theta, \csc\theta: +$
$\cos\theta, \sec\theta: -$	$\cos\theta, \sec\theta: +$
$\tan\theta, \cot\theta: -$	$\tan\theta, \cot\theta: +$
Quadrant III	Quadrant IV
$\sin\theta, \csc\theta: -$	$\sin\theta, \csc\theta: -$
$\cos\theta, \sec\theta: -$	$\cos\theta, \sec\theta: +$
$\tan\theta, \cot\theta: +$	$\tan\theta, \cot\theta: -$

Example 4 *Use reference angles to evaluate functions*

Evaluate (a) $\cos(-225°)$ and (b) $\cot\dfrac{10\pi}{3}$.

a. The angle $-225°$ is coterminal with ____. The reference angle is $\theta' = $ ____ $-$ ____ $=$ ____. The cosine function is negative in Quadrant ____, so you can write:

$\cos(-225°) = -\cos(\_\_\_\_) = \_\_\_\_$

b. The angle $\dfrac{10\pi}{3}$ is coterminal with ____. The reference angle is $\theta' = $ ____ $-$ ____ $=$ ____. The cotangent function is positive in Quadrant ____, so you can write:

$\cot\left(\dfrac{10\pi}{3}\right) = \cot\_\_\_ = \_\_\_$

✓ Checkpoint Complete the following exercises.

Homework

3. Find the reference angle for $\theta = 150°$.

4. Evaluate $\sec 300°$.

13.4 Evaluate Inverse Trigonometric Functions

Goal • Find angles given values of trigonometric functions.

Your Notes

VOCABULARY

Inverse sine

Inverse cosine

Inverse tangent

INVERSE TRIGONOMETRIC FUNCTIONS

- If $-1 \leq a \leq 1$, then the _____ _____ of a is an angle θ, written $\theta = \sin^{-1} a$, where $\sin \theta = a$ and $-\frac{\pi}{2} \leq \theta \leq \frac{\pi}{2}$ (or $-90° \leq \theta \leq 90°$).

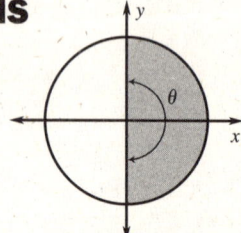

- If $-1 \leq a \leq 1$, then the _____ _____ of a is an angle θ, written $\theta = \cos^{-1} a$, where $\cos \theta = a$ and $0 \leq \theta \leq \pi$ (or $0° \leq \theta \leq 180°$).

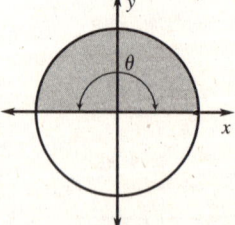

- If a is any real number, then the _____ of a is an angle θ, written $\theta = \tan^{-1} a$, where $\tan \theta = a$ and $-\frac{\pi}{2} < \theta < \frac{\pi}{2}$ (or $-90° < \theta < 90°$).

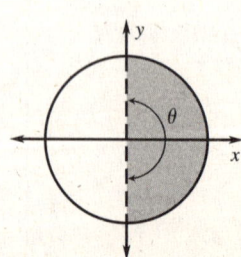

Your Notes

> **Example 1** *Evaluate inverse trigonometric functions*
>
> Evaluate the expression in both radians and degrees.
>
> a. $\cos^{-1} 3$
> b. $\tan^{-1} \frac{\sqrt{3}}{3}$
>
> **Solution**
>
> a. There is _____ whose cosine is 3. So, $\cos^{-1} 3$ is _____.
>
> b. When $-\frac{\pi}{2} < \theta < \frac{\pi}{2}$, or $-90° < \theta < 90°$, the angle whose tangent is $\frac{\sqrt{3}}{3}$ is:
>
> $\theta = \tan^{-1} \frac{\sqrt{3}}{3} = $ _____ or $\theta = \tan^{-1} \frac{\sqrt{3}}{3} = $ _____

✔ *Checkpoint* **Evaluate the expression in both radians and degrees.**

1. $\sin^{-1} \frac{\sqrt{3}}{2}$

2. $\cos^{-1}(-0.5)$

3. $\tan^{-1}(-1)$

Your Notes

Example 2 — Solve a trigonometric equation

Solve the equation $\cos \theta = \frac{2}{5}$ where $270° < \theta < 360°$.

Use a calculator to determine that in the interval $0° < \theta < 180°$, the angle whose cosine is $\frac{2}{5}$ is $\cos^{-1} \frac{2}{5} \approx$ _____. This angle is in Quadrant ___.

In Quadrant ____ (where $270° < \theta < 360°$), the angle that has the same cosine value is:

$\theta \approx$ _____ − _____ = _____

Example 3 — Find an angle measure

Find the measure of the angle θ in the triangle shown.

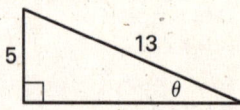

Solution

In the right triangle, you are given the side opposite from θ and the hypotenuse, so use the inverse sine function to solve for θ.

$\sin \theta = \dfrac{\text{opp}}{\text{hyp}} =$ _____ $\theta = \sin^{-1}$ _____ $\approx$ _____

✓ **Checkpoint** Complete the following exercises.

4. Solve the equation $\sin \theta = 0.7$ where $90° < \theta < 270°$.

5. Find the measure of the angle θ in the triangle shown.

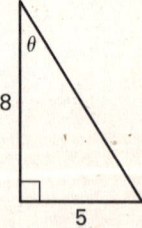

Homework

13.5 Apply the Law of Sines

Goal • Solve triangles that have no right angle.

Your Notes

VOCABULARY

Law of sines

LAW OF SINES

The law of sines can be written in either of the following forms for △ABC with sides of lengths a, b, and c.

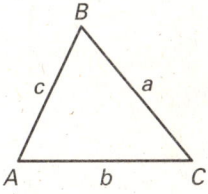

$$\frac{\sin A}{a} = \frac{\sin B}{b} = \frac{\sin C}{c} \qquad \frac{a}{\sin A} = \frac{b}{\sin B} = \frac{c}{\sin C}$$

Example 1 *Solve a triangle for the AAS or ASA case*

Solve △ABC with $A = 28°$, $B = 102°$, and $a = 8$.

Solution

First find the angle: $C = 180° - 102° - 28° = 50°$.

$\dfrac{b}{\sin 102°} = \dfrac{8}{\sin 28°}$ Write equations.

$b = $ _____ Solve for each variable.

$b \approx $ _____ Use a calculator.

$\dfrac{8}{\sin 28°} = \dfrac{c}{\sin 50°}$ Write equations.

$c = $ _____ Solve for each variable.

$c \approx $ _____ Use a calculator.

In △ABC, $C = $ _____, $b \approx $ _____, and $c \approx $ _____.

Your Notes

POSSIBLE TRIANGLES IN THE SSA CASE

Consider a triangle in which you are given *a*, *b*, and *A*. By fixing side *b* and angle *A*, you can sketch the possible positions of side *a* to figure out how many triangles can be formed. In the diagrams below, note that $h = b \sin A$.

A is obtuse.

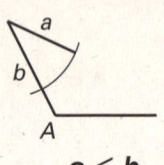
$a \leq b$
_____

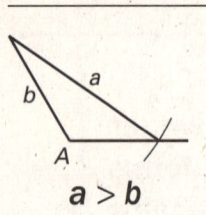
$a > b$
_____

A is acute.

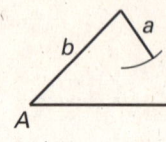
$h > a$
_____

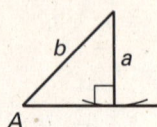
$h = a$
_____

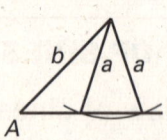
$h < a < b$
_____

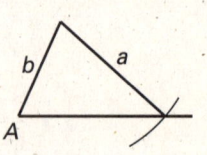
$a > b$
_____

Example 2   Solve the SSA case with one solution

Solve $\triangle ABC$ with $A = 94°$, $a = 18$, and $c = 13$.

Make a sketch. Because A is _____ and *a* is longer than *c*, _____ can be formed. Use the law of sines to find C.

$\dfrac{\sin C}{13} =$ _____   **Law of sines**

$\sin C =$ _____ ≈ _____   **Multiply each side by _____.**

$C \approx$ _____   **Use inverse sine function.**

You then know that $B \approx$ _____ = _____.

$\dfrac{b}{\sin 39.9°} =$ _____   **Law of sines**

$b =$ _____   **Multiply each side by sin _____.**

$b \approx$ _____   **Use a calculator.**

In $\triangle ABC$, $C \approx$ _____, $B \approx$ _____, and $b \approx$ _____.

Your Notes

Example 3 *Examine the SSA case with no solution*

Solve △ABC with A = 77°, a = 6.1, and b = 9.

Solution

Begin by drawing a horizontal line. On one end form a 77° angle (A) and draw a segment ___ units long ($\overline{AC}$ or b). At vertex C, draw a segment ____ units long (a). You can see that ___ needs to be at least _____ ≈ ____ units long to reach the horizontal side and form a triangle. So, it is _____ to draw the indicated triangle.

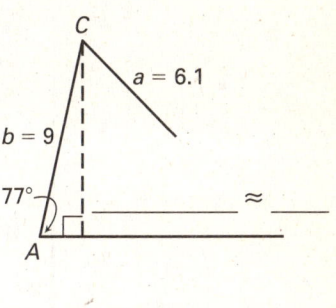

✓ **Checkpoint** Solve △ABC.

1. C = 14°, B = 117°, b = 21

2. A = 56°, a = 24, b = 16

3. B = 122°, b = 5, a = 8

Your Notes

Example 4 Solve the SSA case with two solutions

Solve △ABC with A = 30°, a = 10, and b = 15.

Solution

First make a sketch. Because

b sin A = _____ = _____, and 7.5 < 10 < 15 (h < a < b), two triangles can be formed.

Triangle 1 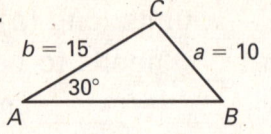   **Triangle 2**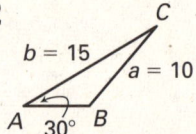

Use the law of sines to find the possible measures of B.

$\dfrac{\sin B}{15}$ = _____   Law of sines

sin B = _____ = _____   Evaluate.

There are two angles B between 0° and 180° for which sin B = _____. One is acute and the other is obtuse. Use your calculator to find the acute angle:
$\sin^{-1} 0.75 \approx$ _____.

The obtuse angle has _____ as a reference angle, so its measure is _____ = _____. Therefore, B ≈ _____ or B ≈ _____.

Now find the remaining angle C and side length c for each triangle.

Triangle 1	Triangle 2
C ≈ _____	C ≈ _____
= _____	= _____
$\dfrac{c}{\sin 101.4°}$ = _____	$\dfrac{c}{\sin 18.6°}$ = _____
c = _____	c = _____
≈ _____	≈ _____
In Triangle 1, B ≈ _____, C ≈ _____, and c ≈ _____.	In Triangle 2, B ≈ _____, C ≈ _____, and c ≈ _____.

Your Notes

AREA OF A TRIANGLE

The area of any triangle is given by one half the product of the lengths of two sides times the sine of their included angle. For △ABC shown, there are three ways to calculate the area:

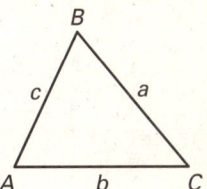

Area = _____   Area = _____

Area = _____

Example 5 *Find the area of a triangle*

Land A piece of land is bordered by three roads as shown. Find the area of the land.

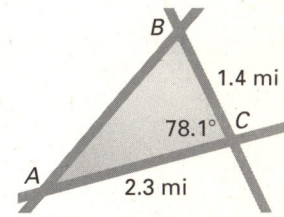

Solution

The area of the land is:

Area = $\frac{1}{2}ab \sin C$ Write area formula.

= $\frac{1}{2}$ _____   Substitute.

≈ _____   Use a calculator.

The area of the land is about _____ square miles.

✓ **Checkpoint** Complete the following exercises.

4. Solve △ABC when A = 35°, a = 11, and b = 14.

5. Suppose the side lengths in Example 5 are 4.6 miles and 2.8 miles. Find the area.

Homework

13.6 Apply the Law of Cosines

Goal • Solve triangles using the law of cosines.

Your Notes

VOCABULARY

Law of cosines

LAW OF COSINES

If △ABC has sides of length a, b, and c as shown, then:

$a^2 = b^2 + c^2 - 2bc \cos A$

$b^2 = a^2 + c^2 - 2ac \cos B$

$c^2 = $ _____

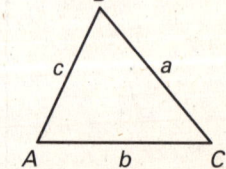

Your Notes

Example 1 Solve a triangle for the SAS case

Solve △ABC with $a = 7$, $c = 12$, and $B = 26°$.

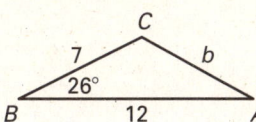

Use the law of cosines to find b.

$b^2 = a^2 + c^2 - 2ac \cos B$	Law of cosines
$b^2 = $ _____	Substitute.
$b^2 \approx $ _____	Simplify.
$b \approx \sqrt{\_\_\_\_} \approx \_\_\_\_$	Take positive square root.

> When you know all three sides and one angle, you can use the law of cosines *or* the law of sines to find the measure of a second angle.

Use the law of sines to find the measure of angle A.

$\dfrac{\sin A}{\Box} = \dfrac{\sin \Box}{\Box}$	Law of sines
$\sin A = \dfrac{_____}{} \approx _____$	Simplify.
$A \approx \sin^{-1} _____ \approx _____$	Use inverse sine.

Find the third angle:
$C \approx $ _____ = _____ .

In △ABC, $b \approx $ _____ , $A \approx $ _____ , and $C \approx $ _____ .

✓ **Checkpoint** Solve △ABC.

1. $b = 15$, $c = 13$, $A = 77°$

Your Notes

> In Example 2, the largest angle is found first to make sure that the other two angles are acute. This way, when you use the law of sines to find another angle measure, you will know that it is between 0° and 90°.

Example 2   *Solve a triangle for the SSS case*

Solve △ABC with $a = 7$, $b = 13$, and $c = 9$.

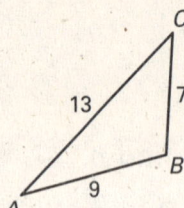

First find the angle opposite the longest side, $\overline{AC}$. Use the law of cosines to solve for B.

$$b^2 = a^2 + c^2 - 2ac \cos B$$

____ = _____ $\cos B$

_____ = $\cos B$

_____ ≈ $\cos B$

$B \approx \cos^{-1}$ _____ ≈ _____

Now use the law of sines to find A.

$\dfrac{\sin A}{\boxed{}} = \dfrac{\boxed{}}{\boxed{}}$ **Law of sines**

$\sin A = $ _____ ≈ _____   **Simplify.**

$A \approx \sin^{-1}$ _____ ≈ _____   **Use inverse sine.**

Find the third angle:
$C \approx$ _____ = _____.

In △ABC, $A \approx$ _____, $B \approx$ _____, and $C \approx$ _____.

✓ **Checkpoint** Solve △ABC.

2. $a = 23$, $b = 18$, $c = 20$

Your Notes

HERON'S AREA FORMULA

The area of a triangle with sides of length a, b, and c is

Area = _____

where s = _____ . The variable s is called the *semiperimeter*, or half-perimeter, of the triangle.

Example 3 *Solve a multi-step problem*

Zoo A triangular path around an exhibit at the zoo is shown. Find the area of the exhibit.

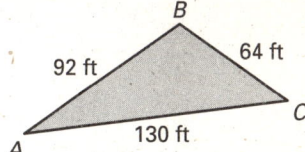

Solution

1. Find the semiperimeter s.

   $s = \frac{1}{2}(a + b + c) =$ _____ = _____

2. Use Heron's formula to find the area of $\triangle ABC$.

   Area = $\sqrt{s(s-a)(s-b)(s-c)}$

   = _____

   ≈ _____

The area of the exhibit is about _____ square feet.

✓ **Checkpoint** Find the area of $\triangle ABC$.

3.

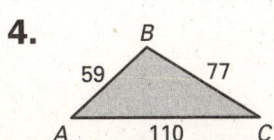

Homework

4.

Words to Review

Give an example of the vocabulary word.

Sine	Cosine
Tangent	Cosecant
Secant	Cotangent
Initial side	Terminal side
Standard position	Coterminal

Radian	Sector
Central angle	Unit circle
Quadrantal angle	Reference angle
Inverse sine	Inverse cosine
Inverse tangent	Law of sines
Law of cosines	

Review your notes and Chapter 13 by using the Chapter Review on pages 898–900 of your textbook.

14.1 Graph Sine, Cosine, and Tangent Functions

Goal • Graph sine, cosine, and tangent functions.

Your Notes

VOCABULARY

Amplitude

Periodic function

Cycle

Period

Frequency

CHARACTERISTICS OF $y = \sin x$ AND $y = \cos x$

1. The domain of each function is _____.

2. The _____ of each function is $-1 \leq y \leq 1$. Therefore, the minimum value of each function is $m = -1$ and the maximum value is $M = 1$.

3. The _____ of each function's graph is half the difference of the maximum M and the minimum m, or $\frac{1}{2}(M - m) = \frac{1}{2}[1 - (-1)] = 1$.

4. Each function is periodic, which means that its graph has a _____ pattern, called a cycle. The horizontal length of each cycle is called the _____.

5. The x-intercepts of $y =$ _____ occur when $x = 0$, $\pm \pi, \pm 2\pi, \pm 3\pi, \ldots$.

6. The x-intercepts of $y =$ _____ occur when $x = \pm \frac{\pi}{2}, \pm \frac{3\pi}{2}, \pm \frac{5\pi}{2}, \pm \frac{7\pi}{2}, \ldots$.

Your Notes

AMPLITUDE AND PERIOD

The amplitude and period of the graphs of $y = a \sin bx$ and $y = a \cos bx$, where a and b are nonzero real numbers, are:

_____ $= |a|$ _____ $= \dfrac{2\pi}{|b|}$

> Notice how changes in a and b affect the graphs of $y = a \sin bx$ and $y = a \cos bx$. When the value of a increases, the amplitude increases. When the value of b increases, the period decreases.

Example 1 *Graph sine and cosine functions*

Graph (a) $y = 2 \sin x$ and (b) $y = \dfrac{3}{2} \cos \pi x$.

Solution

a. The amplitude is $a =$ ___ and the period is $\dfrac{2\pi}{b} =$ ___ $=$ ___.

Intercepts: $(0, 0)$; $\left(\dfrac{1}{2} \cdot 2\pi, 0\right) =$ _____; $(2\pi, 0)$

Maximum:
$\left(\dfrac{1}{4} \cdot 2\pi, 2\right) =$ _____

Minimum:
$\left(\dfrac{3}{4} \cdot 2\pi, -2\right) =$ _____

b. The amplitude is $a =$ ___ and the period is $\dfrac{2\pi}{b} =$ ___ $=$ ___.

Intercepts: $\left(\dfrac{1}{4} \cdot 2, 0\right) =$ _____ ; $\left(\dfrac{3}{4} \cdot 2, 0\right) =$ _____

Maximums:
$\left(0, \underline{}\right); \left(2, \underline{}\right)$

Minimum:
$\left(\dfrac{1}{2} \cdot 2, \underline{}\right) = \left(\underline{}\right)$

Your Notes

✓ **Checkpoint** Graph the function.

1. $y = \frac{1}{4} \sin 2\pi x$

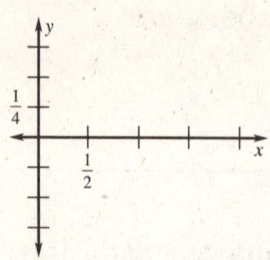

2. $y = 3 \cos x$

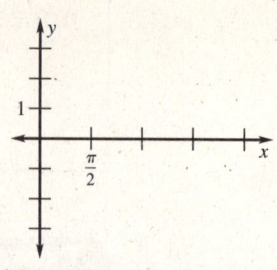

Example 2 *Model with a sine function*

Write a sine function with an amplitude of 3 and a frequency of 1000.

Solution

Find the values of *a* and *b* in the equation $y = a \sin bx$.

The amplitude is 3, so $a = 3$. Use the frequency to find *b*. The frequency is the reciprocal of the period.

$1000 = \frac{b}{2\pi}$

So, $b = $ _____.

The equation is _____.

✓ **Checkpoint** Write a sine function with the given amplitude and frequency.

3. amplitude = 4 frequency = 1500	4. amplitude = 1.5 frequency = 500

Your Notes

CHARACTERISTICS OF $y = a \tan bx$

The period and vertical asymptotes of the graph of $y = a \tan bx$, where a and b are nonzero real numbers, are:

The period is $\dfrac{\pi}{|b|}$.

The vertical asymptotes are at odd multiples of $\dfrac{\pi}{2|b|}$.

Odd multiples of $\dfrac{\pi}{2}$ are values such as these:

$\pm 1 \cdot \dfrac{\pi}{2} = \pm \dfrac{\pi}{2}$

$\pm 3 \cdot \dfrac{\pi}{2} = \pm \dfrac{3\pi}{2}$

$\pm 5 \cdot \dfrac{\pi}{2} = \pm \dfrac{5\pi}{2}$

Example 3 Graph a tangent function

Graph one period of the function $y = 2 \tan x$.

Solution

The period is $\dfrac{\pi}{b} =$ _____ $=$ _____.

Intercept: _____

Asymptotes: $x = \dfrac{\pi}{2b} =$ _____ $=$ _____

$x = -\dfrac{\pi}{2b} =$ _____ $=$ _____

Halfway points: $\left(\dfrac{\pi}{4b}, a\right) =$ _____ $=$ _____

$\left(-\dfrac{\pi}{4b}, -a\right) =$ _____ $=$ _____

✓ **Checkpoint** Graph the function.

5. $y = \tan 4x$

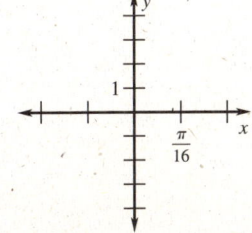

6. $y = \tan \pi x$

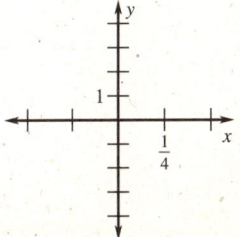

Homework

14.2 Translate and Reflect Trigonometric Graphs

Goal • Translate and reflect trigonometric graphs.

Your Notes

TRANSLATIONS OF SINE AND COSINE GRAPHS

To graph $y = a \sin b(x - h) + k$ or
$y = a \cos b(x - h) + k$ where $a > 0$ and $b > 0$, follow these steps:

Step 1 Identify the amplitude a, the period $\frac{2\pi}{b}$, the horizontal shift h, and the vertical shift k of the graph.

Step 2 Draw the horizontal line $y = k$, called the _____ of the graph.

Step 3 Find the five key points by translating the key points of $y = a \sin bx$ or $y = a \cos bx$ _____ h units and _____ k units.

Step 4 Draw the graph through the five translated key points.

Your Notes

Example 1 *Graph a vertical translation*

Graph $y = 3 \sin 2x + 1$.

Solution

Step 1 **Identify** the amplitude, period, horizontal shift, and vertical shift.

Amplitude: $a =$ ___ Horizontal shift: $h =$ ___

Period: $\dfrac{2\pi}{b} =$ ___ Vertical shift: $k =$ ___

$=$ ___

Step 2 **Draw** the midline of the graph, $y =$ ___.

Step 3 **Find** the five key points.

On $y = k$: $(0, 0 + 1) =$ _____;

$\left(\dfrac{\pi}{2}, 0 + 1\right) =$ _____;

$(\pi, 0 + 1) =$ _____

Maximum: $\left(\dfrac{\pi}{4}, 3 + 1\right) =$ _____

Minimum: $\left(\dfrac{3\pi}{4}, -3 + 1\right) =$ _____

Step 4 **Draw** the graph through the key points.

> Because the graph is shifted up 1 unit, the y-coordinates of the five key points will be increased by 1.

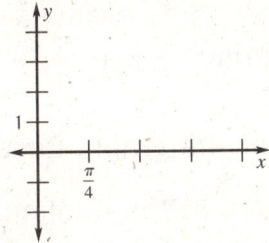

✓ **Checkpoint** Graph the function.

1. $y = 4 \sin 2x + 3$

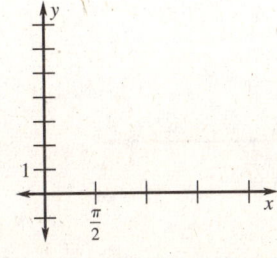

Lesson 14.2 • Algebra 2 Notetaking Guide 355

Your Notes

Example 2 *Combine a translation and a reflection*

Graph $y = -3 \sin \frac{1}{4}\left(x - \frac{\pi}{4}\right)$.

Step 1 **Identify** the amplitude, period, horizontal shift, and vertical shift.

Amplitude: $|a| = $ ___ Horizontal shift: $h = $ ___

Period: ___ $= $ ___ Vertical shift: $k = $ ___

Step 2 **Draw** the midline of the graph. Because _____, the midline is the _____.

Step 3 **Find** the five key points of $y = |-3| \sin \frac{1}{4}\left(x - \frac{\pi}{4}\right)$.

On $y = k$: $\left(0 + \frac{\pi}{4}, 0\right) = $ ___ ;

$\left(4\pi + \frac{\pi}{4}, 0\right) = $ ___ ;

$\left(8\pi + \frac{\pi}{4}, 0\right) = $ ___

Maximum: $\left(2\pi + \frac{\pi}{4}, 3\right) = $ ___

Minimum: $\left(6\pi + \frac{\pi}{4}, -3\right) = $ ___

Step 4 **Reflect** the graph. Because $a < 0$, the graph is reflected in the midline $y = 0$. So, $\left(\frac{9\pi}{4}, 3\right)$ becomes ___ and $\left(\frac{25\pi}{4}, -3\right)$ becomes ___.

Step 5 **Draw** the graph through the key points found.

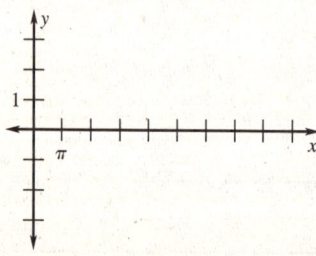

> Because the graph is shifted to the right $\frac{\pi}{4}$ units, the x-coordinates of the five key points will be increased by $\frac{\pi}{4}$.

> The minimum and maximum of the original graph become the maximum and minimum, respectively, of the reflected graph.

356 Lesson 14.2 • Algebra 2 Notetaking Guide

Your Notes

Example 3 Model with a tangent function

Flagpole You watch a classmate lower a flag on a 20-foot flagpole. You are standing 15 feet from the base of the flagpole. Write and graph a model that gives the flag's distance d (in feet) from the top of the flagpole as a function of the angle of elevation θ.

Solution

Use a tangent function to write an equation relating d and θ.

$\tan \theta = \dfrac{\text{opp}}{\text{adj}} = \dfrac{20 - d}{15}$ **Definition of tangent**

_____ = _____   **Multiply each side by 15.**

_____ = _____   **Subtract 20 from each side.**

_____ = _____   **Solve for d.**

The graph is shown at the right.

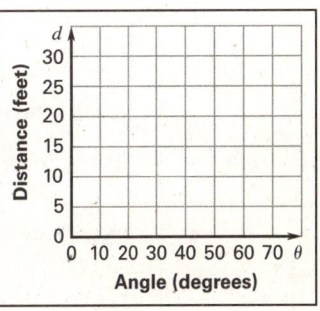

✓ **Checkpoint** Complete the following exercises.

2. Graph $y = -2 \cos(x + \pi)$.

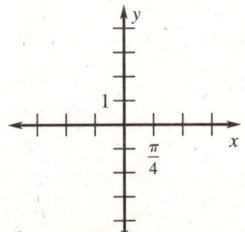

3. Write and graph a model for Example 3 if you stand 10 feet from the flagpole.

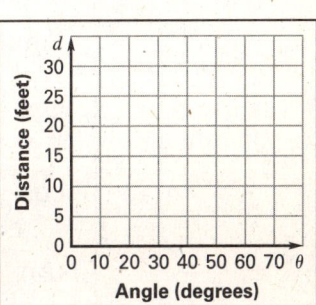

Homework

14.3 Verify Trigonometric Identities

Goal • Verify trigonometric identities.

Your Notes

VOCABULARY

Trigonometric identity

FUNDAMENTAL TRIGONOMETRIC IDENTITIES

Reciprocal Identities

$\csc \theta =$ _____ $\sec \theta =$ _____ $\cot \theta =$ _____

Tangent and Cotangent Identities

$\tan \theta =$ _____ $\cot \theta =$ _____

Pythagorean Identities

$\sin^2 \theta + \cos^2 \theta =$ _____

$1 + \tan^2 \theta =$ _____

$1 + \cot^2 \theta =$ _____

Cofunction Identities

$\sin\left(\dfrac{\pi}{2} - \theta\right) =$ _____

$\cos\left(\dfrac{\pi}{2} - \theta\right) =$ _____

$\tan\left(\dfrac{\pi}{2} - \theta\right) =$ _____

Negative Angle Identities

$\sin(-\theta) =$ _____

$\cos(-\theta) =$ _____

$\tan(-\theta) =$ _____

Your Notes

Example 1 — Find trigonometric values

Given that $\cos\theta = -\dfrac{3}{4}$ and $\pi < \theta < \dfrac{3\pi}{2}$, find the values of the other five trigonometric functions of θ.

Solution

Step 1 Find $\sin\theta$.

$\sin^2\theta + \cos^2\theta = 1$ Write Pythagorean Identity.

$\sin^2\theta + \underline{\hspace{1cm}} = 1$ Substitute ___ for $\cos\theta$.

$\sin^2\theta = 1 - \underline{\hspace{1cm}}$ Subtract ___ from each side.

$\sin^2\theta = \underline{\hspace{1cm}}$ Simplify.

$\sin\theta = \underline{\hspace{1cm}}$ Take square roots of each side.

Because θ is in Quadrant ___, $\sin\theta$ is negative. So, $\sin\theta = -\dfrac{\sqrt{7}}{4}$.

Step 2 Find the values of the other four trigonometric functions of θ using the known values of $\sin\theta$ and $\cos\theta$.

$\tan\theta = \dfrac{\sin\theta}{\cos\theta} = \dfrac{-\frac{\sqrt{7}}{4}}{-\frac{3}{4}} = \underline{\hspace{1cm}}$

$\cot\theta = \dfrac{\cos\theta}{\sin\theta} = \dfrac{-\frac{3}{4}}{-\frac{\sqrt{7}}{4}} = \underline{\hspace{1cm}} = \underline{\hspace{1cm}}$

$\csc\theta = \dfrac{1}{\sin\theta} = \dfrac{1}{-\frac{\sqrt{7}}{4}} = \underline{\hspace{1cm}} = \underline{\hspace{1cm}}$

$\sec\theta = \dfrac{1}{\cos\theta} = \dfrac{1}{-\frac{3}{4}} = \underline{\hspace{1cm}}$

Your Notes

✓ **Checkpoint** Find the values of the other five trigonometric functions of θ.

1. $\cos \theta = \frac{1}{4}$, $0 < \theta < \frac{\pi}{2}$

2. $\sin \theta = -\frac{1}{3}$, $\frac{3\pi}{2} < \theta < 2\pi$

Example 2 *Simplify a trigonometric expression*

Simplify the expression $\dfrac{1}{\sin\left(\frac{\pi}{2} - \theta\right)} \cdot \cot \theta$.

Solution

$\dfrac{1}{\sin\left(\frac{\pi}{2} - \theta\right)} \cdot \cot \theta = $ _____ $\cdot \cot \theta$ _____

$= $ _____ $\cdot$ _____   Cotangent identity

$= $ _____   Simplify.

$= $ _____   _____

✓ **Checkpoint** Simplify the expression.

3. $\dfrac{\tan \theta}{\sec \theta} \cdot \sin \theta + \tan \theta \csc \theta \cdot \cos^3 \theta$

Your Notes

Example 3 *Verify a trigonometric identity*

Verify the identity

$$\sec \theta \cdot \frac{1}{\cos \theta} - \tan \theta \cot \theta = \frac{1 - \cos^2 \theta}{1 - \sin^2 \theta}.$$

Solution

$\sec \theta \cdot \frac{1}{\cos \theta} - \tan \theta \cot \theta = \sec \theta \cdot \underline{} - \tan \theta \cot \theta$

$= \underline{} - \tan \theta \cot \theta$

$= \underline{} - \tan \theta \cdot \underline{}$

$= \underline{} - \underline{}$

$= \underline{}$

$= \underline{}$

$= \dfrac{1 - \cos^2 \theta}{1 - \sin^2 \theta}$

✓ **Checkpoint** Verify the identity.

4. $\dfrac{\cos^2(-x)}{\cot^2 x} = \sin^2 x$

Homework

14.4 Solve Trigonometric Equations

Goal • Solve trigonometric equations.

Your Notes

Example 1 Solve a trigonometric equation in an interval

Solve $2\cos^2 x + 1 = 2$ in the interval $0 \leq x \leq 3\pi$.

Solution

$2\cos^2 x + 1 = 2$	Write original equation.
$2\cos^2 x = \underline{}$	Subtract 1 from each side.
$\cos^2 x = \underline{}$	Divide each side by 2.
$\cos x = \underline{}$	Take square roots of each side.

$x = \cos^{-1}\underline{}$ or $x = \cos^{-1}\underline{}$

$x = \dfrac{\pi}{4}$ or $x = -\dfrac{\pi}{4}$ $x = \dfrac{3\pi}{4}$ or $x = \dfrac{5\pi}{4}$

Therefore, the general solution of the equation is:

$x = \dfrac{\pi}{4} + \underline{}$ or $x = -\dfrac{\pi}{4} + \underline{}$ or

$x = \dfrac{3\pi}{4} + \underline{}$ or $x = \dfrac{5\pi}{4} + \underline{}$

where n is any integer.

> To write the general solution of a trigonometric equation, you can add multiples of the period to all the solutions from one cycle.

The specific solutions that are in the interval $0 \leq x \leq 3\pi$ are:

$x = \underline{}$ $x = \underline{}$

$x = \dfrac{\pi}{4} + 2\pi = \underline{}$ $x = \dfrac{3\pi}{4} + 2\pi = \underline{}$

$x = -\dfrac{\pi}{4} + 2\pi = \underline{}$ $x = \underline{}$

Your Notes

Example 2 — Solve a trigonometric equation in an interval

Solve $d = 20 - 12 \sin \frac{\pi t}{4}$ in the interval $0 \leq t \leq 24$ when $d = 8$.

Solution

$20 - 12 \sin \frac{\pi t}{4} = 8$ — Substitute 8 for d.

$-12 \sin \frac{\pi t}{4} = $ _____ — Subtract 20 from each side.

$\sin \frac{\pi t}{4} = $ _____ — Divide each side by -12.

$\frac{\pi t}{4} = \frac{\pi}{2} + $ _____ — $\sin \theta = 1$ when $\theta = \frac{\pi}{2} + $ _____ .

$t = $ _____ — Solve for t.

On the interval $0 \leq t \leq 24$, d is 8 when
$t = $ _____ $= $ ___ , $t = $ _____ $= $ ___ , and
$t = $ _____ $= $ ___ .

Example 3 — Use the quadratic formula

Solve $2 \sin^2 x + 5 \sin x + 3 = 0$ in the interval $-\pi \leq x \leq \pi$.

Solution

$2 \sin^2 x + 5 \sin x + 3 = 0$ — Write original equation.

$\sin x = $ _____ — Quadratic formula

$= $ _____ — Simplify.

$= $ ____ or _____ — Simplify.

$x = \sin^{-1}$ _____ or $x = \sin^{-1}$ _____ — Use inverse sine.

$= $ _____ _____ — Use a calculator.

In the interval $-\pi \leq x \leq \pi$, the only solution is $x = $ _____ .

Your Notes

✓ **Checkpoint** Solve the trigonometric equation in the interval.

1. $16 \sin^2 x + 5 = 6$; $0 \leq x \leq \pi$

2. $20 - 12 \sin \frac{\pi t}{4} = 25$; $0 < t < 3\pi$

3. $\cos^2 x + 3 \cos x - 4 = 0$; $0 \leq x \leq \pi$

Example 4 Solve an equation with an extraneous solution

Solve $1 - \cos x = \sqrt{3} \sin x$ in the interval $0 \leq x < \pi$.

Solution

$1 - \cos x = \sqrt{3} \sin x$

$(1 - \cos x)^2 = \underline{3 \sin^2 x}$

$1 - 2\cos x + \cos^2 x = \underline{3 \sin^2 x}$

$1 - 2\cos x + \cos^2 x = 3\underline{(1 - \cos^2 x)}$

$1 - 2\cos x + \cos^2 x = \underline{3} - \underline{3\cos^2 x}$

$\underline{4\cos^2 x - 2\cos x - 2} = 0$ Quadratic form

$\underline{2\cos^2 x - \cos x - 1} = 0$ Divide each side by 2.

$\underline{(2\cos x + 1)(\cos x - 1)} = 0$ Factor.

$\underline{2\cos x + 1 = 0}$ or $\underline{\cos x - 1 = 0}$ Zero product property

$\cos x = \underline{-\tfrac{1}{2}}$ or $\cos x = \underline{1}$ Solve for $\cos x$.

$x = \underline{\tfrac{2\pi}{3}}$ or $x = \underline{\tfrac{4\pi}{3}}$ $x = \underline{0}$ Solve for x.

The apparent solution $\underline{\tfrac{4\pi}{3}}$ does not check in the original equation. The only solutions in the interval $0 \leq x \leq 2\pi$ are $x = \underline{0}$ and $x = \underline{\tfrac{2\pi}{3}}$.

Checkpoint Complete the following exercise.

4. Solve the equation in Example 4 in the interval $0 \leq x < 4\pi$.

Homework

14.5 Write Trigonometric Functions and Models

Goal • Model data using sine or cosine functions.

Your Notes

VOCABULARY

Sinusoids

Example 1 *Solve a multi-step problem*

Write a function for the sinusoid shown below.

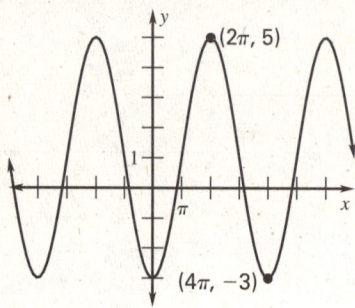

Solution

Step 1 The maximum value M of the function is ____ and the minimum value m of the function is ____.

Step 2 The value of k is the mean of the maximum and minimum values. The vertical shift is

$$k = \frac{M + m}{2} = \underline{\hspace{1cm}} = \underline{\hspace{0.5cm}}.$$

Step 3 When $x = 0$, the function is at its minimum. Use a _____ function whose graph is a reflection in the x-axis with no horizontal shift. So, $h = $ ___.

Step 4 The period is ____ = $\frac{2\pi}{b}$. So, $b = $ ___. The amplitude is

$$|a| = \frac{M - m}{2} = \underline{\hspace{1cm}} = \underline{\hspace{0.5cm}} = \underline{\hspace{0.3cm}}.$$

Because the graph is a reflection, a ___ 0. So, $a = $ ____.

The function is $y = $ _____.

Your Notes

Example 2 Use sinusoidal regression

Temperature The table below shows the average monthly high temperature H (in °F) for Chicago, Illinois. The time t is measured in months, with t = 1 representing January. Write a trigonometric model that gives H as a function of t.

t	1	2	3	4	5	6
H	32	34	43	55	65	75

t	7	8	9	10	11	12
H	81	79	73	61	47	36

Solution

Begin by entering the data in a graphing calculator. Use the graphing calculator's sinusoidal regression feature to get a model.

H = _____

✓ Checkpoint Complete the following exercises.

1. Write a function for the sinusoid.

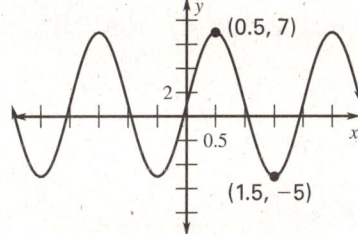

2. The table shows the average monthly low temperature L (in °F) for Chicago, Illinois. The time t is measured in months, with t = 1 representing January. Write a trigonometric model that gives L as a function of t.

t	1	2	3	4	5	6
L	18	20	29	40	50	60

t	7	8	9	10	11	12
L	66	65	58	47	34	23

Homework

14.6 Apply Sum and Difference Formulas

Goal • Use trigonometric sum and difference formulas.

Your Notes

SUM AND DIFFERENCE FORMULAS

Sum Formulas

$\sin(a + b) =$ _____ + _____

$\cos(a + b) =$ _____ − _____

$\tan(a + b) =$ _____

Difference Formulas

$\sin(a - b) =$ _____ − _____

$\cos(a - b) =$ _____ + _____

$\tan(a - b) =$ _____

Example 1 *Evaluate a trigonometric expression*

Find the exact value of $\cos 75°$.

Solution

$\cos 75° = \cos(45° + \underline{\quad})$ Substitute.

$= \cos 45° \underline{\quad\quad}$ Sum formula

$\quad - \sin 45° \underline{\quad\quad}$

$= \dfrac{\sqrt{2}}{2} \cdot \underline{\quad} - \dfrac{\sqrt{2}}{2} \cdot \underline{\quad}$ Evaluate.

$= \underline{\quad\quad}$ Simplify.

Your Notes

Example 2 — Use a difference formula

Find $\sin(a - b)$ given that $\sin a = -\frac{3}{5}$ with $\frac{3\pi}{2} < a < 2\pi$ and $\cos b = \frac{5}{13}$ with $0 < b < \frac{\pi}{2}$.

Solution

Using a Pythagorean identity and quadrant signs gives $\cos a = \underline{}$ and $\sin b = \underline{}$.

$\sin(a - b) = \underline{} - \underline{}$ Difference formula

$= -\frac{3}{5}\left(\frac{5}{13}\right) - \underline{}\left(\underline{}\right)$ Substitute.

$= \underline{}$ Simplify.

Example 3 — Simplify an expression

Simplify the expression $\tan(x + \pi)$.

Solution

$\tan(x + \pi) = \underline{}$ Sum formula

$= \underline{}$ Evaluate.

$= \underline{}$ Simplify.

Your Notes

✓ **Checkpoint** Complete the following exercises.

1. Find the exact value of $\tan \frac{\pi}{12}$.

2. Find $\cos(a - b)$ given that $\sin a = \frac{8}{17}$ with $0 < a < \frac{\pi}{2}$ and $\cos b = -\frac{3}{5}$ with $\frac{\pi}{2} < b < \frac{3\pi}{2}$.

3. Simplify the expression $\sin(x + 4\pi)$.

Your Notes

Example 4 Solve a trigonometric equation

Solve $\cos\left(x - \frac{\pi}{4}\right) + \cos\left(x + \frac{\pi}{4}\right) = 1$ for $\frac{3\pi}{2} < x < 2\pi$.

Solution

Use sum and difference formulas to rewrite the original equation as:

$\underline{\qquad} + \underline{\qquad} + \underline{\qquad} + \underline{\qquad} - \underline{\qquad} = 1$

$\underline{\qquad} = 1$ Simplify the equation.

$\underline{\qquad} = 1$ Evaluate the cosine function.

$\underline{\qquad} = \underline{\qquad}$ Solve for the cos x.

In the interval $\frac{3\pi}{2} < x < 2\pi$, the only solution is $\underline{\qquad}$.

✓ **Checkpoint** Complete the following exercise.

4. Solve $\sin\left(x + \frac{\pi}{4}\right) + \cos\left(x - \frac{\pi}{4}\right) = 0$ for $0 < x < 2\pi$.

Homework

14.7 Apply Double-Angle and Half-Angle Formulas

Goal • Use double-angle and half-angle formulas.

Your Notes

DOUBLE-ANGLE AND HALF-ANGLE FORMULAS

Double-Angle Formulas

$\cos 2a =$ _____ − _____

$\cos 2a =$ _____ − __

$\cos 2a =$ __ − _____

$\sin 2a =$ _____

$\tan 2a =$ _____

Half-Angle Formulas

$\sin \frac{a}{2} =$ _____

$\cos \frac{a}{2} =$ _____

$\tan \frac{a}{2} =$ _____

$\tan \frac{a}{2} =$ _____

Example 1 *Evaluating trigonometric expressions*

Find the exact value of $\cos \frac{\pi}{8}$.

Solution

$\cos \dfrac{\pi}{8} = \cos \dfrac{1}{2}(\underline{}) = \sqrt{\dfrac{1 + \cos \underline{}}{2}}$

$= \sqrt{\dfrac{1 + \underline{}}{2}}$

$= \underline{}$

> Because $\frac{\pi}{8}$ is in Quadrant I and the value of cosine is positive in Quadrant I, the following formula is used:
> $\cos \dfrac{a}{2} = \sqrt{\dfrac{1 + \cos a}{2}}$

Your Notes

Example 2 — Evaluate trigonometric expressions

Given $\sin a = \dfrac{3}{5}$ with $\dfrac{\pi}{2} < a < \pi$, find (a) $\cos 2a$ and (b) $\cos \dfrac{a}{2}$.

Solution

Using a Pythagorean identity gives $\cos a =$ _____.

a. $\cos 2a =$ _____ $- 1 =$ __$\big($ _____$\big)^2 - 1 =$ _____

b. Because $\dfrac{a}{2}$ is in Quadrant I, $\cos \dfrac{a}{2}$ is _____.

$\cos \dfrac{a}{2} =$ _____ $=$ _____ $=$ _____

> In part (b), you can multiply through the inequality $\dfrac{\pi}{2} < a < \pi$ by $\dfrac{1}{2}$ to get $\dfrac{\pi}{4} < a < \dfrac{\pi}{2}$. So, $\dfrac{a}{2}$ is in Quadrant I.

✓ **Checkpoint** Complete the following exercises.

1. Find the exact value of $\sin \dfrac{\pi}{12}$.

   _____

2. Given $\cos a = -\dfrac{7}{25}$ with $\pi < a < \dfrac{3\pi}{2}$, find $\sin 2a$.

Example 3 — Verify a trigonometric identity

Verify the identity $\sin 4x = 4 \sin x \cos x (1 - 2 \sin^2 x)$

Solution

$\sin 4x = \sin(2x +$ ____$)$

$= \sin 2x \cos 2x +$ _____

$= (2 \sin x \cos x) \cos 2x + \cos 2x ($ _____ $)$

$= (2 \sin x \cos x + 2 \sin x \cos x)$ _____

$= (4 \sin x \cos x)$ _____

$= 4 \sin x \cos x ($ _____ $)$

Lesson 14.7 • Algebra 2 Notetaking Guide

Your Notes

> **Example 4**   *Solve a trigonometric equation*
>
> Solve $\cos 2x + \sin x = 0$ for $0 \leq x < 2\pi$.
>
> **Solution**
>
> $$\cos 2x + \sin x = 0$$
> $$\underline{} + \sin x = 0$$
> $$\underline{} + \sin x + \underline{} = 0$$
> $$(\underline{} + \underline{})(\underline{} + \underline{}) = 0$$
> $$\underline{} + \underline{} = 0 \quad \text{or} \quad \underline{} + \underline{} = 0$$
> $$\underline{} = -1 \qquad\qquad \underline{} = -1$$
> $$\sin x = \underline{} \qquad\qquad \sin x = \underline{}$$
> $$x = \underline{}, \underline{} \qquad\qquad x = \underline{}$$

✓ **Checkpoint** Complete the following exercises.

3. Verify the identity $\cos 3x = \cos^3 x - 3 \sin^2 x \cos x$.

4. Solve $\tan \dfrac{x}{2} = \sin x$ for $0 \leq x < 2\pi$.

Homework

Words to Review

Give an example of the vocabulary word.

Amplitude	Periodic function
Cycle	Period
Frequency	Trigonometric identity
Sinusoids	

Review your notes and Chapter 14 by using the Chapter Review on pages 965–968 of your textbook.